AF653012

SECOND HOME TOURISM

SECOND HOME TOURISM

Mahesh Chandra Singh

CENTRUM PRESS
NEW DELHI-110002 (INDIA)

CENTRUM PRESS
H.O.: 4360/4, Ansari Road, Daryaganj,
New Delhi-110002 (India)
Tel: 23278000, 23261597, 23255577, 23286875
B.O.: No. 1015, Ist Main Road, BSK IIIrd Stage,
IIIrd Phase, IIIrd Block, Bangalore-560085 (INDIA)
Tel: 080-41723429
Email: centrumpress@gmail.com
Visit us at: www.centrumpress.com

Second Home Tourism

© Reserved

First Edition, 2010

ISBN 978-93-80540-08-5

PRINTED IN INDIA

Printed at Mehra Offset Press, Delhi

Contents

Preface *vii*

1. Second Home Tourism Impact, Planning and Management 1

2. Place Attachment of Vacation Residents 43

3. Recreation Second Homes 75

4. Second Homes and Coastal Tourism 129

5. Review of Coastal Degradation 213

6. Second Homes as a Part of New Rural Life Style 241

7. Second Homes Ownership and Demand 279

8. Fractional Ownership of Second Homes 313

Bibliography 329

Index 333

Preface

Over the last few years second-home tourism has become more popular, emerging as an important part of the tourism sector in a number of countries. In most cases second homes are located near attractive locations, such as the sea, lakes, mountains or rural areas, whilst often they have a connection to their owners' origins and may be inherited properties.

They offer a peaceful and environmentally friendly holiday home for city dwellers. The USA is considered to be the country in the world with the largest proportion of tourism second homes (Varela et al., 2003). In the European Union the demand for second homes is increasing, notably in southern European countries, and such homes are very often purchased by northern Europeans.

Although initially the demand for second homes was driven predominantly by nationals seeking regions with better climatic conditions, recently there has been an important growth in the sector from foreigners. In Spain the foreign investment in second homes reached 5.7 billion Euros in 2002, which represents a total of 90 000 houses and an average growth rate of 10 per cent. Studies conducted demonstrate that the highest levels of demand come from Great Britain (35 per cent), Germany (31 per cent), France (7 per cent), Italy (5 per cent) and The Netherlands (3.1 per cent).

Second homes have been interpreted as a significant indicator of the development of new patterns of mobility and dwelling in Western countries. However, changes in population distribution, population composition, family structures and tourism preferences pose a reason to challenge the general assumption that second home tourism would continue unchanged in the future. This book reviews representations of the future of second home tourism in the Indian media and policy discourse. Mainstream trends and emerging weak signals are recognized and further analysed in reference to the international context. As a result of the analysis four distinctive themes related to the future of second home tourism are distinguished: dual dwelling, internationalization, alternative forms and regional differentiation. These themes suggest a change in the traditional Indian second home culture, often portrayed as a personal and national utopia. With the exception of dual dwelling, all the themes have so far been overlooked in the official policy discourse.

The book is meant to serve well to the students of tourism, environment and ecology.

—*Mahesh Chandra Singh*

1

Second Home Tourism Impact, Planning and Management

Urbanization and Second-home Tourism

Definitions of Second-home Tourism and Residential Tourism

Second-home tourism deserves special attention from researchers, in revealing what sort of reasons lead someone from elsewhere to decide to spend long periods of time in a particular place, and to constantly return to that place. There are also issues related to the impacts of second-home tourism, and planning implications.

The definition of second-home tourism is based on two main aspects:

1. The type of tourist dwelling where tourists stay, which may be privately owned, rented or cost-free (visiting relatives or friends).
2. Frequent return to the same holiday place.

Generally, second-home tourists live in privately owned or rented dwellings, and have particular characteristics. They return to the same place for leisure time, and thus demonstrate great knowledge of, loyalty towards and appreciation of the destination. They often make friends or have relatives in the location, establish close links with the destination and are committed to the sustainability of the place. Second-home tourists spend long periods of time at the destination where they purchase their house.

Such periods of time are long compared to the other forms of tourism, but are obviously less than a year at a time – otherwise the individuals concerned would not be considered tourists. It is useful here to highlight the difference between second-home tourism and residential tourism, which is based on the period of time travellers stay at the destination.

In the case of residential tourism, the length of stay may be longer than a year – that is, people change their place of residence and in some cases can even get a job at the destination. According to the WTO definition, if that happens the travellers cannot be classified as tourists. This can be the case with aged people living in rest homes. There is, however, an important difference between such travellers and local residents, since the former consume income at the destination whilst their money is generated at their usual place of residence. Distinction between second-home tourism and residential tourism involves consideration of the reasons why second-home tourists become residential tourists.

There are certain socioeconomic determinants or jobs that might facilitate the change of place of residence. According to recent research, climatic conditions, price, political and social stability, cultural factors, etc. are amongst the factors that influence the demand for second homes.

Time sharing is another form of second-home tourism, but in this case tourists do not spend long periods of time at the same destination. It could be considered a particular form of second-home tourism, depending on the way the participants use their tourism dwelling.

The final consideration demonstrates the third characteristic of second-home tourism, which is related to the relationship established between the tourist dwelling and the visitor. Often tourists stay in private dwellings that can be owned, rented, owned just for a period of time (timesharing), or free (the visiting friends and relatives (VFR) market).

Second-home tourism has a considerable impact on the local economy through the economics of the building industry. However, the impact is different from that of the 'classic' tourism industry, as these tourists tend to cook their own meals and often organize their own trips and entertainment. Hence hotels, restaurants, travel agencies and tour operators may not be used, whilst the building industry, agriculture and retail may gain more benefits from second-home tourism demand.

When researching second-home tourism, four main aspects should be considered:

1. The second-home tourists, who are very often characterized by a strong affiliation with and loyalty to the destination.
2. Businesses that provide products and services to this market, including the building industry, which is responsible for the construction of private tourist dwellings and a wide range of decorative and household services.
3. The government and local authorities, whose responsibility is geared towards the provision of adequate levels of services and infrastructure. If second-home tourism is a dominant sector at the destination, there are special needs and services that must be provided by the planning and governmental services. For example, the process of urbanization, generally depending on local government, requires planning and the provision of land and infrastructure.
4. The host community, which often looks on the sector as being responsible for creating employment. It is also important to consider the social and cultural consequences of the interaction between the local communities and second home owners.

As second-home tourism implies long-term commitment from visitors, it is only when all the stakeholders have compatible aims and objectives that coexistence can be peaceful and mutually beneficial. The local authorities therefore need to provide a planning framework that ensures coordination of the activities and the optimization of impacts.

The Socioeconomic and Environmental Impacts of Second Home Tourism: The South Pacific Coast of Nicaragua

Attractive coastal regions of Central and South America have recently experienced a rapid growth of second home developments. Informed by the experiences of Europe and the Americas, this study examines the socioeconomic and environmental impacts of second homes on the South Pacific Coast of Nicaragua. An extensive review of Spanish, French and English academic literature as well as secondary data from the Rivas region were examined. Nicaraguan press releases from the two main national papers, La Prensa and El Nuevo Diario, were scanned to add congruence to the local debates and opinions.

collected. In-depth, semi-structured interviews and participant observation were used to collect additional qualitative data. Twenty-one decision makers and tourism officials were interviewed in the months of January and February 2007. The interviewees were representatives from the local government, Ministry of Tourism and the local tourism industry. The main impacts include conflicts with local and indigenous communities over land use and ownership, seasonal and low-income employment generation, an increased burden of municipal budget to provide public infrastructure, and environmental degradation.

It is argued that the second home tourism sector, strongly driven by private real estate investors, fails to generate tourism activities which are expected to sustain community development. This study further indicates that municipalities concentrating on the second home tourism segment may deprive access to resources to other forms of tourism activities.

Urbanization and Second-Home Tourism

Over the last few years second-home tourism has become more popular, emerging as an important part of the tourism sector in a number of countries. In most cases second homes are located near attractive locations, such as the sea, lakes, mountains or rural areas, whilst often they have a connection to their owners' origins and may be inherited properties. They offer a peaceful and environmentally friendly holiday home for city dwellers. The USA is considered to be the country in the world with the largest proportion of tourism second homes. In the European Union the demand for second homes is increasing, notably in southern European countries, and such homes are very often purchased by northern Europeans.

Although initially the demand for second homes was driven predominantly by nationals seeking regions with better climatic conditions, recently there has been an important growth in the sector from foreigners. In Spain the foreign investment in second homes reached 5.7 billion Euros in 2002, which represents a total of 90 000 houses and an average growth rate of 10 per cent. Studies conducted demonstrate that the highest levels of demand come from Great Britain (35 per cent), Germany (31 per cent), France (7 per cent), Italy (5 per cent) and The Netherlands (3.1 per cent). A number of factors have contributed in the growth of second-home demand in Europe, namely:

- greater confidence in the European Union.
- experience of destinations through frequent visitation.
- the internationalization of the building.

"Tourism & Second Homes Reality Check South of the Border"

By Mitch Creekmore, Stewart International

Wall Street is mired in a downward spiral due to oil and financial stress. On Friday, Washington announced concerns over Ginnie Mae and Freddie Mac with possible government intervention. The two mortgage giants have taken $11 billion in write-downs over the last nine months and their stock fell by 30 percent and 45 percent, respectively, for the week ending July 11. Where are Americans going to invest? Where can we safely put our money to work in a reliable investment atmosphere? Housing had always been one such "safe" venue.

We all wish our domestic financial and residential real estate woes would improve over the next six months. Unfortunately, that is unlikely. They probably won't get much better until we have a new president in the White House and well after the first of the year. News out of Washington and the U.S. Commerce Department in April said new home sales plummeted by 8.5 percent to a 17 year low in the month of March. The report gives little hope the housing market is near the bottom.

The economy expanded at an annual rate of one percent in the first quarter, the Commerce Department said last week. That caps the weakest six months of growth in the last five years.

The world's biggest financial institutions have taken about $400 billion in writedowns and credit losses tied to the U.S. housing slump, according to data compiled by Bloomberg. Eli Broad, founder of homebuilder KB Homes, said in an interview with Bloomberg that with homes sales and prices declining and consumer confidence at a 28 year low, "I don't see it turning around very quickly. This is worse than any recession we've had since World War II." Selling off vacant, unsold homes could take "several years," he said. REALTOR® Magazine reported in a survey in the May issue of *Business Week* that cities like Los Angeles, San Diego, Las Vegas and Phoenix saw sellers reduce asking prices on their residences by more than an average of 20 percent in the last 12 months. The number of Americans in danger of losing their homes to foreclosure rose to the highest level in three decades during the first quarter of 2008, according to data from the Mortgage Bankers Association. "I think housing is going to continue to have a corrosive effect on consumer psychology and the economy in general to a far greater extent than people think, or even far greater than I thought about a month or two ago," Broad said in his interview.

These are stark and worrisome headlines, to say the least, about the challenging plight we'll all face in the coming months. Interestingly, on the same day as the REALTOR® survey, *USA Today* had a front page headline in their Money section entitled "Foreign Buyers Snap Up U.S.

Real Estate." With the continuing decrease of the dollar against the Euro and Pound Sterling, coupled with the reduction in home prices in popular destinations, the U.S. has become a "great buy" for international purchasers that have stronger currencies and greater disposable incomes.

The question now, though on a very cautious and 'wait and see basis,' is: where will *Americans* invest? Where will they look for real estate opportunities, whether it is a second home or a retirement destination? There seems to be no sense of urgency in today's market like there had been in the years from 2000 – 2005. Annualized appreciation in the "big four" second home markets was staggering at over 100 percent in residential values during that same time period, according to the National Association of Realtors.

Today, Americans are concerned about rising oil prices, the cost of gasoline, healthcare issues, the pending presidential election and the overall credit crunch that has crippled the mortgage industry and led to widespread mortgage foreclosures. The subsequent impact all of these factors create on American buying mentality is being felt throughout the U.S., as well as in Mexico and virtually all of Central America. With that said, many U.S. citizens will still look south of the border for second home purchases due to its close proximity, increased airlift capacity, access and affordability (even with higher fuel costs), and a lower cost of living that cannot be attained anywhere in the U.S. – especially on a fixed income!

The biggest unanswered question is, "When?" Like Mexico, the countries of Costa Rica, Panama and the Dominican Republic (DR) have seen dramatic increases in tourism and real estate activity over the past seven years. Mexico is the most important tourist destination in Latin America. According to the InterAmerican Development Bank (IDB), the country receives about 30 percent of its total income from international tourism in the region. Eight percent of Mexico's GDP comes from the tourist sector and accounts for six percent of their nation's employment.

Mexican tourism is heavily dependent on North American visitors, and at the same time, it is extremely vulnerable to U.S. economic fluctuations. A major advantage that Mexico has in the region is fonatur, the National Trust Fund for Tourism Development. Since it's inception in 1974, fonatur has been the public trust and part state-owned entity that has been responsible for the development of Cancun, Los Cabos, Ixtapa, Huatulco and Loreto. The mission statement of fonatur is, "To be the institution responsible for the planning and development of sustainable tourism projects of national impact. To be an instrument of promotion for investment and training of the tourism sector; thus being the national entity that lends its experience to regions, states, and municipalities, along with small and medium businesses." Today, fonatur has additional new master planned projects like the Nautical Ladder in the Sea of Cortez, the Riveria Maya and Costa Maya developments in the State of Quintana Roo, Litibu in the State of Nayarit, and Palenque in the state of Chiapas. During the six-year presidential term of Vicente Fox Quesada, fonatur realized more than six billion dollars in foreign direct investment. For these many reasons, Mexico has continually retained its reputation as the "big enchilada" in tourism and real estate development within the Latin American region.

When the U.S. economy began to show signs of weakness, many speculated as to whether American tourism in Costa Rica, Panama, the Dominican Republic and the rest of the Central American countries also would begin to decline. So far, this has not been the case. In fact, Costa Rica saw one million visitors in the first five months of 2008, according to the Costa Rican Tourism Board (ICT). This represents a 16 percent increase of approximately 133,000 visitors when compared to the same time period in 2007. The Dominican Republic enjoys about 4.5 million visitors each year. Even though Americans have less discretionary income, meaning fewer dollars to spend on vacations both domestically and internationally, they're still willing to travel to these countries. Close proximity to our border makes airline tickets and hotel accommodations more palatable even in the face of rising fuel costs. Tourism will remain one of the biggest generators of GDP for most of these countries. All of these so called "banana republics" of old have tourism boards that are aggressively and strategically marketing to North Americans. Eco tourism and sustainable developments are no longer exclusive to Costa Rica.

Each country has something different to offer with its own rich culture and history, archeological presence and special natural amenities that make the experience unique. Some of the biggest names in the development world from countries like Spain, England, Canada, Mexico and the U.S., to name a few, have world class resorts and master planned projects established or under construction in these nations.

It's worth mentioning that the professionalism and integrity of the real estate agent community in most of these countries has improved as well. It's not as much about "my commission" and a general lack of disclosure as in years past, but instead about creating a greater level of comfort and security for buyers. Title insurance and escrow services have helped push real estate agents to adopt higher standards of service and ethics for the benefit of their customers. As a result, one only needs to determine where they want to be, what geographical amenities they like, and whether they are beach people, rain forest or colonial aficionados.

Guatemala, El Salvador, Nicaragua, Honduras and Belize have something for everyone. Why? Because it's simply the truth! All of these markets will attract a particular buyer based on their personal preference and their price point. The latter criteria will become an increasingly more important component in the selection of where to buy and where to invest in the coming years.

With the tremendous appreciation that Mexico's residential sector has experienced, coupled with that of Costa Rica and Panama, many North Americans will be "priced out" of some international markets. Where a two-bedroom condominium sold for $180K five years ago in a given destination, and was affordable then, that same unit today sells for $400K or more. As a result of this dynamic value appreciation, foreign purchasers will seek a geographic location suitable for their given means and disposable income that will still provide them with acceptable amenities, healthcare, infrastructure, enjoyment and upside investment potential. A lot has been written about the vast inheritance the "boomers" will realize over the next decade. Many, many North Americans will have, and have now, a lot of money that can be invested in something or somewhere.

Why not second homes in any of these countries? Our neighbours to the south are keenly aware of the investment impact this unprecedented group of inheritors can make on their country. Not to mention the impact they'll have on improving the quality of life with new infrastructure, tax revenue and development wherever they invest. Today, that total is over two million purchasers from North America. The perception and viability of owning a home in these wonderful countries has changed a great deal. Foreign buyers now understand and recognize the safeguards that can be provided for real property acquisitions outside the U.S. There is a greater sense of comfort and security with North American buyers. Given the dire second home landscape in America over the next 18 months, and maybe longer, Mexico and Central America will be the places to be, the places to invest, the places to own that second home!

Planning Laws Could Restrict Second Home Ownership

The Government is considering measures that will deter second-home owners from buying properties in desirable rural locations. Around 240,000 people own a second home in England and the detrimental effect of this on rural communities has long been recognised. In some areas property prices have risen beyond the reach of local people and village schools shops and pubs are threatened with closure because properties remain empty for large parts of the year.

Prime Minister Gordon Brown has now commissioned an enquiry that will look at whether local councils should have the power to prevent homes being sold to buyers who will not use them as their main residence. In such cases, planning permission would be needed to convert a property from a full-time home into a second home. Any scheme recommended by the enquiry is likely to be piloted in the areas facing serious difficulties from second-home ownership, such as the Isles of Scilly, South Hams in South Devon, North Cornwall and North Norfolk. In April of this year, Capital Gains Tax liability on the sale of second homes will be reduced to 18%, a move that is being strongly opposed by the Government's Rural Advocate, Stuart Burgess.

Asset Sure News 21st September 2007

The Impact of Second Homes and UK Holiday Homes on Communities

The growth in the amount of disposable income over the last 20 years, achieved by homeowners in the UK has been considerable. As a result many people have purchased second homes to act as a UK holiday homes both here in Britain and in other European popular destinations like Spain and France and Portugal. Britain has fantastic countryside and traditional seaside resorts and scenery that have attracted hundreds of thousands of a people to purchase second properties using the equity they have amassed in their own homes and their disposable income, as the economy has strengthened during the last 10 to 20 years. This has led to house price growth. The amount of land available for new building holiday properties is under immense pressure and at the same time the number of traditional cottages is finite.

Here in the UK, the continued rise in property prices has had some negative effect on local villages and communities popular holiday destinations such as Devon, Cornwall, the Lake District and the New Forest. Residents of these largely rural communities (which rely heavily on tourism from holiday makers) are finding it increasingly difficult to get onto the property ladder because of huge demand for holiday homes pushing up the overall price of property out of their reach. In some extreme areas this has created resentment and bitterness as locals cannot afford to buy property in their own village and they have been indirectly forced out of their own area to look for cheaper property elsewhere.

The problem is widely recognised among local communities, councils and housing authorities. Some local councils have actively sought to intervene to stop holiday home usage. For instance, they have sought to restrict the usage of the property in its local planning guidelines for people that have not lived in the area for a fixed time as well as influence local planning guidelines. Recent proposals by new forest district council to increase the level of council tax above the standard 90 per cent rate for second homes left unoccupied, is currently being considered. The government has also signalled that it may change the law to give councils more flexibility to adjust its own council tax rates to reflect the needs to balance the local economy with the volume of holiday homes in its area. In addition, major new national housing reform is being introduced to bring three million new affordable homes to the UK by 2020, particularly for key workers and first time buyers.

The wider economic impacts on local people migrating from their local town has knock on effects for the economy. Without affordable accommodation key workers have a to migrate away from the local area. Businesses and local services are also on the decline us local people who run these small businesses also cannot afford can to purchase property. The huge decline in some villages in South Wales is a notable example where areas have been left unoccupied as holiday homeowners have left them for the winter. The fact they are left empty for most of the year means spoilt the traditional community feeling and spirit between the old villages that used to rely on coal and industry with strong history and bonds, is now dependant upon tourism from people who do not live there or only visit a few weeks a year. Another obvious example is the Lake District where an amazing 50% of homes in the village of Berwick are empty throughout the year. The problem looks set to continue as more and more of us seek second homes to escape the pressure of a modern lifestyle.

The Impact of Empty, Second and Holiday Homes

Executive Summary

In response to the increasing requirement for public policy to be evidence-based, the Economic and Social Science Research Council (ESRC) has funded a programme of research projects to examine how evidence can be generated in a number of social policy areas. Beyond developing the evidence base in a number of topic areas, the programme aims to develop the methods of systematic reviewing. Systematic reviews are considered to be a key tool for the identification, comprehensive assessment and synthesis of research evidence.

A systematic review aims to provide a comprehensive and unbiased summary of available evidence on a given topic. This is achieved by the use of a clearly defined search strategy to ensure that an extensive range of potential sources of evidence is explored. In addition the use of explicit criteria to appraise the quality of the evidence retrieved ensures that only robust evidence is synthesised in the production of the final review.

This review addresses two questions:

- What are the impacts of privately owned empty or irregularly occupied properties on the sustainability of rural communities?
- To what extent have the policy interventions addressed the effects of empty of irregularly occupied properties on the sustainability of rural communities?

These questions address key national and local policy concerns, notably sustainable communities and housing demand. Furthermore the social and economic impacts of second homes in particular on rural communities are contested, and have been the focus of considerable and often emotive debate over the last three decades.

Methods

An essential first step was to ensure there was no ambiguity around the questions being addressed by the review. The review was concerned with vacant property, second homes and holiday homes (i.e. properties rented out on a series of short term lets) in the private sector located in settlements with populations of less than 10,000. We adopted the ten dimensions of sustainability proposed by Long (2001) as a framework for organising the evidence.

A review protocol was drawn up at the outset of the review, detailing *a priori* decisions about the selection and appraisal of studies, the search strategy, and data synthesis methods. Ten electronic databases and many internet sites were searched. The process produced 1060 references. Of these 273 were relevant to the review. Once the specified inclusion criteria were applied, 30 references remained. Of these, 23 met our quality criteria and finally entered the review. Information was extracted from each study in a uniform manner, and data synthesised to provide a narrative account of the findings.

Evidence-Base

Seventeen of the review studies addressed second home ownership. The studies included in the review were undertaken in various locations across the UK over a period of more than 30 years, using a variety of methods, and various definitions of second or empty homes. The definition of what constitutes a second home has been a perennial problem. Another fundamental difficulty has been the accurate identification of the number of properties that are empty or used as second homes. Different studies have focused on different aspects of empty and irregularly occupied properties. The political problematisation of second homes has led much of the research to have a relatively narrow focus, and second homes have (with some notable exceptions) been studied in isolation from other expressions of external housing demand in local areas, such as retirement and commuting.

The impacts of privately owned empty or irregularly occupied properties on the sustainability of rural communities: key findings.

The evidence was organised thematically around four of the ten dimensions of sustainability proposed by Long (2001). The evidence only addressed the impact of empty or irregularly occupied properties on one of these dimensions – demand for housing/access to affordable housing – in any great depth. There was a smaller literature that addressed impacts of second homes on community cohesion and viability, and the built environment. There is as yet no evidence that addresses the impact of empty or irregularly occupied property on a number of dimensions of community sustainability, notably: reputation or image of the community; crime and antisocial behaviour; social exclusion and poverty; and accessibility of facilities, services and employment.

Rural Housing Markets

- The issue of empty or irregularly occupied properties cannot be considered in isolation from the other processes of change within rural housing, including the undersupply of alternative forms of housing, changes to local economies, loss of industries and transport.
- Although it is widely believed that rural depopulation is a consequence of local residents' inability to compete with incomers in rural housing markets, many studies conclude that outward migration is more closely allied to a lack of employment, education, and leisure opportunities than to a lack of housing.
- Low wage economies, restrictions on the supply of new housing and external demands combine to raise house prices and disadvantage many local people in rural housing markets.
- Second homes remain a localised phenomenon. Certainly their national significance in Wales, at least, has declined over the last decade.

- Second homes are not the sole source of external demand; however they have been subjected to more attention than other external demands such as commuting and retirement.
- Ageing and retirement are the key factors likely to impact on housing markets in the next 25 years.

Community Cohesion

- Early studies indicate that second home ownership was seen by host communities to be part of a wider process of social change rather than a cause of outward migration.
- Attitudes towards second home ownership vary between locations; areas where tourism and recreation have been dominant appear to be more tolerant of second home ownership.
- There is little evidence of conflict between second homeowners and local residents.
- Profiles of second home owners indicate that they are generally middle aged or retired, and wealthier than the national average, however much of the profile data is more than 20 years old.
- It is difficult to compare 'incomers' with 'locals' as few studies profile host communities.
- More recent studies report concerns that the age profile of rural communities is unbalanced, as younger people migrate away and are replaced by older incomers.
- Demand for housing from commuters, the retired and second home owners has changed the profile of rural communities.

Community Viability

- Second home ownership was seen to make a useful contribution to local economies as part of the tourist industry, but differences in levels of contribution between different localities make generalisations regarding the impact of second home ownership problematic.
- Spending on renovation and modernisation of second homes has in the past bought new income into local economies, however these are one-off spends.
- Through payment of local taxes, second home owners support public services in their host communities without creating additional demands.

- There is little evidence regarding the contemporary spending of second home owners on local services such as retail and leisure.
- Early studies suggested that employment related to renovation was created by second home ownership; however, more recent evidence suggests that any additional jobs are low skilled and seasonal.

Built Environment

- Early studies suggested that second home ownership had a positive impact on the built environment particularly with regard to conservation and renovation of previously derelict properties.
- No studies address broader environmental concerns.

The Impact and Effectiveness of Policy Interventions

We identified few studies that had evaluated policy interventions, and these were mainly concerned with empty properties as opposed to second homes. There was, however, a larger literature that investigated the type of local policies that were in place to control second home ownership, and various policy recommendations were presented.

Second Homes – Policies, Policy Evaluations, and Policy Recommendations

- Only a minority of local authorities and National Parks in England and Wales report having a specific policy towards second homes. Where these policies do exist, they usually relate to occupancy controls on new dwellings.
- Recent research in England suggests strong support from authorities for greater powers in respect of second homes, although fiscal measures are preferred over planning controls.
- Evaluations of specific policy interventions towards second homes have been very limited and have focused upon the use of restrictions on occupancy on new development.
- Very little work has been undertaken to assess the impact of local occupancy on rural housing markets; instead research has focused on mechanisms for delivering affordable housing in the countryside.

- Authors' policy recommendations reflected the period in which their research was conducted. Most recently authors suggest planning and policy tools should be used in a focused way and targeted on those communities with the greatest housing pressures, with greater partnership working between local government and rural communities.

Empty Properties: Outcomes of Policy Evaluations

- Policy intervention directed at bringing empty property back into use in rural Scotland appear to offer a way of addressing housing need, especially in remoter rural locations where development of new affordable housing by housing association may prove problematic.

Conclusions

Part of the rationale for undertaking this report was to reflect on the specific benefits that the methods of systematic reviewing can bring to social policy, using the example of an investigation of the impact of empty and irregularly occupied dwellings on the sustainability of rural communities.

Given the often emotive nature of the view of second home ownership as a key driver causing dwellings in rural areas to be empty or irregularly occupied, the approach of 'going back to basics', rigorously searching for material, and considering only empirical evidence (rather than opinion or observations), allows reflection on the topic in a more neutral way. This is not to say that the study can claim objectivity or transparency, but allows the reader to see how and why decisions have been made through the process of this review, and how the available evidence has been handled. In this respect systematic reviewing offers a valuable set of methods in approaching the secondary analyses of existing evidence. However, whether a systematic review is perceived to be more rigorous and valuable in terms of output and findings than a traditional literature review conducted by experts in their field remains an empirical question.

Further, in looking afresh at the empirical evidence contained in existing studies, a systematic review attempts to draw out answers to questions which the original research may not have been designed or set up to answer. This represented a challenge but it is important to note that the difficulty relates to the process of asking research studies to answer questions which are not their primary focus rather than xii to any fault in the original studies. Nevertheless, a defining feature of much of the evidence in relation to empty or irregularly occupied property is its age. A considerable body of work investigating second homes, particularly, relates to UK society over twenty years ago. The value of more recent evidence on second homes lies in highlighting the scale of the issue and the efficacy of possible policy responses. However, in relation to providing a succinct answer to the two questions regarding the impact of empty or irregularly occupied dwellings on the sustainability of rural communities and the effectiveness of policy interventions, the available empirical evidence is limited, and this in itself is useful to know.

Introduction

This introductory chapter describes the background to the development of this ESRC-funded review of the evidence regarding the effects of privately owned empty or irregularly occupied properties on the sustainability of rural communities, and the extent to which policy interventions have mitigated these effects. The chapter explains why a systematic review of this area of public policy is important, and introduces the relevant policy context.

Introducing the Study: Developing Evidence-based Policy

There is a growing requirement for public policy to be evidence-based. A key tool in the formulation of evidence-based policy is the systematic review which seeks to provide a comprehensive assessment of existing knowledge in a given area through extensive searching and critical appraisal of available evidence. The methods of systematic reviewing are commonly used in the fields of health, and education, and are increasingly being adopted to consider social and public policy topics. The ESRC has funded a programme of research projects that aim to develop and refine the methodologies required for the identification, appraisal and synthesis of evidence in the social policy context, and examine how evidence-based policy can be generated in a number of social policy areas.

As part of this ESRC programme, the University of York has established an 'evidence node' in health and social policy, focusing upon the methodology of reviews in social policy and social care. The first review undertaken by the node examined the evidence related to the effectiveness of current public and private safety nets available to mortgagors in unforeseen financial difficulties, attempting to link policy responses or 'interventions' with specific outcomes, notably mortgage arrears and repossessions.

Other reviews undertaken by the York node have addressed how carers access health care and the effectiveness of respite services for careers of people with dementia-type illnesses. A number of other reviews have also been generated by the ESRC programme at other academic centres in the UK. As intended, this growing body of work has helped to stimulate methodological debate and development regarding how systematic reviews can be undertaken in complex policy areas. This review therefore adds to the growing body of work undertaken at the University of York and elsewhere and has two purposes: to provide a rigorous and authoritative account of the evidence in the topic area; and to take forward some of the methodological debates related to undertaking reviews in complex policy areas raised by Croucher *et al.* (2003).

Why Undertake a Review in This Topic Area?

A review in this area of interest is timely. The topic addresses key national and local policy concerns, notably sustainable communities and housing demand. The complexities of the policy context also present particular methodological challenges. Furthermore, the social and economic impacts of second homes, in particular, on rural communities are contested, and have been the focus of considerable, often emotive debate over the last few decades.

Policy Context

As part of its publication *Sustainable Communities: Building for the Future* (Office of the Deputy Prime Minister [ODPM], 2003) the Government has developed the themes that were identified in the Rural White Paper to tackle social exclusion. The policy agenda has set out its intentions with respect to sustainable and inclusive communities principally through the development of affordable housing. Housing is not only the major contributor to the experience of disadvantage in rural areas, but has been described as the principal engine of social change in rural England. At the same time, these policy developments are linked with sustaining and developing rural economies, particularly in relation to tourism, alongside the maintenance of environmental quality.

Vacant or Empty Properties

A fundamental issue in relation to the maintenance of sustainable communities in the countryside is the extent to which the stock of residential dwellings in any community is fully occupied. The government have drawn attention to the issue of stock under-utilisation. Dwellings may be empty or irregularly occupied for a variety of reasons. Research has drawn attention to the need to distinguish between two types of vacant dwellings. The first, *transactional vacants*, are an inherent function of the housing market and represent properties vacant whilst being sold or let. Included in this type are properties undergoing renovation or improvement and which are intended to be reoccupied relatively quickly. In contrast, the second type can be described as *problematic vacants*, and are unoccupied for substantial periods of time and are often in poor condition. There are many reasons for dwellings remaining vacant for considerable periods of time. The consultation paper on empty homes issued by the ODPM (2003) identified factors such as dilapidated dwellings, requiring substantial investment to bring up them to a habitable standard; in extreme cases buildings that have been abandoned by their owners; cases where ownership is unresolved, say if an occupant died intestate; properties held as speculative assets; property held as an investment, say for retirement; and property held by two home owners who begin cohabiting, leaving the other property vacant. The consultation paper noted that the latter two examples are often viewed as second homes. A significant additional factor in the rural context is that vacant properties may arise as a result of the rationalisation of agricultural labour on farm holdings and estates, which has led to a considerable number of dwellings becoming redundant as tied accommodation, although owners have often been reluctant to sell or let these dwellings on the open market.

Second and Holiday Homes

Cutting across these policy areas are the factors of production and consumption in relation to leisure and housing. Increased leisure time and cultural and lifestyle choices can be expressed in the free market through the consumption of property and can act as one component of the drivers of social change in rural areas that the Government is seeking to mediate. A further variable is the use of property for leisure purposes that also coincides with individual strategies in relation to retirement planning and investment. Such dynamics have contributed to an increase in second home ownership and an influx of households into the countryside. An essential feature of such migration, alongside other migration flows resulting from commuting or retirement, is that it is differentiated by income and wealth and throws into sharp relief the unequal capacities within the general population to attain owner occupation in the countryside. As part of these phenomena, second homes have a localised impact in rural localities leading to micro-crises in local housing markets.

Policy Responses

Policy responses to second and holiday homes are centred around attempts to mitigate the impact of demand-led pressures on the rural housing stock. In contrast, policies aimed at tackling vacant dwellings in the private sector are focused upon supply-led considerations encouraging, or compelling, owners to bring properties back into use. The issue of empty homes was the subject of recent policy attention in England in the form of the consultation paper *Empty Homes: Temporary Management, Lasting Solutions* (ODPM, 2003). This paper set out a range of approaches for tackling empty homes, including the potential for new statutory powers for local authorities to take over the management of some private sector empty homes.

A rationale for policies aimed at bringing empty properties back into use in rural areas is that they enable more households to live in these communities. This has a knock-on effect on the viability of local services and facilities such as shops and schools. Further, such schemes often ensure that such properties are targeted on households that need affordable housing. There are a number of examples of schemes at national level, such as the rural empty property initiative in Scotland, or at local level, the farm cottage scheme, run by Kennet District Council, Wiltshire.

Second and holiday homes occupy the interface between the two policy areas of leisure and housing. Tensions between these policy areas were highlighted by the operation of the controversial policy in the Yorkshire Dales National Park whereby a redundant barn could be converted into accommodation for a holiday home, but could not be converted into a permanent dwelling to meet a local housing need. This policy was subsequently revised, and indeed, Yorkshire Dales National

Park recently adopted a policy whereby the sale of new homes or barn conversions will be restricted to buyers who qualify under the scheme as 'local'.

At the same time, the subject of second homes has been increasingly the focus of policy attention at the national level. The Government legislated to reduce the discount on second homes in England with respect to council tax from 50 per cent to ten per cent and Part 6 (Council Tax Provisions) of the Local Government Bill came into force in 2003.

Local authorities can spend any additional funds thus raised on improving public services such as transport, affordable housing or policing. However, it is significant that the discount will not be removed entirely, and will be set at a minimum of ten per cent. It is hoped that this retained discount will provide an incentive for individuals to continue to register their second homes to enable local authorities to monitor the scale and impact of second home ownership within their areas.

This step marks the view that from a policy perspective it is deemed necessary to separate out the impact of second home ownership from other influences upon local housing markets. Similarly, local authorities in Scotland have the new power to reduce the discount on second homes from 50 per cent to ten per cent. It will come into effect at the start of the financial year 2005-06. Any additional income generated by cutting the discount will be retained locally and used to provide new-built affordable social housing Unitary authorities in Wales have had the discretion to charge full council tax on second homes since 1998. The research by Tewdwr-Jones *et al.* (2002) noted that by 2001, all but two of 22 authorities had done this.

Policy attention at local level has also focused upon the issue of second homes. A review of planning authorities in other parts of the UK has noted that a number of authorities are proposing specific second homes policies for their areas. For example, the Draft Unitary Development Plan for Gwynedd Council sets out that any proposal for developments that would lead to an increase in second homes will be refused in communities where the level of second homes has reached ten per cent.

Whilst policy documents in particular note that such use of dwellings on an irregular basis in rural areas may have both positive and negative impacts, the costs and benefits of second and holiday homes have not been elaborated in a systematic way. Further, it is necessary to understand the diverse impacts that vacant, second and holiday homes have upon rural housing markets and economies in the context of sustainable communities.

Methodological Challenges

In addition to the policy relevance, the context for the review is complex and presents particular methodological challenges. A clearly defined question is the essential first step in undertaking a systematic review; the question frames the review, generates the consequent search strategies and study selection criteria. In addressing review questions in complex policy areas, however, it is necessary to resolve the tension between the defined question (and seeking the material to address that question), and the requirement to provide a 'contextual map' in order to understand the question and make the conclusions of a review meaningful.

Croucher *et al.* (2003) recognised that although the focus of their review was on the various safety nets available to mortgagors, the findings of the review had to be seen in the wider context of a complex interaction of factors-economic cycles, interest rates, housing prices, financial regulation and lenders' practices-that impact on sustainable home ownership. The context for this review is similarly complex.

Various factors, such as the growth of home ownership and the 'Right-to-Buy' legislation, changing patterns of employment, and the so-called 'flight from the cities', have resulted in growing housing demands in rural areas from both local people and new residents, high house prices, and a lack of social rented housing. Evidence gathered in the Countryside Agency's annual 'state of the countryside' reports indicate growing housing demand from local people and new residents, high house prices, low incomes, and a lack of social rented housing in many rural areas.

However, demand for housing and the operation of housing markets must be seen against a broader background of on-going socioeconomic and environmental changes occurring in the countryside. A review of the impact of empty or irregularly occupied properties, particularly second homes, must therefore be located in this complex context.

In preparing this review we have not sought to provide a 'contextual map' as time and resources did not allow for the examination of the wider contextual literature. Fortunately the Countryside Agency has recently published a review of countryside issues in England, drawing on the evidence collated between 1999-2003 for the preparation of the annual 'state of the countryside' reports. It provides a valuable portrait of emerging trends across a number of key themes, including: rural demography; health and social care provision; education; transport; environment and recreation; and the rural economy. It provides a valuable background to our review. A further methodological challenge relates to the difficulties of defining key concepts such as 'rural', 'second home', and 'sustainability'. In Chapter Two we present the definitions we have adopted for the purpose of the review. It is important to note latthis point that our thinking regarding sustainability has been shaped by the work of Long (2001).

Indeed the dimensions of sustainability outlined by Long provided a framework for organising the evidence we retrieved. Long presents a series of headings relating to different aspects of sustainability including: housing demand; quality and design of housing; crime and antisocial behaviour; social exclusion and poverty; accessibility and viability of facilities; and community cohesion. We have sought to present the evidence against these headings, in an attempt to distinguish the different ways in which empty and irregularly occupied properties impact on rural host communities.

As noted above the social and economic impacts of second homes, in particular, on rural communities are contested. There are about 100,000 second homes in rural England representing less than 1% of the total stock; nevertheless second homes are widely perceived to be a manifestation of social inequality, and a main cause of rural housing shortages. A review in a contested area such as this may be particularly useful in moving the debate forward.

Report Structure

This report is presented in seven chapters. Chapter Two presents a detailed account of the methods and definitions employed in the review. Chapter Three presents a commentary on the research methods adopted by the studies – highlighting some of the difficulties regarding different definitions particularly of 'second homes', and the range of methods used in the studies that entered the review. Chapter Four presents the substantive findings of the review examining the impact of empty, second and holiday homes upon the sustainability of rural communities.

The nature of policy interventions on empty, second and holiday homes, examining studies that have evaluated policy mechanisms, and also drawing together recommendations for policy, which have been set out by various studies in the review. Chapter Six addresses the particular methodological challenges encountered during the review process. Finally Chapter Seven provides the conclusions from the review, highlighting possible avenues for future research. Substantial appendices are attached for reference, providing more detail on the search strategies, data abstraction methods and studies included and excluded from the review.

Methods

Introduction-What is a Systematic Review?

A systematic review aims to provide a comprehensive and unbiased summary of available evidence on a given topic. This is achieved by: the use of a clearly defined search strategy to ensure that an extensive range of potential sources of evidence is explored; and the use of explicit criteria to appraise the quality of the evidence to ensure that only robust evidence is synthesised in the production of the final review. The review process is guided by a protocol in which the approach to be taken by the review team is explained in some detail, making transparent the basis on which decisions will be made, the source of studies, the reasons why studies will be included or excluded from the review, how quality will be assessed, and on what basis the data will be synthesised. Once a review is underway a greater understanding of the content and type of literature may develop. If it is found that changes to parts of the protocol are necessary, these are documented and justified within the final report of the review.

Systematic reviews are complex (and often costly) studies, but they offer an invaluable means for policy makers and practitioners to make sense of large volumes of evidence that may be difficult and time consuming to locate and of variable quality. In addition they can be used to direct future research towards that which is poorly understood or under-researched. The six stages of the review process are set out in Table.

Table : Review process

1. *Formulate the review question/s.*
2. *Develop review protocol .*
    - *Define appropriate study design,*
    - *Define quality assessment criteria,*
    - *Devise search strategy,*
    - *Devise data abstraction method,*
    - *Decide data synthesis method,*
3. *Document identification and retrieval.*
4. *Application of study selection criteria.*
5. *Extraction and synthesis of data from studies entered into the review.*
6. *Presentation of review findings.*

Location and Timing of Studies

Study inclusion was limited to material in English published in the UK. It was beyond the scope of this review to examine literature from other countries as interpretation of any studies retrieved would require a comprehensive understanding of that country's cultural norms regarding housing markets, finance systems and perhaps leisure trends. It is unknown whether restricting the search in this way omitted any research that included empirical data relating to the UK that was not published in the UK, although this seems unlikely. The resources available to the review did not allow the additional effort required to locate, retrieve and filter literature from outside the UK. In setting the boundaries of a review, it is usually necessary to decide a 'cut-off' point, where evidence from before a given time is considered to be less useful as it addresses concerns or interventions that are too far removed from current context and practice to be meaningful. There was no obvious date that would provide a logical cutoff point for research in this field.

There were no major policy changes that would suggest any prior research was inappropriate (with the possible exception of the 1980 Housing Act that introduced the 'Right-to-Buy' council homes which had significant implications for rural areas) or notable housing market events that would suggest major changes in the field. Gallent *et al.* (2002) note that the theme of second homes flourished in academic literature in the 1970s.

Moreover many of these early studies continue to be frequently cited in more recent reports and publications. Initial scoping searches showed that we would not be overwhelmed with potentially relevant studies and so a decision was taken not to restrict studies on date. Studies were therefore included regardless of when they were published, which produced substantial debate within the review team surrounding the applicability of older research in this field to contemporary policy making, especially when examining dynamically changing housing markets. We return to this issue in Chapter Six.

Study Design

One of the challenges for a review addressing policy is deciding on the type of 'evidence' that will provide the most trustworthy answers to the review question/s, and this was a central concern for this review. We are aware there are lively debates about what constitutes 'good' or 'good enough' evidence when promoting evidence-based or evidence-informed policy and practice.

For the purpose of this review we took evidence to mean any contribution that is based upon primary empirical material as part of the study – be that qualitative or quantitative. Any study setting out views or opinions that could not be substantiated by its own empirical data was not included in the review. We recognise that there may be other types of 'evidence' that could have informed this review, however given that second home ownership is a highly politicised and emotive subject, we were keen to ensure that the evidence we included could be grounded directly in empirical research.

We also recognise the use of hierarchies of evidence in many systematic reviews – particularly in the health care field-that privilege experimental over other types of study design, as they are deemed to provide the most robust internally valid results when assessing the effectiveness and outcomes of health care inventions. For reviews in complex policy areas however, such hierarchies are less useful, in part due to the (almost complete) lack of experimental studies, but also because 'evidence' is more broadly defined and drawn from a range of research paradigms.

Study Selection Criteria-Quality Appraisal

One strength of systematic reviewing is the consistent critical appraisal of the evidence-base. It examines what is known about a subject and how confident we can be in this knowledge. It also ensures that the conclusions and recommendations derived from a review are based on evidence in which the research design and its conduct can be assumed to offer a reasonable level of confidence in the results. Studies of poor quality are therefore excluded. A quality criteria tool developed by Croucher *et al.* (2003) was chosen to establish whether a study met the quality threshold. Although there is little consensus over the use of appraisal tools in reviews, this tool has been successfully adopted by other reviewers since its development. It was also utilised in this review as reviewer and readers alike can readily understand it; it includes guidance on its practical application; it offers prompts to aid reflection on the study and is not resource intensive.

These criteria were applied to each study that met the initial inclusion criteria. As noted by Croucher *et al.* (2003), those criteria marked as essential are those with the potential to alter the findings of the research, and the reviewers had to be confident that studies going forward to the review had addressed these criteria satisfactorily. Those criteria marked as desirable aid interpretation of results and may help explain variance in findings.

Devising the Search Strategy

The aim of a search is to identify as comprehensive a list as possible of studies that relate to the review questions, reducing the potential for bias that may arise from too narrow a consideration of the field of investigation. A search strategy should therefore aim to be as inclusive as possible of the range of sources of primary studies, within the confines of resource constraints of the review. This section details how our search was conducted.

The subject of vacant and irregularly occupied property has relevance to a variety of different policy areas such as housing, planning, recreation and environmental health. Further, in an academic context, both housing and rural studies can be characterised as having a strong interdisciplinary focus. These features suggest that the search strategy needed to have a very broad focus. Research evidence was identified using a number of channels.

Table : Identifying Research

- *Searches of appropriate electronic databases.*
- *Reference checking of all articles received.*
- *Checking relevant internet sites.*
- *Hand searching of journals.*
- *Contact with a sample of local authorities with high concentrations of second homes.*

The review team included an Information Scientist from the NHS Centre for Reviews and Dissemination (NHS CRD) who developed and conducted the electronic search strategy working with the research team to establish key search terms, and potential sources of studies. The search terms included in the search strategy are set out in Appendix One. Recognising that many social science databases do not allow for sophisticated searching, the aim was to develop a strategy that would be highly sensitive, and facilitate identification of the greatest number of potentially relevant studies in the subject area.

Electronic Databases

Electronic databases represent a powerful source of references for a review. However different databases are constructed in different ways, and tend to specialise in certain types of data sources, or particular topics or disciplines. In addition, some are better indexed and contain more detailed abstracts than others. It is therefore important to utilise a range of databases within any one review. The requirement to search a range of databases is increased in a complex area of study, where different disciplines may have been involved and a range of approaches may have been taken to addressing research questions. As noted by Croucher *et al.* (2003), electronic databases do not appear to be as valuable a source of references for social policy reviews as for reviews on social care or health topics. Very few of the studies retrieved from electronic databases entered this review, nevertheless the studies provided a valuable source of additional references from which a number of included studies were drawn.

A full list of the databases searched is presented in Appendix One. A total of 10 were searched including the key social science databases (e.g. Social Science Citation Index and ASSIA), as well as the databases for related disciplines like economics (EconLit) and planning (Planex), and those covering grey literature (SIGLE). The inclusion of databases covering grey literature was thought to be particularly important as a significant number of the studies eventually included in the review conducted by Croucher *et al.* (2003) were retrieved from indexes of grey literature. Hansard was also searched for evidence cited in government sources.

The majority of databases were searched for no cost, as they are available through the University of York resources, or access to them at the British Library has been financially supported through the ESRC Evidence Network.

Only some databases were sophisticated enough to run a complex search. Those where this was possible include: Sociological Abstracts, SIGLE, ASSIA, Econlit, PAIS, SCCI and SSHICP. The remaining databases were searched using a simplified version of the search strategy. To ensure consistency in searching procedures, the search strategies were designed and undertaken by a specialist Information Officer from the NHS Centre for Reviews and Dissemination. The search strategies are presented in Appendix Two.

Internet Web Sites

Internet web sites can prove a valuable source of up-to-date material and grey literature. A number of websites were browsed for relevant documents. The websites searched in this review cover a range of national and local government sites, academic research institutes, professional organisations, and research funders. A list of these websites is presented in Appendix Three. As noted by Croucher *et al.* (2003), not all websites incorporate search engines or allow easy navigation. Although a number of potentially relevant references were found on the web (n=11), only one went forward for inclusion in the review.

Hand Searching

Electronic databases may be incomplete or not up to date in their coverage of the field so some hand searching was included in the search. Croucher *et al.* (2003) noted that in their review on safety nets for home owners that hand searching proved a fruitful source of studies for their review. Appendix Four includes a range of journals from policy and academic fields with a remit in the housing and rural 17 studies area that were hand searched for papers that may not have been catalogued on databases or cited elsewhere.

Reference Checking

The reviewers checked the reference lists of all retrieved literature for additional references, including unpublished material. Each new reference identified in this way was also searched in turn for new references until this process was exhausted. Citations in retrieved studies were an important way of tracing older studies. In this particular review, reference checking provided more that half of the studies that were finally included.

Local Authority Contacts

Local authorities are charged with undertaking comprehensive assessments of their local housing markets, although until recently this has primarily concentrated on the needs and requirements for social housing. Nevertheless, it was thought that certain local authorities may have undertaken research into empty or irregularly occupied dwellings, given the reported level of interest in this issue and recent policy changes concerning the council tax reductions for second homes.

It was thought too onerous to canvas each rural local authority in the UK; therefore, a sample of authorities in England and Wales, identified by FPD Savills (2004) as having in excess of three per cent of dwelling stock used as second homes, were contacted and asked about research in their area. A list of the authorities contacted is presented in Appendix Five.

If more time had been available the comprehensiveness of the review would have been improved by contacting authorities in similar positions in Scotland and Northern Ireland. One Welsh county council provided major reports by key researchers that had not been identified elsewhere, however other local authorities did not appear to possess significant unpublished research.

Document Identification and Retrieval

The search process produced 1060 references. Once duplicate references were removed, a total of 963 remained. All references were entered into Reference Manager, an essential tool to ensure that the progress of each reference at each stage of the review is tracked and recorded. The number of studies retrieved at each stage of the review, broken down by source of reference. If studies were unavailable within the research unit or University of York's library then they were obtained from the British Library Documents Supply Centre or other university libraries and inter-loans arranged. We were unable to obtain some studies and these are detailed in Appendix Six.

Applying the Selection Criteria

The initial reference set of 1060 reports and studies became the 23 included in this review. After the lead reviewer scanned each reference, 273 were identified as being potentially relevant and copies of the reports retrieved. If the relevance was uncertain because of the absence, or quality, of the abstracts then the report was retrieved anyway. The reports were then examined in more detail and checked against the inclusion criteria. Studies that looked likely to pass the inclusion criteria were then subjected to the data extraction process using the form in Appendix Seven, which was created with Microsoft Access. At least two reviewers checked the decisions made regarding the application of the inclusion criteria and quality appraisal, with disagreements decided by consensus within the whole review team. This left 30 studies that met the inclusion criteria but 7 of these did not meet the quality threshold, meaning a total of 23 studies went forward to the final reDetails of the seven studies that did not meet the quality threshold are included in Appendix Eight. Three of these were conducted for Masters or Diplomas in Town Planning, and, although they demonstrated sufficient understanding of the topic and research methods, were not adequately robust to meet the quality threshold of this review. One other study did not use methods that were sensitive enough to capture data relating to second homes, or other empty or irregularly occupied properties, as acknowledged by the authors. Two further studies did not contain enough information about the methods used in the study to convey any confidence in the findings reported. Although this may have been due to poor reporting rather than poor research, it was nevertheless problematic. Finally one study mainly reported an unsystematic literature review; although there was some new research reported in addition to secondary data, again this was not reported in sufficient detail.

Wallace *et al.* (2004) report how some authors express concern at the reduction of such large initial reference sets to the small numbers of studies that go forward for review, suggesting that a large quantity of relevant evidence is being lost in the process. The two most common reasons for studies not passing the inclusion criteria were that they did not address the issues of empty or irregularly occupied property or were not based upon empirical research. Many studies did not pass the inclusion criteria in the review of assistance for mortgagors in financial difficulties for very similar reasons, either they did not pass the inclusions criteria or were not empirical studies.

As reported in Arksey *et al.* (2004) the table should be treated with some caution when assessing the utility of different databases for the review. Once the initial references were received the duplicate entries from different databases were removed according to a hierarchy of databases relevant to this review. The less sophisticated databases, such as Planex or IBSS, were deduplicated against the more specific ones, such as SSCI, SSHI, SocAbs, SIGLE, Econlit or ASSIA. Nevertheless, it is interesting to note the dominance of grey literature databases and reference checking as sources of studies for this systematic review. As in Croucher *et al.* (2003), the academic peer-reviewed databases were less helpful as a supply of studies that were worth consideration for the review. It is apparent that journal articles are not the prime publication source of primary research in housing. Those journal papers that were retrieved were usually excluded in favour of the main report to the commissioners, as they included more detail about the substantive topic and the research methods.

Document Retrieval

Most retrieval was conducted through the British Library Document Supply Centre (BLDSC), which generally worked very well. However, 35 reports were found to be potentially relevant but were unavailable through the BLDSC, the research commissioners or other libraries. These studies are listed in Appendix Six. They were mostly from the 1970s and generally evenly split between those focusing on second homes and those focusing on general rural housing issues. One of the reports dated from the 1960s, 14 from the 1970s, 5 from the 1980s, 10 from the 1990s and 1 from 2000 onwards. The 1970s reports were more concerned with second homes, and the 1990s reports with general rural housing issues. Many of these studies were produced at the local authority level, and not deposited within the public domain which may account for the difficulties in locating them. Emails and letters were sent to the rural authorities with the most concentrations of second homes, but apart from one authority where a particularly interested information officer was employed, this resulted in few studies being identified, despite local authorities being charged with conducting local housing market area analysis. The information officer with whom the review team was in contact actually supplied some key studies that were not identified through any databases but that were included in the final review. It is also of concern that fifteen studies conducted in the 1990s and 2000s were also unavailable. One of these was produced for a private client who would not agree to the full report being released, but others were requested from libraries and commissioning organisations with no success.

From the patterns of decisions made as the other reports went through the review process, it may be surmised that many of the reports would not have met the inclusion criteria for the review because they were not based upon empirical research. In addition many of the reports that focused on general rural housing issues may not have included work on empty or irregularly occupied properties, as it is likely that they may have only have addressed the supply of social housing or planning concerns, for example. It is likely, however, that the earlier studies on second homes would have been the most rewarding to have found, albeit that they are several decades old.

Data Abstraction and Synthesis

An electronic data extraction form was designed: to ensure a uniform and structured set of data was extracted from each study; to record the reasons for including or excluding studies from the review; and to aid comparison between the studies. Reviewers completed a form for each of the studies that passed the relevance criteria for the review. An Access database was used to manage data extraction forms. Over and above the bibliographic and descriptive data extracted from each study, these forms were used to record the different strands of evidence relating to the impacts of empty and irregularly occupied properties on the different dimensions of sustainability set out. In regard to policy initiatives data were abstracted regarding the structure, process, and outcome of policy.

Two matrices were developed. The first matrix charted the evidence from each study concerned with the impacts of empty and irregularly occupied properties on rural communities onto the different dimensions of sustainability. We drew on raw data from the studies and the interpretations of the authors of the studies. The second matrix charted different types of policy interventions – planning, fiscal, housing market, environmental – and evidence relating to their structure, process and outcomes. These matrices enabled us to organise the evidence around particular themes, and compare findings across different studies.

Achieving an actual synthesis of the findings has been problematic. In particular it has been a challenge to draw conclusions from evidence on housing markets. Housing markets are dynamic systems and change considerably across both time and location. In addition, the disparate nature of the studies, in terms of case study areas, time when research was conducted, various methods adopted, and inconsistent definition across studies means the review relies heavily on a descriptive account of study findings. The review team are aware of the debates surrounding methods in narrative synthesis but recognise that more empirical testing of various approaches is required to develop these methods further.

Conclusion

The review has presented particular methodological challenges. These are further explored in Chapter Six. We are confident however that the rigour of the search ensures that very little evidence has been overlooked, and that through the application of study selection criteria only robust evidence has been synthesised and presented in the findings of this review view. Definitions of empty, second and holiday homes.

The definition of what constitutes a second home or holiday home has been a perennial problem. This is an issue in all aspects of the research as it impedes comparison between studies and has the potential to cause confusion.

Although individual studies may provide a clear definition of the types of accommodation that were included or excluded, it is unclear whether studies that compared evidence from other research findings to each other or to the Census material were talking about the same phenomena. For example, a study that reported the growth in second home ownership in local areas may have recorded the growth in purpose built holiday villages, rather than existing dwellings in villages, smaller settlements or dwellings that stand alone in remote countryside.

A degree of permanence relating to the dwelling physical structure was often included in definitions of second homes. However, other studies included chalets, log cabins and static caravans. Their inclusion could be problematic as the analysis did not always disaggregate the findings for these distinct parts of the second homes market. It was therefore capable of overestimating the number of second homes in a locality with potential as permanent first homes for local people. Local demand for residence in holiday parks, with chalets, log cabins or static caravans, appears to be generated by lack of other housing opportunities rather than housing preferences, although residency in Park Homes may be more long term. Exploring these differences would have added some clarity to any analysis of the degree of competition in the local housing market between locals and second home owners.

Several studies were careful to draw a distinction in principle between second homes and holiday homes, Tewdwr-Jones *et al.* (2000), Pyne 1973, South West Economic Planning Council, 1975, Bennett, 1979, Davies and O'Farrell, 1981, Capstick, 1987). However, difficulties with differentiating between a second and holiday home were readily acknowledged by a number of the studies. Bielckus also noted that where households owned two properties, it was not always clear which could be defined as the first home or second home, since the way in which such properties were used, and also length of occupancy in the different residences were not always clear cut.

Distinctions were also blurred between the dwellings used as holiday homes and second homes, as second homes were sometimes let to defray costs associated with ownership. One study defined holiday homes as a reduction in supply and conceptualised them as part of the tourist stock of accommodation, such as hotels. This may also be problematic if looking comprehensively at demand in local housing markets as they remain dwellings unavailable for use as permanent residence for local people but have been removed in the analysis of total dwelling stocks.

Some definitions emphasised the use made of the dwelling for leisure or recreation. As there are changing patterns of employment for some, with home-working, tele-working and dual income households, the distinction may today be less clear. One partner may use the 'other' dwelling to work from whilst the other does not, as household and working arrangements become more diverse. This pattern of changing housing consumption has yet to be explored in research concerning second or holiday homes.

Identifying Empty and Irregularly Occupied Property

A fundamental difficulty that studies have sought to address is the identification of an accurate figure of the number of empty, second homes and holiday homes, either nationally, or in case study areas. As has been noted above, this difficulty relates in part to the definition of the types of dwelling that constitute empty, second and holiday homes. A further difficulty stems from the way that empty, second and holiday homes are identified in sources of data, and potential confusion over the precise use to which dwellings are put. Subsequently, these factors have implications for the comparison of the number of empty, second and holiday homes between studies and over time.

The Census provides a readily accessible source, in that it attempts to measure the number of empty, second and holiday homes. The Census has provided data on second and holiday homes every ten years since 1981 – prior to this, second homes were not recorded in the Census. However, whilst the 1981 and 1991 Censuses differentiated between second homes and holiday homes, the 2001 Census only included an aggregate figure including both second and holiday homes. Furthermore, studies have highlighted that it is likely that the Census undercounts the actual number of second homes. Second/holiday homes were identified in the 2001 Census as being distinct from vacant dwellings either by the enumerator or from a household completing a Census form for an address that was not their principal residence. Households that returned a form where all household members are visitors are classed as second or holiday home. Unoccupied dwellings are classified as a second or holiday home if at least one of the household spaces within it (or the single household space if the dwelling is unshared) is a second or holiday home. However, as Gallent *et al.* (2002) point out, enumerators exclude properties that are not known to be secondary residences or holiday homes, and this is where an undercount may occur. These authors also noted that it is not known to what extent second homes are enumerated as occupied accommodation on Census night.

Difficulties in accurately distinguishing between empty, second or holiday homes was also noted by Murie *et al.* (1995) who described problems in the way in which properties are recorded as empty by surveyors as part of surveys of empty properties in Scotland. A number of properties recorded as empty were in fact second or holiday homes, which casts doubt on the way these are recorded. For example, the Post Census Survey of Vacant Properties (PCSVP) was conducted in 1991 by the General Register Office for Scotland as a follow up survey of properties classified by Census enumerators as being vacant on Census night. It did not include households spaces identified in the Census as not used as main residence or occupied household spaces where the household was absent on Census night. The qualitative research conducted by Murie *et al.* (1995) noted problems with the classification between these two categories and the truly vacant category and suggested that it was probable that some vacants were student housing or were second or holiday homes. Other research on empty properties in Scotland has reinforced this finding. The evaluation of the Scottish Empty Homes Initiative found that many properties identified as empty were in fact being used as holiday homes.

A further concern about the Census is that it only provides data every ten years, and thus the figures soon date. Studies subsequently need to have recourse to other sources to obtain current numbers between Censuses. Historically, rating registers have provided an important source of data for studies of second homes. The majority of the studies undertaken in the 1970s drew upon rating registers for this purpose. However, the registers did not identify second home owners directly, and instead noted which owners had an address outside of the county. Thus they only indicated the possibility of dwellings used as second homes. Surveys were then required to identify which properties were actually used as second homes. However, in line with the identified drawbacks of the Census, a number of studies recognised that such methods might lead to an undercount of the actual number of second homes. As highlighted by the De Vane (1975) study, the work by Tuck (1973) and Pyne (1973) estimated that the rating register undercounted second homes by about ten per cent.

To attempt to mitigate this undercount, a number of studies used alternative sources to identify second homes to complement the figures drawn from the rating registers. Thus Coleman (1982), Bennett (1976), Bollom (1975), De Vane (1975), the South West Economic Planning Council (1975), Tuck (1973) used a case study approach to draw on alternative sources to corroborate the figures identified from the rating register. These studies used the local knowledge of local residents to try and identify second homes in their respective settlements. Bollom (1975) and the South West Economic Planning Council (1975) also used the electoral register as a method of identifying possible second homes. Other studies used field surveys such as Davies and O'Farrell (1981) – an approach which may offer the potential for additional accuracy, but which would be a costly method to reproduce in future research.

Recent research such as Gallent *et al.* (2002) identifies council tax returns as the most promising source of data on second homes, although these authors also highlighted drawbacks. To a certain extent confusion arises from the way that properties may, or may not, be registered by owners for council tax. At the time that the research by Gallant *et al.* (2002) was undertaken, a 50% discount for properties used as second homes was available, and the authors point out that, individuals may not necessarily have claimed the discount of 50%, even though they may have been eligible, thereby removing themselves from any count. Murie *et al.* (1995) also noted that in Scotland, although the majority of dwellings that qualified for two discounts for council tax were second homes, this number was not wholly accurate as a count for second homes specifically. Greater clarity over second home numbers may develop as local authorities in Scotland develop their monitoring and identification of second home owners as part of the billing process.

Which Methods Have Studies Used?

The authors of the various studies had employed a mixture of methods, primarily surveys, interviews and discussion groups with various key respondents. Some also utilised secondary data sources such as previous research or market surveys. The summary table in Appendix Nine includes a brief description of the methods employed by each study.

Surveys

Many of the earlier studies undertook large-scale postal surveys of second home owners. Second home owners were usually identified through rating registers. Two smaller studies also surveyed much smaller samples of second home owners. Questions posed to second home owners addressed a variety of topics across the different studies; for example, location of primary residence and distances travelled to second homes, seasonal use of property, frequency and length of visits, amenities used, average expenditure, age and socioeconomic status of second home owners, as well as questions about the location, age and state of repair, and amenities in the properties used as second homes. Other studies surveyed rural officers in local authorities, and local estate agents.

Case Studies

Nearly all the studies investigated second homes in different case study areas although the location and connection between the case studies varied. Only one study considered case study areas across the UK. Others used case studies in particular nations or other 31 defined geographic areas such as a National Park. These multi-area case studies were very useful to illustrate the diversity in the experiences of the same phenomena displayed in different local housing markets. Only two studies considered second homes in a single location.

Key Informants

A key feature of this body of research was collating the views, experiences and judgements of key informants on various aspects of empty, second and holiday homes through surveys or interviews and discussions. However there was some variation across the studies regarding the type of respondents that were considered as key informants, reflected to some extent the shifting focus of the research.

As noted above, a feature of studies investigating second homes in rural areas in the 1970s and 1980s was a focus on assessing impacts by surveying second home owners themselves. With the exception of one study, all the studies also presented local residents' views regarding second home owners and, sometimes, local housing demand, usually via interviews/discussion groups with local residents, although an alternative approach used by many of the studies was to examine impacts of second homes by contacting local key informants. In some instances, these informants included local contacts, such as police, local businesses, members of the clergy. Some studies reflected methods of gauging local feelings that would now be considered inappropriate for research. Examples include using village gatekeepers such as the clergy, police officers, postmasters or teachers. With greater commuting and turnover in employment, the ability of such professions to talk on behalf of a community may be more limited today. Moreover, it may be more acceptable to actually the hear the voices of those who are the subjects of that part of the study, for example, holding focus groups of villagers. On a similar theme, no studies interviewed or surveyed first time buyers in rural areas, and yet their ability to enter owner occupation underpinned many assumptions about the problems second homes may be causing.

One study held a focus group of young people, but they were not engaged in the process of registering or searching for property to rent or own at that time. Although, one study did make the point that the ability of households to trade up as household circumstances change is also vital for sustainable communities and so retaining existing homeowners is a problem in areas of high house price rises. Inclusion of data from those making house searches in case study areas would be beneficial for comprehensive analysis, to highlight similarities or differences between the type and price of property they are seeking to buy.

A considerable proportion of the studies also interviewed professionals in the public and/or private sectors. Many studies used the knowledge of housing and planning officials or staff from housing associations to gauge knowledge about local housing markets. However, many local authorities did not have housing needs assessments and some were out of date. Few had conducted comprehensive housing market analysis and so the ability of these people to comment on the local housing market was drawn mainly from their local knowledge and experience of the areas where they worked. Government and regulatory pressure has recently been exerted on local authorities to conduct more comprehensive analyses of local, sub-regional and regional housing markets, and so it is hoped that local policymakers will have a more robust evidence-base on which to draw in the future. There are already richer sources of contemporary data available now relating to house prices and neighbourhoods. These data are available at small output levels, such as the Census and other official statistics and market research tools such as Mosaic.

Some studies presented data based on interviews with estate agents; however, it was unclear whether a range of local agents had been sampled and the how the data were analysed. Greater use could have been made of key players – estate agents, lenders and solicitors – in the private market to provide more information about market processes and gauge levels of inward and outward migration.

Other studies interviewed key informants such as local tradesmen, planners and local residents to gauge the impact of second home ownership on local economies. These interviews were rarely supported with financial information.

Secondary Data

Some studies also drew on secondary data such as government report and market research data, Census, employment and labour market statistics, statistics on vacant properties, and Local Plans in Wales, Scotland and England.

Limitations of the Studies

The political problematisation of second homes has, in effect, led to the focus of the initial questions posed and research commissioned perhaps being too narrowly defined. The issue of second homes has been, with notable exceptions, studied in isolation from other expressions of external demand in local areas, such as retirement and commuting.

The study of second homes in isolation from other drivers of housing demand meant that it was difficult to separate impacts attributed to second homes from other factors, although authors continued to attribute shortages of affordable housing for local people and external competition in housing markets to second homes. One author did, however, decide to abandon the aim of assessing the impact of second homes on house prices as it was not possible to identify contrasting areas with high and low levels of second homes where direct comparison between housing markets could be achieved.

Where the issue of second homes was set within a wider economic and social context, authors drew on data from multiple case studies and examined other sources of external demand. For example, Gallent *et al.* (2002) noted that assessments of the economic impact of second homes in rural areas need to consider broader impacts such as e-shopping and the role of supermarkets in changing shopping habits of residents in rural areas. The multitude of factors from which housing market imbalances emerge should be included in any future analysis of rural housing markets.

The issue of second homes would be interesting to explore in the context, not only of the impacts on local housing markets, but as part of changing patterns of housing consumption, housing wealth and subsequent housing inequalities. The point of how home is interpreted was raised briefly in the evidence, but exploring this further in relation to use of second homes would be interesting, given changing patterns of work and residence.

Measures that have been taken to intervene in local markets have been poorly evaluated, such as those to restrict occupancy in National Parks, for example. Greater evaluation might shed light on the directions in which policy should develop in this respect.

2

Place Attachment of Vacation Residents

Introduction

Many different conceptions of the bond between people and places have been hypothesized and studied. The most widespread terms include place attachment, sense of place (SOP). One consistent thread woven throughout most recent research on place attachment deals with the importance of time spent at a. While both researchers and writers have made the case that time and experience in a place are important for deepening the meanings and emotional ties central to the person-place relationship, little in-depth research has studied these factors and their role in forging this connection. Accordingly, this study sought to provide a greater understanding of why and how time influences visitors' and residents' connections to places in Grand Teton National Park (GTNP) and Jackson Hole, WY.

Place Attachment Concepts and Time—Theory Overview

Place attachment, as defined as one's emotional or affective ties to a place, is generally thought to be the result of a long-term connection with a place. This is different from saying a place is special because it is beautiful, which is often a simple aesthetic response.

For example, one can have an emotional response to a beautiful (or ugly) landscape or place, but this response may sometimes be shallow and fleeting. This distinction is one that Schroeder (1991) labelled "meaning" versus "preference." He defined meaning as "the thoughts, feelings, memories and interpretations evoked by a landscape," and preference as "the degree of liking for one landscape compared to another". For a deeper and lasting emotional attachment to develop—in Schroeder's terms, for it to have meaning—an enduring relationship with a place is usually a critical factor. Research has generally focused on describing two main aspects of place attachment, place identity and place dependence. Place dependence emerged from a framework proposed by Stokols & Schumaker (1981) and is described as the person's perceived strength of association with the place. The focus of place dependence has been on the functional aspects of one's connection to place: does it meet some functional or useful need? Length of association with the place, as well as past experiences, both play a role in creating and strengthening place dependence. Stokols and Shumaker (1981) argued that endurance and frequency are two critical objective properties of person-place association.

Endurance refers to the length of place association, while frequency refers to the number of times the person and place are associated. Therefore, the person-place bond always encompasses a temporal element. The concept of place identity was first elaborated upon with Proshansky et al.'s (1983) framework, and later modified by Korpela (1989), who proposed that it is a product of active environmental self-regulation, whereby an emotional attachment lies at the core of place identity. Thus, place identity has been defined as a more emotional, or even symbolic, dimension of place attachment that is also formed and strengthened over time.

Relph (1976) and Tuan (1977) also discussed timerelated concepts (insideness; rootedness) related to connections to places. Hummon's (1992) synthesis of works on community attachment found that long-term residence increases attachment feelings, partly through familiarity and experiencing significant events over time, but possibly even more importantly, through local social involvement. Studies of recreation places have also found that time seems to play a role in place attachment. Moore and Graefe (1994) quantitatively examined place attachment, dependence, and identity to recreational trails. They found that longer length of association, more frequent use, and greater proximity to the trails contributed to stronger scores on these measures of place attachment. They also noted differences in how these attachments form, with place dependence possibly developing quickly, while the more affective place identity required longer periods of time. Other studies have found similar relationships between place attachment and various measures of length of association.

Change in Meanings Over Time

One issue has been that few studies have separated a place's significance to an individual from how attached the individual is to the place and its meanings. As Stedman (2002) noted, place attachment (a measure of strength) is different from the place meanings (the what and why) to which one is attached. While a person's place attachment is in part based on the meanings attributed to a place, he argued the constructs should be separated.

Some researchers have noted that place meanings may be influenced by one's length of association with a place. For example, Kiteyama and Markus (1994) suggested that a person's sense of place may change over time, with the salience of different features changing over the course of their time in a place. They proposed that newcomers might view their connection to a region as based more on environmental features, whereas those who have been in the region longer tend to view their connection more in the context of their social relations at the place. This hypothesis was partly supported by Mitchell et al.'s (1993) study on recreational users of a national forest. Cantrill (1998) and Cantrill & Senecah (2000) also found some evidence for this hypothesis in residents of a community in Michigan. Interview respondents who had lived in the community for less than 15 years were more likely to discuss the natural/environmental features of the area when describing their sense of place, while residents who had lived in the area for more than 15 years were more likely to reference their social relations. This reinforces the findings from various community studies.

Lingering Questions

Quantitative studies have found that length of association with a place—through time—seems to play an important role in place attachment. But these studies provide less insight into how and why time is involved in the process of forming place attachment. Qualitative studies have begun to address these relationships. For instance, studies using interviews have pointed to aspects of time that influence the attachment process through the development of different place meanings, changes in those place meanings over time, and the role of continuity in strengthening person-place bonds.

Study Purpose

In the present study, quantitative methods were used to confirm and further describe the role of time in place attachment, and qualitative methods were used to describe the underlying process of why and how time can influence the formation of place attachments and their associated meanings. Based on previous research, the key research question explored was: 1) Do people who have a longer length of association with a place (in Grand Teton National Park (GTNP) and elsewhere) express more emotional or social meanings when describing that important place? In contrast, do people who have a shorter length of association refer to either the physical setting or an activity as more important when they describe their connections to that important place? In other words, is a person's length of association with a place related to the nature of his/her attachment to it?

METHODS

Study Area

Jackson Hole (JH) was the broad area of focus for this project. JH is located in northwest Wyoming, and encompasses the town of Jackson and Grand Teton National Park (GTNP). GTNP is one of the most recognized mountain areas in the world, offering incredible mountaineering, hiking, rafting, skiing, and other outdoor pursuits. GTNP receives over three million visitors a year, the majority during the summer. The town of Jackson, WY, has a year-round population of about 8,000 people (as of 2000), is located about 15 miles from the heart of the park, and is heavily dependent upon tourism revenues. In addition, over 95 percent of the immediate area is public land, protected by various degrees not only in GTNP, but also in National Forests, Wilderness areas, and the National Elk Refuge.

Data Collection

Two methodological approaches, a drop-off/mail-back questionnaire and personal interviews, were used to collect data for this study. A stratified random sampling approach was used to distribute the questionnaire to one adult in private vehicles entering GTNP from July through October 2000. To increase the response rate, follow-up procedures were used based on Dillman's Total Design Method. The questionnaire collected information on the visitor's length of association with GTNP. Questions addressed both frequency and endurance of this connection: 1) length of stay (in hours or days) on this visit to GTNP, 2) number of visits to GTNP, and 3) the number of years they had visited GTNP.

The survey also collected information on respondents' special places in GTNP and elsewhere in an open-ended format. Visitors were asked to list up to three important places in the park, describe the reasons why those places were important, and estimate how much time they had spent at each place. This open-ended approach was used in order to capture the depth of meanings, while the use of a survey allowed for a multitude of responses to better identify the range of visitors' experiences of GTNP.

The personal interviews were conducted with a purposive sample of visitors to GTNP and year-round residents of JH. Selection of individuals was based on key variables of interest for place attachment. Criterion sampling was used to access a diversity of visitors based on variables that included number of visits to the park and whether individuals had special places in GTNP.

Nine separate interviews were conducted with GTNP visitors in August and September of 2001, four of which were "couple" interviews, where both members of the couple participated, for a total of 13 people participating in GTNP visitor interviews.

In addition, 29 personal interviews were conducted with JH residents between August and November 2000. The key variable of interest was length of residency in JH; the number of years that these interviewees had lived in JH varied from 1½ years to more than 65 years. A snowball sampling approach was used to identify potential participants.

A total of 38 JH resident and GTNP visitor interviews were thus conducted, involving 42 individuals. These interviews were semi-structured in format and used an interview guide approach. The interviews included discussion of an important or special place in the JH valley, and then of an important or special place elsewhere.

A key objective was to ensure that interviewees used their own words or meanings to describe their connections to places. The GTNP visitor interviews lasted 20-45 minutes (averaging about 30 minutes), while the JH resident interviews lasted 30-60 minutes.

Creative Analysis

The survey data provided a broad view of the role that time played for a large number of people. The interview data were then used to explore in-depth the meanings of places and the role of time. The majority of places examined in this study were recreational places, but other types of places such as homes and communities were also described.

Survey Data Analysis

Analysis of the survey data took two forms, both quantitative and qualitative. Place meaning questions were first analysed qualitatively. First, the GTNP places that were listed were categorized into 86 distinct places, based on the name of the place or the type of place.

The types of places mentioned by respondents as special in GTNP varied greatly in terms of scale, from specific (Inspiration Point, the Chapel of Transfiguration), to more general, to very broad, such as the whole park. Respondents could list multiple reasons for the importance of places, resulting in a total of 1,299 reasons cited. Reasons for a place's importance were first coded in NVivo (QSR*NUDIST Vivo 1.0, 1999), a qualitative data analysis software program. To establish codes, an inductive approach was applied to develop categories of codes based on respondents' meanings. These categories were refined as analysis progressed.

After initial coding, a total of 36 separate categories of place meanings were identified. A reliability analysis was then conducted, and after further refinement and collapsing of these categories, coding based on 17 separate categories was finalized. These codes were next transferred to SPSS for further analysis. All respondents who had mentioned a type of place categorized by place code were identified (for instance, "environmental setting or characteristics"), and then these cases were compared with those who had not identified this place code. Thus each place code was measured on a nominal level referring to the presence or absence of a code for each respondent. Certain meanings were double (or even triple) coded, as it was sometimes impossible to exclude overlapping meanings based on some of the respondents' answers. Responses that were double coded were placed in both coding categories during analyses.

T-tests, cross-tabulations, and Chi-square statistics were used to analyse statistical relationships between the time (length of association) variables and the place meaning codes; all results reported here were statistically significant, $p<.05$.

Interview Data Analysis

Personal interviews were tape recorded with the permission of the interviewees and transcribed into a Word document, which was then also transferred into NVivo. The unit of analysis in this step was the words and phrases expressed by the participants. The interviews were first coded inductively, allowing the codes to emerge from the data, rather than being set *a priori*. After the first interview was coded, the coding scheme was then used for the next interview, which was then built upon and refined during this process. Each successive interview led to more categories and helped to distinguish and elaborate the overall coding scheme, as refined codes were applied to earlier interviews. Clusters and categories of codes were also established as the coding continued: NVivo allows for creating a hierarchical "tree" of codes.

Results and Discussion

A total of 649 questionnaires were distributed during the sampling period in GTNP. Of these, 493 visitors returned completed questionnaires, yielding a 76 percent response rate. In addition, the analysis included questionnaires returned by the local and visitor interviewees. In the following sections, results from the questionnaires and interviews are presented and discussed. First, differences in visitor characteristics are examined between people who had a special place in GTNP and those who did not, focusing on length of association. Differences in place meanings based on length of association are then explored. Finally, results from interviews are discussed in light of the findings from the questionnaires.

Who had a Special Place in GTNP?

Forty-eight percent of visitors said specific places in GTNP were special or important to them. Statistically significant differences between those who had a special place and those who did not were found based on trip characteristics including visitors' frequency of visits, endurance of association, and length of stay. Those reporting a special place had a statistically significant longer length of stay (3.4 days vs. 2.2 days, $t=3.134$), greater number of visits to the park (9.6 visits vs. 2.0 visits, $t=6.352$), and longer association with the park (16.1 years vs. 9.7 years, t=4.317). Statistical significance also was found between repeat visitors who had a special place and firsttime visitors who did not. Of repeat visitors, 75 percent reported a special place, while only 45 percent of first timers did (*X2*=44.72). To further assess if numbers of visits made to GTNP was related to special places, respondents were also categorized in terms of four groups: 1) first visit, 2) two to four visits, 3) five to nine visits, and 4) ten or more visits.

Statistically significant associations were found, indicating that as the number of visits increased, so did the likelihood of reporting a special place. Of particular note, 97 percent of visitors who had visited ten or more times reported a special place in the park (*X2*=54.53). This finding is consistent with the results of past research that longer lengths of association are associated with stronger measures of place attachment. While this study did not measure strength of place attachment, the finding that people who reported more visits and had more years of association with GTNP were more likely to report a special place lends support to prior findings and the proposition that greater association with a place leads to place attachment.

Frequency, Endurance, and Place Meaning

Visitors described a variety of place meanings, as represented by the definitions of place meaning codes present. The most common meanings were: 1) the physical setting, 2) outdoor recreation activities, 3) emotional connections, 4) wildlife viewing, 5) escape, 6) social ties, 7) special moments, 8) the undeveloped nature of the park, and 9) tradition/time spent.

Statistically significant differences were found between visitors' length of association and the place meanings they reported. Using Chi-Square analysis, repeat visitors were significantly more likely than first time visitors to report the following place meanings as important (generally on at least a two-to-one ratio): outdoor recreation, solitude, social ties, special moments, and time or tradition. Differences were not found for such place meanings as the physical setting and visitors' emotional connections to places.

T-tests were also used to test differences between place meanings and the variables associated with time. In relation to number of visits, place meanings significantly associated with more visits (frequency) included outdoor recreation (t=2.465) and the physical setting (t=2.295).

Certain place meanings were more likely to be reported by those who had been coming to GTNP longer (endurance) and thus had stronger connections with park places: outdoor recreation (t=3.434), social ties (t=3.117), special moments (t=2.091), time or tradition (t=2.181), and lodging (t=1.984).

Taken together, these findings only partly support previous research. Both theory and research evidence suggest that longer associations with a place may shift the basis of attachment from physical aspects of the place to social aspects of the place. In support of previous research, repeat visitors (frequency), as well as those who had been coming for more years (endurance), were associated with more reports of social connections to places in GTNP. While the overall category of emotional connections found no differences between repeat and first-time visitors, the repeat visitors were more likely to report "special moments" and "solitude," both of which have emotional connotations. Contrary to expectations, no differences were found between repeat and first-time visitors in regards to reports of the physical setting; this meaning was the most commonly reported one, across all visitors.

In addition, those with more visits (frequency) were also more likely to report meanings involving the setting as well. Interestingly, repeat visitors, more visits, and more years visiting were also associated with higher reports of outdoor recreation, a meaning that could be hypothesized to be closely tied to the setting. One likely reason for these differences may be the type of place studied in the present research. Most previous research of this type was based on community studies, not recreation destinations or national parks. The physical setting was most frequently reported by all visitors as the reason that GTNP was special, regardless of length of association.

GTNP is a vacation destination of great scenic beauty, and also a place where outdoor recreation is important for visiting. Therefore, it is not surprising that most people repeatedly return to GTNP because of the park's scenic values and opportunities to recreate. This finding suggests the importance of considering the type of place under study and its relation to development of different place meanings. This relationship needs further study, given that the kind of place appears here to be a factor in the kinds of meanings people assign to that place and the process of place attachment itself.

Interview Results and Discussion

Interviews with Residents

In analyzing the interviews from the JH residents, every important place mentioned was a place where that person had a high level of "intensity" of visitation in terms of length of association; this use of the term "intensity" is similar to the concept of "experience use history" described by Schreyer et al. (1984). Intensity of visits describes how frequently a person visits the place in a certain number of years, and attempts to capture both the frequency and endurance of one's connection to a place.

Each place discussed by interviewees was given an intensity ranking of low, medium, or high. For instance, examples of low intensity of association for interviewees might include a person visiting a place five times over 30 years, or two times over five years, while examples of high intensity of association might include a person visiting a place 50 times over 25 years, or 10 times over two years. Likewise, places outside the JH area were ones with which local interviewees had at least a moderate, if not high, level of intensity of association.

Interviews with Nonresidents

The visitor interviews also revealed the role of time in place attachment. Eight of 13 interviewees described a special place in GTNP, whereas the other five did not have a special place. In looking at the intensity of association with GTNP, the intensity varied much more among visitors than locals.

This would be expected because for the nonresident interviewees, GTNP is primarily a vacation destination (albeit a special one for some of them) and therefore not a place where they have spent a great deal of time, especially in comparison to the residents. In terms of intensity of association with GTNP, of the eight visitors who described an important place, one was high; one had a high level earlier in her life, but recently was low; two were medium; and four were low. And for the five visitors who did not describe a special place, the intensity of association also varied: two were high, one was medium, and two were low.

However, when asked to discuss an important place outside the JH area, all of the visitor interviewees except one could easily think of a place, and four of the thirteen described their homes or a place where they had lived, revealing the importance of home places. The other interviewees talked about favourite or cherished vacation spots, and all were places they had visited a number of times, again revealing at least a moderate intensity of association in their connections to special places they discussed.

Discussion of Interviews and Place Meanings

Moore and Graefe (1994) hypothesized that the ways in which different types of place attachments form also differ. Place dependence seemed to develop comparatively quickly, while the more affective place identity seemed to require more time. Similarly, others have hypothesized that over time, social connections to places become more salient and important; whereas in the beginning, it is often attributes related to the physical setting that are important.

These hypotheses were supported by the results of the interviews. One distinction made by a number of interviewees was that their feelings about a place changed over time as they gained experience with the place. They noted that the reasons for first moving to, or visiting places in, JH changed or had grown as they lived in the place and spent more time there. They seemed to be distinguishing between "preference" and "meaning", and this difference is presented in the next section as one of "attraction" as opposed to "attachment."

Attraction vs. Attachment

A number of the people interviewed for this study described how they became attached or connected to special places, both in JH and outside the valley. Many interviewees acknowledging place connections generally described differences in the meanings of places between their initial impressions of attraction to a place and their lasting attachment to that place (at least 12 interviewees explicitly discussed this difference, and another five implicitly alluded to it). They often said that the beauty of the physical setting was the first thing they noticed.

However, this attraction was quite different from the meanings and stronger emotional attachments that developed through living in a place for a longer time, and it was this lengthier attachment that resulted in more meaningful emotional and social connections to that place. While many interviewees described this phenomenon in various ways, several quotes will serve to briefly illustrate this idea.

IC, a 25-year female who lived in JH 1½ years and has since moved away, commented that, "… I took the job here because I knew that I loved this place, in the sense that I loved the scenery. I mean I had no attachment to it yet." Another interviewee also discussed this difference between attraction and attachment in a similar fashion.

OT, a 48-year old married woman who had lived in JH for 12 years, commented: Well certainly while visiting, one can't help but be amazed by the whole thing, it is a beautiful and all that—blah, blah, blah. So when we knew we were moving to Jackson of course we were excited. I tell you it is really different, I have a completely different feeling about Jackson than that feeling. Like the feeling I would imagine what a visitor feels like when they come here and it's just so beautiful. But now I feel, I feel attached, I feel responsible, you know it feels more like family and not just 'I'm on vacation' having a visit. It's just a really different feeling, and it grew slowly. No one can come here and not love this place in some ways. But the attachment feeling now for this place has definitely grown over time. You know it took years really. I think it probably started leaking in maybe after about five years, that I really felt like this was totally a home base.

For OT, as well as other interviewees, being in a place, spending time there, and having experiences there is critical for a place to become emotionally significant, rather than just another pretty place—it becomes a place marked with personal and socially shared memories and events.

These examples affirm earlier research and hypotheses emphasizing that over time, one's connections to places tend to expand beyond a focus on environmental or setting features to valuing deeper emotional or social aspects of the place.

Conclusions

The importance of time in connecting people to places was affirmed in the present study. The results from the questionnaires lend some support to prior findings and hypotheses that length of association with a place is an important factor in the development of place attachment. People who reported more visits and had more years of association with GTNP were more likely to report a special place than those with shorter lengths of association. The questionnaire findings also indicated that length of association affects the meanings of place attachment. The results revealed consistencies as well as discrepancies in regards to the research question addressed. Findings indicated that it is important to consider the type of place when assessing meanings—a critical consideration for recreation managers.

In regards to the interviewees, an important distinction a number of them noted was that their feelings about a place changed both over time and because of their experiences at the place. This aspect of person-place relationships was referred to as "attraction vs. attachment" in this study. Others have noted these kinds of changing place meanings over time, theorizing that different types of place attachments develop in different ways. Over time, more emotional or social connections to places seem to become more salient, in contrast to early stages of one's connections to places, when physical settings are often most important. Based on their interrelated conceptions, these frameworks suggest that every person-place bond has its locus within an ever-changing temporal scale that provides a critical context affecting that bond. Attitudes of local residents towards the development of tourism in Slovenia: The case of the Primorska, Dolenjska, Gorenjska and Ljubljana regions

Long Term Planning in Tourism

Long term planning in tourism is associated with the reactions of local residents to it. Tourism can develop and grow when local residents have a positive attitude toward it and when they see their role in the process of the tourism development. At the point when a tourism destination is born, the quality of the life of the local residents goes through radical changes, which are not necessarily negative. It is true that there can be more people around, traffic can become difficult, crime rates can increase, and the pollution of all environment resources is possible. Additionally, tourism brings changes that affect traditional way of life, family relations, the nature of the local structures functioning and many not predictable problems. Conversely, new jobs emerge, old towns, facilities and places are revitalized and social life significantly improves. Local residents do see new business opportunities in tourism and are motivated to explore them. At the same time, they know that some negative physical, cultural, social and economic impacts will emerge. The most complex problems that accompany tourism development, reside in the relationship between tourists and local residents. Furthermore, there are limits of tourism growth that are closely associated with the place capacity and with the quality of life in the local community.

When these limits are exceeded, local residents develop negative attitudes towards tourism. When negative attitudes become beliefs, tourism development obstacles appear. The beliefs of the local residents become the most reliable indicator of the limits to the growth of tourism. Tourism can even become "[...] the scapegoat for all the problems in the certain place not regarding that they were there before tourism developed. It is easy to blame tourism for all social and other problems".

Founded on Pearce's (1996) model of tourism community relationship and supported by literature review, the present study proposes an integrated approach to understanding the factors that shape the attitudes of local residents towards tourism. A principal components analysis is used to build a perceptual map, which provides a clearer understanding of the framework and the regression analysis shows the association between tourism development, the impacts of tourism and the role of tourists in it. The implications of this study are apparent in defining management strategies well-suited to the factors that play important role in the general perception of tourism development in a local community.

On the Research of Local Attitudes and Tourism Development

Farnum et al. (2005) claim that today there is a far greater consensus regarding the constituent elements of a sense of place. At the same time, they are convinced that there is still a fair amount of ambiguity regarding the term of place. This ambiguity is exacerbated by that definitions of sense of place and related constructs are often dependent upon how they are approached. The sociological meaning of place is set by the attributes of the local residents, which are the result of the experiences with the place, the result of the social interaction in the place, and the result of the emotional attachment to the place. The meaning of a place is therefore a complex structure consisting of physical, behavioural, social and psychological processes.

In the eyes of local residents the physical place that they live in is an authentic and natural environment. Tuan (1977) observes that places involve meanings and values that facilitate intimate relationships with particular geographical areas. At the same time, a place should be distinguished from the general environment. The 'general environment' refers to the biophysical components of the land, components that exist regardless of the types of human connections to them. Additionally, the sense of place consists of the entire set of cognitive, affective sentiments and the meanings one attributes to such areas and that are part of a particular geographic locale.

Physical place is the local environment for a variety of social activities, and often the arena for activities in which tourists are involved. Local residents socially interact at the local place, maintain friendships, discuss common issues, resolve problems and even create new entrepreneurial opportunities.

Social interactions are sustainable, durable and strongly emotionally induced and the emotional power of these interactions is a result of historical, cultural, and social experiences and the result of the immediate social context. According to Williams and Vaske (2003), place attachment is equivalent of the geographer's sense of place. Sometimes it is related to the whole set of phenomena (place dependency, place identity, place satisfaction, place rootedness) as proposed by Kaltenborn (1998).

The term 'sense of place' is often used in narrower sense in recreation and tourism. The power of a sense of place is related to the extent to which an individual values or identifies with a particular environmental setting. Furthermore, in the term of strength, it is a component of the attachment to the particular place, and this attachment is generally presumed to be positive. Place attachment necessarily involves emotion. As a concept, a sense of place can be thought of as a collection of place meanings, which express attachment to a place in a very broad sense. For this research, the meaning of the place is most important as it appears as a symbolic and evaluative set of ideas, beliefs and values that order the opportunities of the tourism development.

Place attachment itself has received considerable scholarly attention. All agree that it is a complex phenomena and only one of the attachments within the larger context of human attachments. As previously emphasized, the attachment to place may be based on social relationships or processes that are more important than particular physical landscape characteristics. Beckley (2003) claims that even if the landscape changes, the sentiments do not change. However, the notion that the physical characteristics of the place may change challenges the attachment of the local resident. Dixon and Durrheim for example claim that the place identity is a component of the self-identity and the reference to how one sees oneself is made in relation to the environment (2000: 28). Rowles in this sense (1983) distinguished between three senses of 'insideness', expressing different aspects of his respondents' interaction with their surroundings.

'Physical insideness' designated their 'body awareness' of their environment, expressed as a kind of tacit knowledge of the physical details of place: "Social insideness designated their sense of connection to a local community, recognition of their integration within the social fabric" (1983: 302). Finally, 'autobiographic insideness' designated their idiosyncratic sense of rootedness. In tourism place, identity and place dependency is a commonly used concept.

Some scholars view place identity and place dependency as the two fundamental but distinct dimensions of place attachment. Place dependency and place identity scales are the most used to assess place attachment in recreation and tourism. However, when we look at place attachment from the tourist point of view, we see a different picture. Tourists interact with the certain place only for a short time, which is not enough to develop a sense of that place and depend on it. Nevertheless, when tourists interact with a certain place for a long time, they develop some kind of place dependency.

The place may even become a part of their identity. When this happens, they develop the desire to visit the place again. There is even a chance that the place becomes a second home for a tourist. Second homes are an integral component of tourism in rural and peripheral areas and this is also evident in some eastern parts of Slovenia. Place satisfaction, introduced by Stedman (2002; 2003b), is perhaps the most relevant to tourism. As an attitude, place satisfaction is closely related to the quality of place and to the quality of service. Local residents who are highly satisfied and highly attached to the place do not want any changes. Only the residents that are highly attached to the place and are not satisfied with it will try to change it.

Development of Local Residents' Gaze

Changes in the physical and cultural environment that mainly result from mass tourism have their impact on values and traditional way of life in the local community. Even family relations and the structure of the local community are affected by these changes. Constant changes demand great effort from the local residents to cope with them. At the same time, changes force local residents to be actively involved in the operations of the tourism planning and development of the tourist destination.

Relationships between local residents and tourists have been part of thorough research for many years. Less research has been aimed at the dynamics of the relationship between local residents and tourists as a source for the shaping and development of the local residents' attitudes and attributes towards tourism and tourists.

The attitudes of local residents are crucial for the construction of their beliefs about tourism development. Local residents hold highly divergent meanings about the growth of the tourist destination. Some researchers even hold the view that the meanings are formed out of social categories and people share them between themselves, empirically and potentially. In addition, these meanings are free from restraints, when residents explain them and use them to construct the meaning about tourism development.

Social groups in the local community form their own meanings and attribute them to the certain destination. The power of a social group strongly determines the impact of the groups' meanings on the process of tourism development. Dominant classes determine tourism politics and distribute the meanings that support it. At the same time, local residents separate the meanings of the physical and social space from the meaning of the tourist destination. A symbolic concept of a certain physical and social space that consists of attributes from different social groups is a foundation for the abstract concept of the tourist destination.

Tourist Lifestyle Development

Tourism is one of the core processes where the dissolving of the social classes can be observed. Age, sex, nationality, racial identity, political attitudes and some other features are substitutes for class identity in post-modern times. New concepts have their roots in the individuation and pluralisation of life styles. Some researchers like do not agree with such a radical distinction and Boegenhold (2001: 829) for example argues that social status and social praxis are still connected with the lifestyle of an individual. Zapf et al. (1987) similarly describe lifestyle as a relatively permeable pattern of organization of everyday life and this has been indicated also in my own previous research.

The lifestyle of the tourist has been a focus of research for many decades. Many typologies of tourists have evolved through time. The aim of tourist lifestyle research is to explain the crucial behaviour patterns of tourists. Murphy (1985) identified two general categories of a tourist lifestyle: interactional and cognitive/normative. Lowyck et al. (1992) also differentiate general types from tourist types. Cohen (1972) was convinced that tourist typologies add to the understanding of the tourist self-concept, his values, needs, motives and beliefs, while the interactionist concepts reveal the tourists' motives that attract them to the tourist destinations. Plog (1991) even developed distinctive scale to measure the personal characteristics of tourists in the frame of cognitive-normative categories, while Urry (1990) and Bauman (1992) developed the phenomenological concept known as the 'tourist gaze', which differentiates between tourists that gaze collectively or individually when they travel.

In my previous research, I researched the tourist type that visits the Slovenian coast regularly and this work was based on the tourist phenotype developed by Jokinen and Veijola (2002: 23). It is important to argue that tourist typologies do not have a common denominator and are based on the goals of the researchers. The weakest part of the developed tourist typologies are the small samples of the respondents. There are also very few studies that study the attributions of the local residents towards the different types of tourists although this could be one of the core elements of the successful planning of the tourist development on the local level.

The 'tourist gaze' concept explains the development of the meaning that tourists attach to the objects and subjects in the environment they gaze upon. This concept, combined with the concept of the accelerating mobility, is essential in shaping the vision of the tourism potential of the local residents and tourists. The gaze is collectively based, and the beliefs that are built on emotions, expectations and imagination in the process of gazing to construct the tourism destination potential. The Western meta-narrative, which is the essence of the tourist gaze of western tourists, is rooted in semiotics. Tourists and local residents alike look for signs in their environment. They learn how to appreciate their meaning and participate in their exchange. In this way, the tourist experiences the general cultural sphere as well as in specific political, ideological, economic, and social practices. The same learning takes place in the heads of local residents in interpreting the signs that are associated with the tourist type that visits their place.

Attitudes of Local Residents Towards Tourists

Most tourism researchers are strongly convinced that a good relationship between local residents and tourists is essential for the long-term development of a tourist destination but the attitudes of local residents towards tourism and tourists are strongly differentiated. Milman and Pizam (1988) discovered that local residents have positive attitudes towards tourists. At the same time, they found out that majority of them mentioned negative impacts of tourism. Alcohol, drugs, traffic problems, criminal acts and conflicts between tourists and local residents were most frequently mentioned. Simultaneously, they recognized employment opportunities, income from taxes and increased quality of life as a positive impact of tourism. Although in the early days of mass tourism researchers emphasized only the positive impacts of tourism, the negative social, economic and environmental impacts have been thoroughly researched over thelast thirty years.

Duvall (2002) confirms the empirical findings of other researchers, but states that they frequently give priority only to the negative impacts of tourism. His studies in Mazatlan in Mexico reveal different tourism realities Local residents in Mazatlan want to attract tourists because the majority of them earn their living from it. Some of them own hotels, bars, restaurants and recreational facilities for tourists. Taxes and prices in this area are high. Locals search for less expensive services and facilities and drink in 'normal' restaurants.

Tourists in Mazatlan are welcomed because they bring fun, entertainment, different and more open cultural patterns as well as the desire to learn. There is no vacation for the residents of Mazatlan. Locals need to learn languages and be creative during their leisure time. There are some negative impacts of tourism, too. Tourists have fun and locals have to work long hours to earn money. Older local residents are against American tourists who seek sexual experiences. The locals sometimes try to minimize their feeling of inferiority by insulting tourists and mocking their behaviour. They even rob the tourists, claiming they are taking back what was taken from them. Locals are frequently forced to show folk customs that are staged to please tourists. In spite of this, they encourage their children to interact with American tourists to adopt their attitudes in order to succeed in life and marriages between locals and tourists are not uncommon in Mazatlan.

Researchers used negative and positive attitudes towards tourism to address specific psychological states empowered by perceptions and beliefs about certain reality. These beliefs are related to the deeply rooted values and personal dimensions that cannot be easily changed and can be used as a measure of tourism development. Crompton (1987) measured cultural capital (the place of birth, the amount time of residency in the certain place) as an indicator of attachment to the local community, while McCool and Martin (1994) researched the correlation between attitudes towards tourism, the time of residency, tourism development and emotional attachment to the place.

Williams, McDonald, Riden and Uysal (1995) similarly measured attachment by time of residency in the certain place and correlated it with age and with income of residents and Jurowski (1998) correlated the quality of life of local residents with the satisfaction with their life in local community.

Mansfeld (1992: 377) examined the perceptions of local residents who live in the suburbs of the big cities and see the negative impacts of tourism every day. He confirmed that people with higher incomes from tourism hold more positive attitudes towards tourism and he established a model of development phase of tourism and tourist destinations, which is based on the characteristics of the tourists. The researches by Choy (1992) and Murphy and Pritchard (1997) also revealed that emotional states and attitudes affect the perceptions regarding that destination more than the tourist infrastructures of a destination.

Theoretical Model and Research Problem

The presented research is founded on the hypothesis that tourism development is associated with the experiences of the tourism impacts, which form the positive or negative attitudes of local residents towards tourism. Additionally, the tourist type is of the highest importance in this process. A different type of tourist triggers different tourism impacts and in some regions some types of tourists are not wanted and tourism development is not based on their participation. Further, it could be expected that the younger population is more confident with tourism development in comparison to the elder population, which is more strongly attached to the place where they live and do not want the many changes that tourism brings.

Their scepticism towards tourism development might be related to their perception of tourism as a probable source of income and survival. Figure 1 shows the hypothetical model that proposes interactions among the constructs of tourism development and the impacts of tourism. The choice of each component of the model was based on the literature review. The model's contribution depends upon the interaction between attitudes about tourism development and the experiences with various tourism impacts, tourist types, tourism and leisure infrastructure and a local resident's place attachment.

The aim of this study is to provide insights in flexibility of residents' beliefs including perceptions and impacts toward tourism development. These insights reflect local residents' demands for active participation in the tourism development.

On the Research and Analytical Methods

In order to test the proposed hypotheses the survey with six sections was conducted. The first section tries to measure place attachment, while the second measures the attitudes towards tourism development. In the third section, the perceptions of a tourist type are examined. The fourth, the fifth and the sixth sections measure cultural, negative and positive impacts towards tourism.

Local residents' attitudes were assessed by a five-point Likert-type scale. This scale ranged from 'extremely disagree' (1) to 'totally agree'. The academic study took place in the regions of Gorenjska, Primorska, Ljubljana and Dolenjska. These regions were chosen because they served the goal of researching the differences between the cognitions of local residents regarding tourism and tourists. The differences were observed on the level of tourism development.

Attitudes towards tourism are difficult to measure, because they are often the result of the short interactions with tourists and not the result of their profound experiences with tourism and tourists. Nevertheless, the interactions of local residents with tourism and tourists could be a good source for the development of their attitudes towards tourism and tourists as well as a solid background for the development of their attitudes towards tourism development.

The are two main stages of statistical data analysis in the report. The first stage entails the reduction of the data through the application of PCA to the set of assessed sections. An exploratory factor analysis was undertaken, using Principal Component Analysis with Varimax rotation. Factor analysis can only reflect patterns of scores on items selected by a researcher, and in this instance, the items were selected assuming a conceptual model constructed by the researcher.

To assess the pertinence of using PCA in this research, the Kaiser-Meyer – Olkin (KMO) statistic was computed. The reliability of the obtained factors was measured by a Cronbach's Alfa coefficients. This analysis was carried out with the Statistica statistical package version 7.

A regression model was estimated in the second stage in order to assess the relationship between the dependent variable (tourism development) and a set of independent variables proposed by the theoretical concept in this research.

Results

The reduction of the initial 20 place attachment attitudes into six new factors, together accounting for 57.7% of the total variance (KMO = 0.71) was obtained through PCA with normalized varimax rotation. Considering the meaning of the place attachment attitudes with high loadings, they were labelled as natural environment quality, tourism and leisure infrastructure, service accessibility, place satisfaction, quality of living and safety living. Natural environment is the first factor and the strongest factor and is specifically related to the need to take pleasure in intact natural environment.

The reduction of the initial five tourism development attitudes into a single factor, together accounting for 44 % of the total variance (KMO = 0.67) was obtained through PCA with normalized varimax rotation. The single factor was labelled tourism development. Knowledge about tourism activities, destination image and variety of tourism services, tourism development and the need for better tourism organization are included in this factor. It seems that the destination's image is the most important item in the set of attitudes about tourism development.

The reduction of the initial 20 tourist type perceptions into five factors, together accounting for 44 % of the total variance (KMO = 0.67) was obtained through PCA with normalized varimax rotation.

Culture seekers as a tourist type prevail in the perceptions of the local residents. They account for 24% of the variance. They are perceived as the most frequent tourist type in the places where this research was conducted, or the culture seeker is the most desired tourist type in these places.

The reduction of the initial 14 change perceptions into two factors, together accounting for 36 % of the total variance (KMO = 0.80) was obtained through PCA with normalized varimax rotation. It can be concluded from the results that tourists play an important role in the process of cultural interaction. In contrast, local residents perceive them as troublemakers and as participants in criminal activities.

This perception is often related to escapism, which is usually the way to run from the unpleasant and stressing everyday environment. As matter of fact, escapism is a part of the behaviour pattern of the post-modern tourists. They want to escape from the mundane world of everyday life and seek new experiences that often disturb the life of local residents.

The reduction of the initial 13 negative tourism impacts into one single factor accounting for 46 % of the total variance (KMO = 0.90) was obtained through PCA with normalized varimax rotation. Local residents are afraid that tourism development would disturb their calm environment, bring traffic problems and air and environment pollution. Constant crowds and higher criminal rates are also expected.

The reduction of the initial 14 positive tourism impacts into one single factor accounting for 46 % of the total variance (KMO = 0.91), was obtained through PCA with normalized varimax rotation. Local residents expect better services, tourism development and development of new occupations and better future prospects for young people from positive tourism impacts.

However, despite the fact that these studies provided important contributions in order to define local residents' attitudes towards tourism development in some places in Slovenia, they do not examine the interactions among them.

In order to examine the main hypothesis, the hierarchical regression in one step was conducted. The findings confirm the hypothesis that the attitudes of local residents toward a tourism development depend on place attachment and of the overall perception of tourism impacts.

Predictor variables of tourism impacts and place attachment have moderate effects on tourism development ($R2 = 0.37$; $p<.000$***). Results indicate that positive tourism impacts ($\beta = 0.21$, $p<.006$***), cultural tourism (β = 0, 19, $p<.013$**), natural environment quality ($\beta = 0.16$, $p<.012$**), and tourism and leisure structures (β 0 0, 14, $p<.037$**) positively influence perceptions of a tourism development. The length of residency ($\beta = -0.19$, $p<.026$**) negatively influence perceptions of tourism development.

Discussion and Conclusion

The theoretical model proposals offer a logical sequence of the formation of local residents' perceptions. The empirical study proves that perceptions of tourism development by local residents are based on what kind of tourism they prefer and what its impacts are. Place attachment represented by natural environment quality, tourism and leisure facilities and length of residency play a significant role in their perceived tourism development.

In the model, the relationship between negative impacts, cultural change impacts, service accessibility, place satisfaction, quality of living and safety of living and tourism development is not significant, and that proves that local residents are more supportive of tourism development when they are newcomers and when they clearly perceive positive tourism impacts.

The relationship between the length of residency and tourism development in the model is negative. Long time residents are generally less favourable to tourism development. These findings tend to confirm that attached residents who are favourable toward tourism may be expressing ties to the overall development of the place more than ties to the community. In places that seem to evoke strong emotional responses, managers should be especially aware of how place attachment will influence attitudes of local residents toward tourism development.

It seems that sense of place is an important factor in the forming of tourism development attitudes. Previous studies, along with this study, confirm its role in tourism development. Still, there is enough evidence to suggest it should be of at least moderate importance to recreation and tourism managers and planners. How integral may depend on such variables as the perception of a desired type of tourism, the magnitude of perceived positive impacts to the area and of perceived threats to the natural environment as well as to the accessibility of the tourism and leisure structures by local residents. Locallybased place meanings make tourism policy development and processes difficult to manage.

It can be concluded that sense of place, place attachment, and other places-related concepts are factors strongly related to recreation and tourism. Thus, research in local residents' attitudes toward tourism development can be helpful as managers face and often struggle with resource allocation issues that affect recreation and tourism resources and opportunities.

The major findings of this study have some significant tourism development implications. The study shows what local residents know about and believe about tourism, including perceptions and impacts. The study also embraces future development tourism in the places in this study and reveals some facts for the control and development and other relations to the other aspects of social and community life.

Flexible attitudes toward tourism development along with the belief that tourism will bring prosperity to the area are a solid basis for the tourism development. In some of the researched places, there is a shortage of tourism and leisure facilities and that could cause significant problems in the future tourism development. The quality of the natural environment is clearly an asset and its protection should be carefully considered when tourism development is planned.

The findings of this study confirm my previous research findings, which state that the local community should play the primary role in the tourism development process in the field of community-led and entrepreneur-led tourism development.

Second Homes-Vacation Homes and Investment Property Now 1/3 of Market

A report issued last week by the National Association of Realtors (NAR) indicates that the second home segment of the housing market is much bigger than anyone had previously suspected. In fact, it is a stunner.

NAR cites two new studies showing that second home purchases are not only growing, but represent a different market segment than previously thought.

The studies show that 36 percent of all homes purchased last year were *second homes*; a total of 2.82 million second home sales. This was an increase of 16.3 percent from the 2.42 million logged in 2003. But, what surprised the researchers was the stated purpose of these purchases. The lion's share of second home purchases had always been considered to be for recreational purposes. The new figures show that investment home purchases represented 23 percent of the total sales during the 203-2004 period, while only 13 percent were vacation homes.

In real numbers, there were 1.80 million sales of investment properties in 2004, up 14.4 percent from 1.57 million in the previous year. Vacation home sales were 102 million last year and 850,000 in 2003. Have purchasing patterns changed? More likely it is the research methodology.

David Lereah, Chief Economist for NAR said that earlier studies had underestimated the number of second home sales because the methodology was flawed. Surveys conducted by mail of home buyers resulted in a small percentage being returned by the Post Office, apparently from non-owner occupied properties. "...this is the first time," Lereah said, "that anyone has come up with a methodology for capturing a representative market share for vacation and investment home owners."

NAR's second-home study was based on two surveys. The organization mailed an eight-page questionnaire to 100,000 homebuyers who purchased between mid-2003 and mid-2004. The survey generated 8,205 usable responses. "Data in this report includes only survey data from respondents who indicated that they purchased a vacation home or investment property; this data was underrepresented in the overall sample due to smaller return rates."

A second survey was used to determine market share and to extrapolate sales date. This was conducted by email and captured data for 3,371 home purchases in 2003 and 2004. Data were weighted to correspond with demographic findings in the mailed survey. Because the findings of this survey showed a much higher volume of second home sales than anticipated, U.S. Census Bureau data were employed to extrapolate the information collected through survey research.

Citing Census Bureau statistics from 2003, NAR states that there are 43.8 million second homes in this country; 6.6 million are vacation homes and 37.2 million are investment properties. There are a total of 72.1 million owner occupied homes. That would indicate that 62% of the housing stock in the United States is owned by persons who own other homes or housing units

Earlier studies had indicated that 6.6 million housing units were second homes. Note that figure is identical to the number of homes the Census Bureau considers to be vacation homes. Thus, earlier studies may have overlooked the purchase and ownership of investment units. Census data indicates the latter may total 37.2 million units.

"In essence, our definition of second homes has changed with the buyer shift toward investment property," Lereah said. "... Second homes are a much larger share than the conventional mind-set of them being mostly vacation homes." There is probably an overlap between the investment and vacation home categories. For example, 14 percent of vacation home buyers rent their property as do 79 percent of investment buyers. Ten percent of investment buyers intend to use their second homes for recreational purposes. One does not know how the Census Bureau or NAR defined their terms in collecting information or how respondents may view their second home ownership. Like most surveys, conclusions may be somewhat at the mercy of respondent definitions and perceptions.

Regardless of the number of second, third, and fourth homes Donald Trump or Martha Stewart may own, second home buyers are not necessarily in the high roller category. The typical vacation home buyer is 55 years old, earned $71,000 in 2003 and spent $190,000 on a single-family, 1,290 square foot get-away property. 37 percent said that their recreational property is bigger than their principal residence. Surprisingly, vacation homes have appreciated only 12.8 percent since 2001. (Just a guess, but this may represent the large numbers of mobile homes purchased as recreational retreats in Sun Belt states.)

Investment buyers are younger and a little more affluent. Their median age is 47 and they have a median income of $85,700. They typically purchased a single family home with a median square footage of 1,700. Their investment may have made them even wealthier: investment properties have increased in value 25.4 percent in the last three years. 30 percent of buyers cited as a reason for their purchase a desire to diversify investments while 28 percent were looking for rental income. Only 10 percent were looking for a personal or family retreat or a vacation spot. Nearly 20 percent of second home buyers intend to convert the properties to their primary residence after retirement.

Investment buyers, probably keeping all of those warnings about being an absentee landlord in mind, tend to buy properties within 18 miles of their principal residence. Vacation homes buyers ventured farther away, buying second homes 49 miles from their primary residence.

But, apparently, some people went a lot farther a field in search of a vacation home.

A 2003 study conducted by California-based EscapeHomes named the top 10 emerging second home markets. They are not where one might expect. Only a few are near the ocean and ten it is the frigid part. Only about half are located in areas that can be considered even remotely temperate in climate. Apparently skiing and shivering are a lot bigger attractions that one might have thought,

The Top Five

1. Burnside Kentucky (encompassing Lexington & Frankfurt, Kentucky; Nashville & Knoxville, Tennessee;)
2. Caribou Maine/Quebec, Canada;
3. Ely/Grand Rapids, Minnesota;
4. Island Park, Idaho (including Bozeman, Montana and Jackson, Wyoming;
5. Ketchikan, Alaska (including Juneau and Seattle, Washington).

Thumbnail

Second homes constitute a much larger part of the housing market than anyone expected. Investors, apparently, have never been considered as a major piece of that market.

Second Homes: A Flavor for Every Taste

As you scour the Internet and the travel publications year after year in search of a vacation rental, do you ever wish you owned a getaway of your own? Thousands of people do, and whether you're looking for a place that's exclusively your own, or contemplating renting your second home to help make ownership more affordable, you can choose from a world of properties of every type, size and location.

Second Home Market Offers Buying Opportunities

If you're considering the purchase of a second home, now's a great time to see what the market has to offer. According to the National Association of Realtors® (NAR), the pace of investment and vacation home sales softened a bit in 2006, still representing a respectable 36 percent of all residential sales, but off four percentage points compared to 2005.

Sales of vacation homes actually rose last year, while sales of properties purchased purely for investment fell, primarily due to the exit of speculators from the real estate market. That's good news if you're looking for a property at a fair price, seeking a respectable return on your investment over time, and plan to make it available for your own use, either full or part-time, now or in the future.

The Who, Why and Where of Vacation Home Purchases

According to a NAR survey, typical buyer of a vacation home in 2006 was 44 years old, with a median household income of $102,200. When it comes to deciding how far a getaway would be, 42 percent purchased vacation homes closer than 100 miles from their primary residence, 32 percent were 500 miles or further. Sales of vacation homes are predicted to remain strong, as significant numbers of potential buyers reach prime buying age for these properties.

The 2006 National Association of Realtors® Profile of Second-Home Owners survey asked current owners what they desired most in a vacation home. Not surprisingly, a connection to nature and the pursuit of an active lifestyle were typical responses; 66 percent wish to be near water, nearly 40 percent with access to recreational activities, 38 percent in proximity to vacation or resort areas and over 30 percent near mountains and other natural attractions.

When giving their reasons for the purchase of a vacation home, a large majority (nearly 80 percent) planned to use the home for vacation or as a family retreat, followed by the desire to diversify their investment portfolio; for use as their primary residence in the future; for the tax benefits; use by a family member, friend or relative; simply because they had extra funds available. Renting to others trailed the respondents list of reasons, at 18 percent.

When describing the location of their vacation home, 29 percent were situated in rural areas, 24 percent in resorts, 22 percent in a suburb and 10 percent in a city or urban area. Detached single-family homes accounted for 67 percent of the total, 21 percent condos, 8 percent town homes, and 4 percent "other".

Buyers of vacation homes tend to be in it for the long term, planning to keep their homes a median 10 years; the largest number of owners responding to the survey, 38 percent, expect to own their vacation home for 11 years or more.

How does your mental picture of the perfect vacation home fit these survey results?

Investment Home Buyers Paint a Different Picture

According to the NAR survey, buyers of homes purchased solely for investment last year were somewhat younger and less affluent than vacation home buyers, with a median age of 39 and a median household income of $90,250. As you might expect, their investment property was close to their primary residence, a median distance of 22 miles.

The reported reasons for purchasing a home for investment purposes differed somewhat as well; 46 percent sought rental income; 43 percent wished to diversify their investment portfolio; 23 percent primarily for the tax benefits; followed by use for vacations or a family retreat; as a place to put extra cash to work, for use by a family member, friend or relative. Eventually using the property as a primary residence trailed the list, at 12 percent.

Buyers responding to the NAR survey reported that over 37 percent of investment homes are in a suburb, 22 percent a rural area, 18 percent urban or central city, and 7 percent in a resort area. Detached single-family homes made up 63 percent of the total, 26 percent condos, 6 percent townhouses, and 5 percent "other".

According to the survey, buyers of homes for investment purposes plan to keep them for a median period of five years; 33 percent plan to hold them for six years or more, and 12 percent plan to sell within a year of purchase.

Let the Search Begin!

Once you've settled on a potential location, start looking for your getaway. Search the Internet, classified ads in the local newspapers and talk to the locals. We highly recommend working with a real estate professional in your area of interest. A professional Realtor makes it their business to listen to your needs, help ensure that you are buying at the right price and may know of properties that are just about to come onto the market.

Before you make an offer on a property, it's also a great idea to visit the destination and return on the typical day and time you expect to visit. You'll get a much more realistic idea about travel time, and potentially save yourself a lot of frustration. If you're thinking about making your getaway your primary residence in the future, now's the time to take a realistic look at how access and mobility issues in the future could affect your enjoyment of a particular property.

Financing Considerations

As with a primary residence, there are financing programs designed to suit many income levels and financial goals. Consult your financial advisor and a lending professional to find a financing option that meets your needs. If you've built sufficient equity in your current home, it can be a potential source of funding for your vacation getaway-consult your financial advisor and a mortgage professional for advice.

Should you Rent Your Second Home?

Many buyers of second homes consider renting for all or part of a year to help defray expenses and perhaps even produce a profit. Renting is an option, here are some aspects of being a full or part-time landlord that may help you decide. Note that you should always obtain competent legal, financial and tax advice before you proceed.

Estimate Rental Income – Include a realistic estimate of the number of weeks the property will be likely to be rented. Calculate monthly costs such as mortgage, insurance, taxes, advertising, maintenance and projected repairs. A real estate professional can help you estimate the income potential of your property.

Look at Tax Consequences – Ask a tax professional about what how projected rental income will affect your net financial picture.

Research the Rules & Regs – Consult your legal advisor to determine whether local laws, deed covenants, homeowner association regulations or other restrictions affect your ability to rent the property.

Consider Hiring a Property Manager – If you are unwilling or unable to take a hands-on approach to the considerable effort involved in renting and maintaining your getaway, consider using the services of a property manager, especially if you're purchasing a vacation property that isn't near your primary home. Your real estate professional can be helpful in identifying a reputable property manager.

A Final Word about Renting

If you purchase a second home in a seasonal recreation area, keep in mind that rental demand for your getaway is likely to be highest during the same period that you'd like to be there.

3

Recreation Second Homes

Recreational Properties

Many of us have fond childhood memories of dad loading up the station wagon or van and heading out of town for a long weekend. For some the destination was a lakeside campsite, but for many it was the summer cottage or cabin by the lake. For others it was a Winter activity that brought with it the long-anticipated excitement of driving up to the favourite mountain and throwing open the doors to a modest old ski lodge that one could call home for the next week or so. But unless one was lucky enough to inherit dad's cabin, the thought of purchasing one piece of recreational paradise can be daunting for most young families.

With prices still on the rise and demand for vacation homes brisk notwithstanding the general slowdown in real estate, there are a few bright lights for homeowners looking to pick up a second home or recreational property.

The Canadian Mortgage And Housing Corporation has instituted recently a new program that will provide Homeowner Mortgage Loan Insurance for borrowers with more than one residential property. This means that Purchasers can now obtain a mortgage insured by the Canadian Mortgage And Housing Corporation on a recreational property with as little as five percent down.

Traditionally getting institutional financing for a vacation property was a challenge, because lenders typically based their lending decisions on the risk of reselling this type of properties. As many second homes are located outside urban centres and, more often than not, in remote rural or coastal areas they might have limited resale potential, which from a mortgaging point of view increased the risk of financing. To mitigate this risk, lenders would require borrowers to put up more money down-as much as thirty-five percent or more, in fact. Even well-known and popular destinations such as Whistler, British Columbia required a minimum of twenty-five percent downpayment.

But lifestyles are changing and these changes affect decisions that real estate consumers make regarding how and where to live. So the Canadian Mortgage And Housing Corporation has made a move to put vacation properties within reach of more people. With a constant and steady increase in demand for this type of properties, the Canadian Mortgage And Housing Corporation has determined that the market is such that it is willing to insure lenders against potential losses. This is welcome news for those who have been longing to get a recreational property but did not want to wait until retirement to come up with the downpayment. All Canadian Mortgage And Housing Corporation's products are permitted to be used with the Homeowner Mortgage Loan Insurance and since most major institutional lenders already have their own recreational property mortgage products, consumers have the flexibility to choose the type of financing that is right for them.

However, as with most types of financing, there are some key limitations that is important to be clear on. The purpose of the Homeowner Mortgage Loan Insurance is to make it more feasible for consumers to purchase a second home. It is important to distinguish between a second home and a rental property. The Homeowner Mortgage Loan Insurance is not intended to allow an investor to purchase a rental property with five percent down. The guideline states that at initiation the real capital asset that secures a mortgage insured by Canadian Mortgage And Housing Corporation must be intended for occupancy at some point during the calendar year by the borrower or a relative of the borrower on a rent-free basis. If a rental income is anticipated from the property at a future date, it will not be calculated for the purpose of assisting the Purchaser to qualify for the loan. The location of the property is not restricted to major resorts or popular vacation spots, but there are some general requirements that apply as well. For instance, the recreational property must be suitable for and available for year-round occupancy. Properties that are constructed for seasonal use or have seasonal access are not eligible. As such, vacation cottages located on an island must have year-round bridge or ferry access. And finally, timeshare interests, life leases and properties in rental pools are not eligible.

Luigi Frascati

Luigi Frascati is a Real Estate Agent based in Vancouver, British Columbia. He holds a Bachelor Degree in Economics and maintains a weblog entitled the Real Estate Chronicle where you can find the full collection of his articles on Real Estate Economics and Finance. Luigi is associated with the Sutton Group, the largest real estate organization in Canada, and is based with Sutton-Centre Realty in Burnaby, BC.

Recreational Boaters of California [RBOC] is a nonprofit governmental advocacy organization that works to protect and enhance the interests of the state's recreational boaters before the legislative and executive branches of state and local government.

RBOC was formed as a statewide organization in 1968 and from that date forward has continued its commitment to promoting the enjoyment, protection, and responsible use of our waterways.

- Protecting your fuel tax dollars from diversion.
- Ensuring more dollars for boating law enforcement.
- Supporting education over regulation of boaters.
- Promoting legislation to fight growing infestations of invasive species clogging waterways.
- Saving interest deductions on boats as second homes.
- Reviewing all proposed legislation that affects boaters.
- Guiding and supporting local issues affecting your recreational boating and marina.
- Working in partnership with Boat U.S. on national boating legislation.

Recreation Properties Captivate Albertans

Mario Toneguzzi, Calgary Herald

Albertans are among the most willing in the country to make changes to their finances or lifestyle to own a cottage. And despite the economic downturn, many Canadians are still dreaming of owning a recreational property, both as a long-term investment and to enjoy with family and friends, adds a national real estate report released Thursday.

The 2009 Royal LePage Recreational Property Report said Canadians are willing to make sacrifices to own a cottage and more of them want to use their cottage, cabin or chalet year-round as a recreational property, although some want it as their primary residence.

"In Alberta, 69 per cent of residents agree that a cottage is a good long-term investment. At 62 per cent, Albertans are among the most willing in the country to make changes to their finances or lifestyle to own a cottage. One in five Albertans would purchase a fixer-upper, the highest score in the country, and 15 per cent would purchase a property with friends or family members," said the report. For Albertans, the three most important features of a cottage or recreational property are access to utilities (60 per cent), peace and quiet (51 per cent) and four-season use (33 percent). Access to boating and fishing (28 per cent) and proximity to amenities (22 per cent) also ranked high for Albertans.

Sixty per cent said a cottage on a lake would be their first choice, but 11 per cent would choose a resort condominium and another 11 per cent would choose a property in the woods, both significantly higher than the national average. In a report also released Thursday, Adrienne Warren, senior economist and real estate market specialist with Scotia Economics, said rising equity in principal residences and rising stock market wealth appear to have put second-home ownership within the reach of more Canadian families.

"Demand for second homes/ vacation homes could slow over the coming decade as the large baby boom generation moves past its peak cottage buying years, and wealth gains fail to replicate the outsized increases of the past decade," she said. Warren said this suggests some easing in the steady upward pressure on recreational home prices seen over the past decade, but at the same time, the available supply of listings is likely to remain fairly tight. Royal LePage's nationwide survey showed the dream of owning a getaway property on the water to escape the pressures of city life is still alive and well across the country, said Phil Soper, president and chief executive of Royal LePage Real Estate Services. "Beyond the obvious lifestyle benefits, however, our research demonstrates Canadians see recreational property as a smart and safe long-term investment." Northwest Sonoma County and Southern Mendocino County Recreational, Second Homes, Retreats and Estate Sites All we do is country.

How we Operate

In effect, a Buyer or Seller or Both hire us. Our function is to bring information to a qualified prospect so they can make an intelligent decision. We try to create a package which gives you the information we would like if we were looking. Sometimes we also put together a brief package on another office's listing because of their not creating one or to correct inaccurate information. We offer good credibility without puffery.

We specialize in North Sonoma County and Southern Mendocino estate or recreational properties. We handle the majority of sales of large properties in this area. All of this area is under 3 hours from San Francisco. Appreciation has been strong. We have owned property here since 1975. We have the toys (four 4x4's, light stepping all-terrain vehicles with rubber tracks), the hindsight and a few skills like being able to fly airplanes or helicopters to help you buy or sell. Living in the centre of our market in the country, helps. We have over 300 acres adjacent to Lake Sonoma. Our neighbours are deer, pigs, quail, etc. Our water supply is a spring.

The properties in this area vary from remote weekend retreats to estate sites. The terrain varies from very rugged to rolling Sonoma Mountains. Most have spectacular views. The weather is very good. Very little fog. Rainfall from November through February is heavy. Between storms is possibly the nicest time of the year. Many do not have PG&E. We can show you what the alternatives are.

The more you can paint me a word picture of what you see in your minds' eye of yourself needing or enjoying, the more I can help. I do see everything that is available in this area.

We will go out of our area as a Buyers Broker. Typically it is for a client who is strong on finances and short on time looking for a large property with a specific criteria such as hunting. I am capable of evaluating any property but it typically has been in the western United States. These are done with a separate contract covering the Buyers objectives and my income and expenses.

What does the Recreational Vehicle Supply List Look Like

If you are a person who loves vacationing and long distance travel, then you would be the right type of person who would love to have a recreational vehicle, since this would provide you with the basic comforts and amenities required for you to live on wheels. A well-maintained RV is actually as good as a second home; with the advantage that you can take it anywhere you like to go.

What Type of Recreational Vehicle Supply Do You Know About?

The RV is usually designed to become a second home for people who travel for indefinite periods, in hostile habitats, and/or rural places where accommodations are not easy to find. This will provide all the regular amenities of a home, such as gas stove, bed, bath, toilet, kitchen, fridge, DVD, music system and so on.

Depending on the budget and the RVs also come equipped with their own pedal power generation system, water harvesting system, radio communication, dish antenna and TV, computer with internet and other such amenities that can enable your independent function despite the local provisions.

When you decide to go for the purchase of a RV it would be good if you run a perfunctory glance at the recreational vehicle supply available in the market. Besides the different types of self-contained motor homes there are three different options.

First, the travel trailer is a type of RV that is usually bigger and heavier than all the other RVs. It is usually pulled along with the help of a special hitch connection with the car/ truck you are driving.

Second, the truck camper is attached to the body of the car by means of a cradle; but it is smaller and becomes part of the body of the car/ truck

Finally, there is the fifth wheel travel trailer. As the name suggests, this type of RV is suspended over a fifth set of wheels while the front is attached to the main vehicle.

The type of recreational vehicle supply available in the market of a certain region is very dependent and limited to the demand of that region. The choice of recreational vehicle supply also depends upon the regions natural habitat. When the natural habitat is friendly and invites tourists, people tend to come and plan for longer stays, time during which some people decide to buy an RV. This too, in whatever small measure it may be, influences the recreational vehicle supply of the area

Recreation Property Market Expected to Regain Ground

A lack of interest in recreation or resort property is a "temporary condition," says a planning firm executive.

The issues clouding the property sector can be traced to a lack of consumer confidence based on current economic conditions, says Joe Miotto, vice-president of planning for NORR Architects and Planners. It will take a couple of years before the industry regains much of the ground it has lost, he says. Miotto was one of several industry insiders speaking at the recent Canadian Resort Investment Conference in Calgary.

Several projects have gone into receivership, or been shelved or cancelled, in the wake of the global recession and the reining in of spending by consumers.

"In many cases, the prospective real estate purchasers have the funds, but have become more conservative about real estate investment, perhaps due to worries associated with job loss, falling stock market prices and similar economic factors which reduce their confidence in real estate spending," says Miotto.

While the U.S. recreation property and resort segment has been pummelled, Canadian projects have not escaped unscathed, he says, adding that people are not losing interest in having a second home or recreation property, It's just the supply-demand curve at work. The market has been saturated with resort real estate product where supply has simply outran demand and real estate price continued to skyrocket.

"This has led to a need for a catch-up and price adjustment period which we are presently experiencing— which is more likely to occur, albeit slowly, over the next couple of years, especially with some of the price discounting that has been going on," says Miotto. There are three main reasons why he feels there will always be a strong demand for resort or recreation property.

- Because recreation property is usually in a limited supply due to the difficulties associated with land availability, lengthy land use approvals, and typically high infrastructure costs.
- Because of an "ever-present desire to improve lifestyle opportunities as a result of more frantic and challenging work environments."

- Because owning resort real estate typically represents a good investment. Values per square foot are usually very high compared to traditional real estate.

As the industry continues to improve along with the economy—and the level of consumer confidence —Miotto says there are two demographic markets that will show interest in second home or reproperty ownership.

The first is the baby-boomer crowd, those with money and time and living much more active lifestyles. The other emerging market is the children of the boomers—Generation X. Between 25 and 40 years old, these people are high-energy individuals, some with families, who are looking for a connection to the outdoors. They also stand to inherit significantly from their boomer parents, so they also have the income to invest in resort property.

As for the industry, itself, Miotto says it will be much more conservative in the future "as the recent years' phenomenon was not representative of normal market conditions."

Bottom of form

The basic need of the world is to save time for the own self and for their family members. There are also some of the people who see their children in week ends only!! Recreational Vehicles are specially made for those who never go for the vacations with their families for the burden of works. Recreational Vehicles facilitate them the facility and the room to make their jobs and to perform whatever they feel to and still the vehicle moves on. So, it's a road vehicle with the splendid services that any of the homes requires. So, RVs are the second option for the housing facilities and recently the Government of some states have made it legal to attend the RVs as the second homes. So, the RVS are becoming more and popular in the trend. People have started understanding the value of the time spending with the families and also the drawbacks of the lives of the people who were and are just living like a clock!!

But, there are so many different types of RVs and they are available in various models and also in various sizes. Motor homes are the most reputed types and people who are wishing to have a luxurious staying while driving can select the option of Motor homes. Motor homes for sale are the vehicles with the great superiority and spontaneously. They are also available in the online business and people are highly desperate in saving their time and money by owning the motor homes for sale.

Actually, all the RVs and the Motor homes are quite costlier option and they are available in the higher prices that are unbelievable. So, people have started demanding the used and second hand RVs that re cheaper in the rated and reasonable in the qualities. The Used RVs are better option for those who have lower cost of budget and still a good quality of the vehicle for the using.

So, to have the best of your life's experience, you should definitely go for the Recreational Vehicles that are better for the driving and journey purpose and best for the staying and accommodations purpose. They also are better for the money saving purpose of accommodations. Also they are better for the home liking purposes and give a good feel even on the wheels. So, the RVs and Motor homes are the most appropriate and affordable options for the longer picnic with the families and also while going the country side. Have them, you'll have the comfort!!

Consider a Second Home as an Investment Property

Arizona has long been the preferred vacation destination for northerners looking for a break from the bitter cold of winter. Some of these tourists even purchased a second home in Arizona for their part-time residence. But second homes in Arizona are not just for the average "snow bird", and these second homes don't have to be a typical retirement property.

More and more people are considering a second home for an investment property. In fact, sales of second homes accounts for a third of all real estate sales in the last year. Unlike the typical retiree property, many second home properties are used as rental properties for investment gain. These home owners realize income from the rental, as well as tax benefits and appreciation in value.

As the population ages, there is a significant increase in the number of people considering a second home for investment potential. Many people consider these second homes as short-term investments, and long-term retirement potential.

These second-homes aren't necessarily small single-family properties or small apartment-like condominium. Instead these investment properties are often properties the investor can picture themselves living in long-term. This means the properties may offer amenities that are for more custom and appealing to a very active population. Investment properties are located close to golf courses and recreational properties, feature spectacular view, easy access to spas, right property in the right location can mean a steady stream of executive renters, and a great rental income. This second property can not only bring in income, but pay off the mortgage long before retirement.

Real estate investment is an excellent way to grow wealth. These second homes give owners a unique opportunity to accrue value. In Arizona, real estate prices have appreciated at a truly spectacular rate. While prices have cooled down from the lightening-hot rates of the past year, appreciation still remains extremely strong. When compared to other investment opportunities, it's clear that real estate is a stable and profitable investment.

There are a number of mortgage options that are quite unique to the second home market. For investors that are would like to pursue a second home, a quality mortgage agent can show you a number of options that make the second home not only possible, but extremely profitable.

European Cities: Towards a "Recreational Turn"?

Concepts and the Oretical Framework: Cities as Places in a "Regime of Dwelling"

Several concepts need to be defined and examined for their adequacy: "city," "recreation," "tourism," and "recreational turn." These concepts establish a theoretical horizon, in which the *spatial* dimensions of society are seen as crucial. As such, the concept of space as allowing cognitive operations of orientation, distance, arrangement, spatial organization, placement, recognition of various spatial qualities and so forth is a central point of analysis.

More precisely, it stems neither from an approach where space is seen as "naturally" built and explained by "natural laws" or closely related (such as in classical approaches of "distance decay"), nor from an approach in which space is seen as the material "surface" or Cartesian *res extensa* on which the social is projected. Rather, it is an approach where the central perspective is that of an actor-and practice-oriented "geography making" by various types of actors. More precisely, it is an approach whereby this geography making stems from practice in everyday life, in which the multifold relationships to space are at stake. This "doing with space," which I call "dwelling" (*Wohnen* in German and *habiter* in French), is addressed within a phenomenologically informed practice-based approach rooted in 20th century developments of social theory. The following concepts should be seen within this broader theoretical framework, in which actors fabricate space through their actions, while being embedded in situations where spatial dimensions—from the local to the global level, and from material to meta-geographical constructions—are Approaching the tourist dimensions of cities raises the question of the *kind* of places concerned, of their *quality*. How can the concept of "city" be defined in contemporary Europe? How can we speak of "cities" without speaking of places that are not cities?

This classical scientific problem is particularly difficult with regard to urban places because of confusion and difficulty in drawing adequate distinctions. One important question, often raised since Lefebvre (1974) or Castells (1973) in the late 1960s and early 1970s is: can we still speak of "the" city, or has the urban phenomenon become too manifold to assign one word to it? Many problems remain unsolved: 1) the urban/rural opposition: is the countryside an urban place for residence and recreation? 2) the "culturalist" definitions of the city in context: is there still a "European" city in the sense of a culturally different urban place, or do processes on the global level affect cities in Europe, Asia, Africa and South America in the same manner, thus no longer allowing us to give culture-based definitions of urban spaces? 3) the delimitation of city in comparison with agglomeration or "urban region", 4) the differentiated urban qualities of places, between global cities and small cities, industrial agglomerations, countryside, tourist resorts etc.

Within the framework of dwelling, a city is seen here as a place of specific qualities with which its inhabitants cope—i.e., mobilize as resources within their actions, recognize as problems within their practices, or give sense to by encoding a certain meaning through their practice. This meaning is constructed through the intentionality that guides the performed practice. Depending on the situation (the city is practiced in one way by the tourist and in another way by the resident), the individual experiences the city and the city makes sense as a place for specific practices. It is therefore the quality of the place, mediated through the specific situation, which is important for dwelling. The problem of defining the city, then, lies in the definition of a certain quality of place, as compared to other kinds of places (urban or non-urban), that is mobilized during an action.

Without probing deeper, we can use three important elements for the current purpose: (1) the distinction between different types of places where urbanness exists, at all levels of scale, making "city" one urban place among others; (2) on a local level of scale, seeing the "city" as designating the densest and most diverse organization of the urban; and (3) in comparison to tourist resorts, approaching cities as places with centrality that often have a poly-functional structure of urbanness (more diverse than resorts).

Tourism as a subsystem of dwelling and as a specific kind of recreation How do touristic dimensions contribute to the quality of the European city? How can tourism be defined? In order to fit into the actor-centred approach, the definition of tourism is one in which *tourists* are seen as essential. In fact, three interrelated issues are raised here: the definition of tourism, the question of recreation and the question of tourist places.

First, tourism is defined as a system of places, actors and practices, which has emerged in order to allow for inhabiting *other* places for the purpose of recreation. More narrowly, tourism could be defined as evolving in a sphere delineated by the various combinations of *displacement* and *recreation* of individual actors. It is therefore distinguished from other definitions of "visitors" for such multiple purposes as conferences, business and pilgrimage, visiting friends etc. The distinction is drawn between the everyday and the non-everyday, where the break with routine constitutes the essential experience.

This has been called "de-routinization" by Elias (1986). Tourist practices are therefore seen as a kind of de-routinization *based upon* a specific relationship with space: Through a displacement, a change of place, where alterity allows for a more efficient break with routine and recursive practices. This allows for an understanding of different practices implying mobility, where familiar / other places and recursive and non-recursive practices are distinguished from each other. From a historical viewpoint, it seems important to see tourism as a relatively autonomous "sphere" or "domain" that has progressively emerged over time, between 1800 and 1850. It is this emergence of a new domain in human societies that contributes to understanding its relative importance in contemporary cities.

Second, recreation should be understood here as a break with the everyday in order to attain "controlled relaxing of self-control" through various practices. At this point of the argument, it should be acknowledged that this dichotomy of recreational practices does not fit numerous recreational practices: going frequently to a second home, or to visit a friend or a family, are practices where the strangeness of place is mediated through a familiar "technology." We might also question the relative importance of tourist practices in an age of mobility, where recreational displacement is no longer rare, such as in bourgeois and middle class tourism between 1850 and 1950. Thus, it might be more adequate to conceptualize a continuum of recreational practices, where the otherness plays a greater or lesser role.

Third, tourist places are nowadays highly differentiated places. Their touristic quality of space emerges not only through markers—through space designed *for* tourists—but also through the situated action of tourists. A tourist place can be defined as a place for tourist situations in the sense that the presence of tourists in a non-tourist place does not immediately transform the latter into a tourist place. Rather, the tourist place is a temporary result of the emergence and stabilization of tourist practices. As a first step towards a more differentiated approach, three elements might help to distinguish four fundamental types of tourist places.

The distinctions are threefold: the tourist site (*site touristique*) is distinguished from other tourist places by its lack of capacity to receive staying visitors (bed capacity). The tourist post (*comptoir touristique*) is distinguished from the resort and city by the absence of the local population in the former and its presence in the latter. Finally, the tourist resort (*station touristique*) is distinguished from the tourist city (*ville touristique*) in that the latter has diverse urban and tourist functions, while the former has monofunctional characteristics. One element is therefore important in order to pinpoint a city where tourism is important: we need to look for diverse urban functions and centrality. The tourist city is therefore a specific kind of urban place and a specific kind of tourist place, defining a certain mode of urbanity.

The "recreational turn" is defined here as four interrelated processes: (1) the presence of tourists in urban places; (2) the desire, by local authorities or enterprises, to have tourists in their territory; (3) the rejection of tourism (i.e., a negative attitude towards tourism); and (4) a general interpretation scheme—a "gaze" in the Foucaldian sense—based on tourism, with which to interpret the world. It expresses itself in two main modalities, usually termed tourism and leisure.

This "recreational turn" could be related to the works of scholars like Dumazedier (1988) on the "civilisation of leisure" (*civilisation du loisir*) or Schulze (1997) on "society of experience" (*Erlebnisgesellschaft*). As the latter points out, the "aesthetic" is a certain way of giving meaning to numerous practices. As such, recreation is a way of giving meaning to practices through a particular stance and attitude. Indeed, we observe that although an "effort" is made, for example, climbing a mountain or going to an exhibition, that is not seen as work, but rather as "fun" and "relaxation." This attitude is by no means "natural"—in the nineteenth century, British alpinists were seen as "fools" by the indigenous inhabitants of Switzerland—but rather corresponds to the emergence of a new social value for practice. In this way, we can also understand that the activity of "shopping" is a playful one, whereas the veryday task of buying is not.

"Recreational turn" is therefore an expression that tries to back up the hypothesis of a greater importance of different forms of recreation in contemporary society, and more precisely in European cities. The fundamental idea is that of a change in the quality of the urban space affected by recreation. European cities develop a new quality by the relatively increased importance of recreation, and more specifically of tourism. The quality of urbanness depends to a great extent on the presence of tourists, of tourist-related business, of images informed by tourism. A "real" city –a place defined by a certain quality of urbanness – is essentially defined by its touristic quality.

The Context of the "Recreational turn" of European Cities

Several elements can be seen as essential in the ongoing process of recreationalization of urban space. Changing time budgets (working time down, leisure time up, especially the holiday: between four and six weeks a year, with the 1997 laws of reduction of labour time in France, even up to 11 weeks for senior executives), changing financial budgets (general rise in living standards between 1950 and 1970 in Europe), but also new ways of practising space, related to acquired tourist practices (more frequent but shorter holidays) are important elements. That means the longterm holiday —the German *Sommerfrische* or the French *villégiature* of the 19th and first half of the 20th century— of one or two months is being replaced by more differentiated recreation practices: one or two weeks' holiday, short trips for the weekend, long weekends, shorter but more frequent, year-round holidays, etc. The tourist industry is aware of this change, and advertises products such as "city breaks" or "short breaks". This new organization of the tourist practice is one important element of the rise of cities as places of recreation. This, by the way, invalidates the widespread thesis of tourist practices as "flight" from the cities to the countryside, mountains or seaside, developed by Enzensberger (1962) and widely acknowledged in the academic literature on tourism. What about the "flight" from the city to the city, or more precisely, from the (residential) suburb to the (touristic) centre of the city?

In press, *Hagar. Studies in Culture, Polity and Identities.* Preprint – please cite from local level, we find a huge discrepancy between different figures, and varying assumptions and counting principles from one source to another. For example, the cities, which are neither complete nor reliable. The research group on tourism in European cities, based in Vienna, tries to address this problem. For Europe as a whole, the European Commission estimates 2.2 billion bed nights (ECT, 2001), the most important countries being Italy, Germany, Spain, France and the United Kingdom. These figures have the advantage of coming from the same source, but the disadvantage of being contradictory to other sources: for example, the statistical surveys of the United Kingdom count respectively 204 million foreigners' bed nights and 490 million nationals' bed nights, a figure well above that given by the European Commission; French surveys count 567 million foreigners' bed nights, which exceeds the overall figure and is five times higher than that for foreigners given by the European Commission.

Furthermore, these figures do not allow for a regional or local breakdown. Nevertheless, we can establish a cartographic construction known as a "cartogram" based on those figures. It constructs the cartographical surface of countries depending on the importance of tourism, rather than the area of the national territory. It allows for a visual appreciation of the importance of tourism in European countries. Irrespective of the problem of exact figures, the conclusion drawn is that the scale of European tourism has increased significantly. The elementary counting unit is nowadays the million bed nights in an increasing number of European cities.

Apart from those cities where tourism plays a key role, there are numerous cities where tourism is present, but on a much smaller scale. Yet, establishing the recreational turn by counting tourists or bed nights is not sufficient. As tourism can be defined as a system of places, practices, representations and actors with a relative autonomy, other elements besides beds, bed nights and flows would be required in order to establish the contemporary context of tourism in European cities.

Processes of Recreationalization

Several processes lead to the increased and differentiated recreational quality of European cities, following — and this is the main hypothesis— the initial quality of the place. Indeed, the initial quality can be that of a tourist resort or an industrial agglomeration or it can be tourist-oriented since the 19th century (Paris, Venice) or only recently (Bilbao). This historical element contributes to difference between European cities. Although there is no coherent theoretical framework for addressing these issues, the following processes can be observed. Festivalization Festivalization is one of the processes of the recreational turn in European cities. Festivals can be defined as musical, operatic or theatrical events, taking place every year, at the same place and at approximately the same time.

The concept has been extended to incorporate the question of "events". We find two kinds of urban places that are important in that scheme: capitals (Edinburgh, Budapest, Istanbul, Vienna, Berlin) or medium-sized cities (Aix-en-Provence, Salzburg) and smaller tourist cities (Granada, Orange) or quasi-rural places where the festival is the dominant urban attribute (Marciac Jazz Festival). Festivals are also used to boost "anciently constituted" tourist resorts: Garmisch-Partenkirchen, San Sebastian, Verbier, Gstaad, Montreux, Baden-Baden. As a consequence, "festive cities" are created on the basis of *fêtes*: Paris (*Nuit Blanche* or *Paris-sur-Seine*), Reykjavik, Dublin, etc., directed not only towards the city's inhabitants, but, because of the increased geographical accessibility in terms of cost and time, to metropolitan inhabitants at the national and European levels too. Probably, the inspiring model for conceiving of an urban space as festive space is the case of Ibiza.

More generally, the attempt to create what are called "events" is more and more important, and is seen by promoters as one way to generate profit or to play with the image of the city. Sports events are exemplary for this process, because professional sport has grown in importance since the 1950s. Sportsmen and sportswomen have developed from amateurs to professionals, creating performances to be experienced as a spectacle by an ever greater audience. The "sports system" is now a huge industry, with virtually no break throughout the year, and performing on a global scale. The pattern of distribution of sports events points to metropolises and anciently constituted tourist resorts.

In press, *Hagar. Studies in Culture, Polity and Identities.* Preprint – please cite from the original manufacturing has been replaced by tourism. This can be observed more and more in those cities or urban regions where a decline of the manufacturing sector has occurred since the 1950s. The most spectacular examples are British and Irish cities: Dublin, Glasgow, Liverpool, Manchester, Sheffield and Birmingham have made enormous efforts to change the city's image and/or its infrastructure and the practices of people. But also in France (Lille), Germany (Ruhr, Hamburg), Italy (Genova, Torino) and Spain (Barcelona, Bilbao), the effects of a new recreational dynamic can be grasped. The processes taking place are differentiated, spanning from the constitution of industrial heritage to festivals, from sports to the display and imitation of lifestyle.

Liverpool is an interesting example because of the redefinition of what heritage might be: a malleable concept that can apply to virtually every situation. In the case of Liverpool, heritage defines the 19th century harbour facilities. It coincides with the urban regeneration towards the constitution of a tourist space. Two main operations were conducted: the preparation and recognition of parts of the city – the port and adjacent areas – as a "World heritage site" by UNESCO and the nomination as European Capital of Culture in 2008. The share of the hotel and catering sector in employment is about 5 %-which is relatively small compared to Benidorm, where it is 50%.

Barcelona is perhaps the model for all those transformation processes where tourists from all over Europe come to experience the leisure of the Barcelonese, and to stroll like them along the main street, the Ramblas. This was made possible through a politics of urban regeneration, "boosted" by the hosting of the Olympic Games in 1992.

Another process can be observed: the "heritageing" of inner cities. The result is what Ashworth and Tunbridge (1990) call "tourist-historic cities". This process is not entirely new and has its roots in the 19th century tourist development of Venice/Italy, Brugge/Belgium and Rothenburg ob der Tauber/Germany. It has expanded throughout the 20th century to more cities to the extent that few European cities are exempt from branding and image-construction through the slogan of "cultural heritage" This labelling raises the issue of a landmark that is worth visiting and fits in MacCannell's (1976) theory of a marker for a "thing" becoming a tourist attraction. The actors of this process are no longer local or the tourists themselves, which used to be the case in the 19th century. There are global or national actors, such as the UNESCO natural and cultural heritage project – roughly 1'000 "natural" or "cultural" sites are labelled, not to forget national laws for heritage protection.

Nevertheless, the UNESCO labelling and accompanying discourse raises the problem of an adequate distinction between "cultural" and "natural". Due to the aesthetic, tourist and heritaged gaze, the bio-physical elements, *e.g.* the Chinese karsts become cultural, because of the definition, by a special board of actors, of it *as* worth while seeing. Therefore, all those labelled things have become cultural. 15 This process of heritageing is most important for small and medium-sized cities and transforms profoundly the quality of space, such as in Trier/Germany, Toledo/Spain, Pisa/Italy, In press, *Hagar. Studies in Culture, Polity and Identities.* Preprint – please cite from the original Carcassonne/France. This process has extended to cities of the whole spectrum of the urban hierarchy, where more or less adequate historical layers are invented in order to display them to visitors. Nevertheless, this process of heritageing is not self-evident and creates conflicts on which elements of cities are "heritageable" and which are not.

Approaching the Modernity of Metropolises

The contemporary practice of short visits to cities – advertised as "short breaks" or "city breaks" – a trip lasting usually for a long weekend, is one element of the presence of tourists in cities. One observation or question can be made: those tourists being mostly "urbanites" themselves, how could we understand that they visit a *similar* place? Besides the experience of heritage, Duhamel (2006) identifies another fundamental process in the touristification of cities from the point of view of the tourist: to experience elements standing for *modernity*.

Since the London and Paris of the 19th century, the modernity of metropolises has been at the centre of the tourist agenda. Experiencing the urbanness of the city seems to constitute the key difference with resorts and heritage cities: the touristic practice of the city is based on its very urban, as a total experience, not of one element of it. This also allows for an understanding of the multiple ways of residing in a metropolis as a tourist: exchange of apartments or staying with inhabitants rather than in hotels are forms of contact with the otherness of the place. The objective is to experience the city not as an "outsider", but as an "insider", thus transforming the other place into a familiar place.

It is different to seeing the tourist city as a collection of tourist sites. From resorts to cities: a specific kind of urbanization Finally, there is another kind of city which can be called a "tourist city": ancient tourist resorts – or "anciently constituted tourist resorts", as Knafou (1996) calls them more precisely–becoming cities through the development of centrality and diverse urban functions.

This is one kind of urban place completely overlooked in the literature, because it is either addressed as a "resort" or as a "normal" city without grasping the specificities of such a city with ancient tourist elements. They can be described as a development of a mono-functional resort into a more diverse city, where tourism continues to play a key role, often embedded in what Soane (1993) terms "resort regions". In Europe, there are two kinds of such "tourist cities". The bigger ones, such as Nice/France, Brighton & Hove/United Kingdom, Wiesbaden/Germany, and the smaller ones, such as Garmisch-Partenkirchen/Germany, Saint-Malo/France, Montreux/Switzerland etc. They have in common their emergence as tourist sites *before* the more recent rise of mass tourism.

This corresponds to the first and second periods of tourism's development: the first between 1780 and 1830, the second between 1830 and 192016. The process of urbanization is an interesting one:

the diversification of recreational practices develops alongside population growth – both permanent and second homes – and the emergence of centrality in former non-central places. Vacation Home Sales to Surge, Study Says-Second Homes: Ecologists concerned about increased demand for resort properties in 1990s as baby boomers move into the age group that typically buys them.

In the next 10 years, droves of baby boomers may be heading for the hills. And for the mountains. And for the beaches. According to a new survey financed by the real estate and resort-development industry, demand for second homes may surge in the 1990s as baby boomers move into the age group that typically buys vacation properties. Demand for vacation properties may soar from its current level of about 135,000 purchases a year to as many as 450,000 a year, according to the study's authors. "Baby boomers generally are reaching that point in their lives where people historically have purchased vacation homes," said Steven S. Miner, research director of Eugene, Ore.-based Ragatz Associates Inc., which conducted the survey.

But the shift of development to the nation's hinterlands already is a matter of grave concern to environmentalists, who worry that more people and more traffic in once-pristine areas will damage wilderness areas. Now, in a new twist, some are advocating that the federal government take a new look at the ways in which it is helping to accelerate the process.

A U.S. Forest Service report, based on public hearings and backed by environmental groups, has suggested that the federal government should reconsider the tax breaks it gives to people who buy vacation homes in such ecologically important areas as New England's Northern Forest.

"The federal tax provision to deduct the interest on second-home mortgages may encourage the demand for recreational development and could be partially responsible for the increased rate of land conversion threatening the Northern Forest," the report said. "While the purpose of the deduction is to stimulate growth and construction, it may be having other effects in the Northern Forest." For many within the real estate industry, the mortgage-interest deduction is a key issue. Under current law, people who own second homes can deduct from their taxable incomes the mortgage interest they pay on the properties. In other words, depending on a household's tax bracket, the federal government will subsidize up to one-third of the cost of owning a vacation home.

Policy Document o Preserve it

The IRTRC policy was adopted on the 18th of December 2007 as a variation to the 2005-2011 Waterford County Development Plan.

Amendment to Existing Tourism Policy as per the County Development Plan 2005-2011

Proposals to develop low density residential developments for permanent accommodation or holiday home use removed from designated settlement centres were previously contrary to the policies of the Development Plan as set out in Chapter 3 (Settlement Strategy), Chapter 6 (Economic Development) and Chapter 9 (Development Standards). However it was considered that the development of golf courses, hotels, race courses and other tourist developments/leisure facilities located in rural unzoned areas, which provide an important local/national amenity, may form the basis for justifying limited on-site residential development. To allow this, however, some of the policies as set out in the County Development Plan 2005-2011 had to be amended as follows:

Rural Settlement Strategy

Should Read as Follows

The success of the County Settlement Strategy will be dependent on the ability of the Local Authority to channel development into the identified zoned settlements.

Whilst the measures outlined in Section 3.6 will promote this, a key factor in the success of the County Development Strategy will be the degree to which development outside of the designated nodes can be controlled. To do this, it is necessary to establish a Rural Settlement Strategy, which will set out how it is envisaged that development will take place outside of the zoned areas.

The Rural Settlement Strategy, as set out in the Plan is based on the National Spatial Strategy 2002-2020, the Regional Planning Guidelines and the Sustainable Rural Housing Guidelines for Planning Authorities issued by the DoEHLG. The strategy is also linked to other key elements such as the Housing Strategy, demonstrated development pressures, and associated projections such as future population levels, etc.

This strategy will be implemented in parallel with the policy on the provision of housing in association with Integrated Rural Tourism and Recreational Complexes and medium sized tourism development and on tourism zoned lands.

Rural Tourism

It is recognised that the growth of the tourism industry is critical to the economy of the county. This is particularly true in the rural areas where employment opportunities are reducing and traditional employment levels in agriculture are in decline. While seeking to ensure that most tourism development with associated accommodation facilities, is located in or close to towns or villages or on tourism zoned lands, the council recognises that, by its nature, some tourism developments may require other locations. In this regard consideration will be given to the provision of Integrated Rural Tourism and Recreational Complexes *and* Medium sized developments at appropriate locations throughout the county.

Integrated Rural Tourism and Recreational Complexes

In recent years, there has been an increase in the demand for, and development of, Integrated Rural Tourism and Recreational Complexes and Golf Courses. Associated with this has been the demand for housing, either for temporary letting as holiday homes or for permanent residential use. It is acknowledged that the provision of accommodation of an individual unit nature, (self contained apartments, lodges, chalets or houses) is emerging as an integral element of the Integrated Rural Tourism and Recreational Complex (IRTRC). An Integrated Rural Tourism and Recreational Complex can be defined as a high quality tourism development located in a rural location which includes the following:-

- A quality hotel (min 50 beds); and
- A leisure centre/spa, conference centre or similar and
- Other facilities such as a 18 hole golf club or a similar major public facility such as an Adventure centre, marina, indoor recreation centre.

Such proposals may also include tourism related residential developments, which are ancillary to the main tourist attraction. The council also recognises that an element of permanent housing may be considered to balance seasonal fluctuations in population associated with such tourism developments, and to support the initial economic viability of such proposals, which will be important generators of employment in rural areas.

Consideration will be given to the provision of IRTRCs where the developments comply with the following criteria:-

- Complies with the Scenic Landscape Evaluation and coastal development and landscape policies;
- Relates to the scale and level of activity in the locality;
- Will not have a significant adverse impact on the character or siting of settlements or the amenity of existing residents;
- Will not have a significant adverse affect on the character or appearance of the County's countryside and will generally retain the open nature of the land;
- Will not impact on road safety or the free flow of traffic;
- Will not have a significant adverse impact on sites of nature conservation value or archaeological importance or the built heritage;
- New dwellings are of a good standard of design and are sympathetic to the landscape in terms of their siting, design and materials;
- Include a phasing plan for the provision of the proposed facilities.

An IRTRC proposal should be a sustainable development, which demonstrated long term viability. Overall there should be an emphasis on innovation in design and layout providing for an integrated development linking units to open space and facilities. Existing site features, including trees and hedgerows should be retained as far as possible to form a comprehensive landscaping scheme.

Applications for IRTRCs containing holiday homes should be accompanied by details of an agreement that the overall development will be retained in single Management or as a time share, short term letting of similar arrangement. In No instance shall the holiday homes/

holiday units be sold for or used as permanent dwelling places. Permanent residences may be permitted in association with an IRTRC application and the criteria as set out in Section 9.4.2.

Medium Sized Tourism Developments and Associated Holiday Homes

Medium sized tourism developments of a local scale may have the capacity to accommodate holiday homes. A smaller tourism development may consist of the provision of any of the following:-

- a quality hotel (minimum of 50 bedrooms), or
- a golf course, or
- a major equestrian centre, holiday camp (similar to Trabolgan), marina, adventure centre, sporting activities with a maritime/ estuarine location or
- similar type facility of regional attraction.

It is recommended that the paragraphs on 'Tourist accommodation and facilities', 'Holiday homes and second homes' and associated policies be amended as set out below:-

The paragraphs on 'Tourist accommodation and facilities', 'Holiday homes and second homes' and associated policies is amended as follows:

> *The development of tourism accommodation is crucial to the effective development of the tourism industry in the county. Apartment type developments are best located within the existing established tourism centres. Clustered holiday home developments will also be most appropriate in these centres, or in other settlements throughout the county where facilities and services are available or on tourism zoned lands or as part of IRTRC or medium sized tourism developments. In settlement areas outside of established tourism centres, it is important to ensure that holiday home developments will not impact negatively on the existing residential community (e.g seasonal fluctuations in population levels and the closure of services during winter months).*

In keeping with the Sustainable Rural Housing Guidelines for Planning Authorities, there will be a presumption against holiday home/ second home development in areas outside of settlements, in Visually Vulnerable and Sensitive Areas, and along Scenic Routes as designated in the Scenic Evaluation Map. However, consideration will be given to the development of appropriately scaled holiday homes on tourism zoned lands or as part of IRTRC or medium sized tourism developments. The council will encourage suitably scaled clusters of holiday homes in settlements and in IRTRCs, and will facilitate tourist houses in areas where such development will not contravene the council's Settlement Strategy as outlined in Chapter 3 and/or the Rural Tourism policy.

ED7: To support the development of appropriately scaled holiday home/second home development within existing settlements or on tourism zoned lands or in association with IRTRC or integrated into medium sized tourism developments in accordance with the Settlement Strategy set out in Chapter 3 or the Rural Tourism policy.

ED8: To support the development of appropriately scaled permanent home development in association with IRTRCs.

Tourism Development

The section of the Development Standards, which sets out the criteria for the assessment of residential tourism development, is amended as follows

The Council requires that planning applications for developments of this nature to demonstrate that the development provides for all year round usage. Any residential tourism development must demonstrate that it:-

- Does not place unsustainable demands upon the existing or planned infrastructure capacity of the area;
- Does not conflict with the maintenance of the natural and cultural heritage of the area;
- Is located within or adjacent to an established settlement node, on tourism zoned lands or in association with an IRTRC or a viable tourism facility; or medium sized tourism development.
- Reinforces the provision of non-residential tourism facilities in the county either through integration with established facilities or by the provision of new facilities; and
- Minimises the need for additional vehicular journeys to/ from visitor facilities in the immediate environs.

Development of an IRTRC and Housing on a Green Field Site

On a green field site, consideration shall only be given to the provision of dwellings/tourist accommodation units, where it is demonstrated that they are in accordance with the relevant criteria set out hereunder.

Development of Holiday Homes in Association with an IRTRC on a Green Field Site

The following standards shall be applied to holiday home development on green field sites:-

- The provision of holiday homes will only be considered where the total landholding is not less than 100 acres (40ha).
- The number of holiday homes permitted will be dependence on site specifics – area of site, location, degree of visibility, natural screening, scale of tourist facilities available/to be provided. Each case will be assessed on its merits.
- The building height/scale of the units shall be relative to the complex, the topography and screening of the site, etc.
- The holiday homes/units shall be clustered in an open plan layout with shared amenity space.
- The IRTRC and associated holiday homes/accommodation, excluding any related limited provision of permanent housing, should be developed and managed as a single unit.
- The holiday homes shall be used for short term occupation only and not used for permanent residential use. Where holiday homes are sold or transferred in ownership, the new owner shall be required to enter into a legal agreement with the Planning Authority that the unit shall not be used as a permanent home.
- The developer will be required to pay a special financial contribution towards the provision of social and affordability housing which will be calculated using a similar methodology to that applicable under Part V of the Planning and Development Act (2000-2006).
- All development shall have regard to the Scenic Landscape Evaluation and specific site suitability for development – drainage, access, etc.
- Provision of adequate water supply to serve the development and safe treatment and disposal of sewage, which would not prejudice the ground water quality in the area.

Development of Permanent Homes in Association with an IRTRC on a Green Field Site

The following standards shall be applied to permanent residential development on green field sites:-

- The provision of dwellings will only be considered where the total landholding is not less than 100 acres (40ha).
- The number of dwellings permitted will be dependence on site specifics – Location, topography, degree of visibility, natural screening, etc. Each case will be assessed on its merits. However in no case shall the number of dwellings provided exceed 1 unit per 8 acres (3 ha).
- Detached dwellings only will be considered (to avoid urban/ suburban patterns of development which would be unsuitable in a rural setting).
- Minimum site size of 0.5 acres (0.2ha).
- All development shall be required to comply with the minimum development standards as set out in the County Development Plan 2005-2011, except where in conflict with the above specified standards.
- The developer will be required to pay a special financial contribution towards the provision of social and affordability housing which will be calculated using a similar methodology to that applicable under Part V of the Planning and Development Act (2000-2006).
- All development shall have regard to the Scenic Landscape Evaluation and specific site suitability for development – drainage, access, etc.
- Provision of adequate water supply to serve the development and safe treatment and disposal of sewage, which would not prejudice the ground water quality in the area.

Development of an IRTRC and Housing in Association with a Protected Structure

Consideration shall only be given to the provision of holiday homes and permanent dwellings where the Protected Structure or group of structures within the curtilage and/or attendant grounds are being refurbished and adapted for sustainable use. Such a decision shall be based on a full appraisal of the structure and setting. Appropriate subdivision of a structure may be also be an option.

For both permanent and holiday home development of the Protected Structure or structures within the curtilage and /or attendant grounds of a Protected Structure, the standards set out above for green field sites will applied, in addition to the standards set out below:-

- The immediate grounds of the main structure/complex and the avenue/driveway/entrances of the main structure/ complexes shall be maintained free from housing development and associated works.
- New housing shall be screened from the Main Structure/ complex by either the topography of the site or existing mature landscaping. Where there is no existing screening arising from either topography or planting, a minimum separation distance of 500m will be required to be maintained (this is a minimum guideline only and a greater separation distance may be required in certain circumstances).
- The building height of the dwellings shall be relative to the complex, the topography and screening of the site, etc., but in no case will the building height of exceed that of the protected structure.
- Consideration could be given to the conversion of existing stone stable buildings/courtyard building to high quality tourist accommodation.

However, it should be borne in mind that these are indicative maximum thresholds and not the minimum expectation of the developer. Regardless of the above criteria, some sites may not be suitable for such development. The suitability of the site will be determined by the Planning Authority and will be based on reports, and the potential impact of the proposed developments on the character of the Protected Structure and its setting (if applicable).

Guidelines for Development of an IRTRC and Housing in Association with a Protected Structure

In all cases, prospective developers will be required to hold pre-planning discussions with the Planning Section, the Conservation Officer and the Heritage Officer. Preplanning with Bord Failte would be advisable. Information to be submitted with any such application should include:

- A Cultural Heritage Impact Assessment report of the Protected Structure, which may include a Building Conditions and Conservation Report; (This is dependent on the site and level of proposed development);
- Description of intervention works necessary to consolidate the PS;
- Description of proposed works necessary to ensure continued use of the building (change of use will be considered where appropriate);
- Description of proposed dwellings, including site specific designs of the proposed housing which demonstrates that regard was had to the topography, landscape features and the built heritage of the site.
- Assessment of impact of proposed housing on the Protected Structure, its curtilage, setting and its landscape features.
- Assessment of the impact of the proposed development on the natural heritage of the site. This may include a tree survey and flora and fauna survey. (In some cases, this may be included in the Cultural Heritage Impact Assessment).
- A Masterplan for the holistic approach to the development of the site is necessary as careful management of the house, gardens and demesnes, which should be considered assets, will benefit public and developers alike.

The complexity of the reports required would be dependence on the specific site and the level of development proposed. Prospective developers should comply with:-

- Appendix B; Architectural Heritage Impact Assessments, The Architectural Heritage Protection, Guidelines for Planning Authorities, DoEHLG, 2004.
- 'Guidance Notes for the Appraisal of Historic Gardens, Demesnes, Estates and their settings', Cork County Council, April 2007. This will be superseded by guidance notes, which are currently being prepared by our Conservation Officer.

Development of Medium Sized Tourism Developments and Associated Holiday Homes on Unzoned Lands

The following criteria would have to be complied with for the development of a medium sized tourism facility with associated holiday homes:-

- The provision of holiday homes will only be considered where the total landholding is not less than 30 acres (12ha).
- The number of holiday homes permitted will be dependence on site specifics – area of site, location, degree of visibility, natural screening, scale of tourist facilities available/to be provided. Each case will be assessed on its merits.
- A business plan shall be submitted with any application to demonstrate the long term viability and sustainability of the tourism development and associated holiday homes.
- The tourism development should not detract from any existing tourism facilities in the area.
- The tourism facility and any associated holiday homes shall be built and managed as a single unit by a management company.
- No permanent dwellings shall be permitted in association with the tourist facility/development.
- The developer will be required to pay a special financial contribution towards the provision of social and affordability housing which will be calculated using a similar methodology to that applicable under Part V of the Planning and Development Act (2000-2006).
- All development shall have regard to the Scenic Landscape Evaluation and specific site suitability for development – drainage, access, etc.
- The building height/scale of the holiday homes shall be relative to the topography and screening of the site, etc.
- The holiday homes/units shall be clustered in an open plan layout with shared amenity space.
- All development shall be required to comply with the minimum development standards as set out in the County Development Plan 2005-2011, except where in conflict with the above specified standards.
- The facility and units should be accessible to all, and fully compliant with Part M of the Building Regulations.

Regardless of the above criteria, some sites may not be suitable for such development. The suitability of the site will be determined by the Planning Authority during the planning application stage

Recreational & Second Properties Cabin Fever? Mortgaging for Recreation Properties

All across Canada we're seeing the recreational property market continue to go through the cedar-shingled roof. Industry experts predict another year in which buyers seeking a property may outnumber the recreational properties available. The boomers are in their peak income years and have benefited from an unprecedented climb in the valuations on their primary homes. And across the country, they're scouring every lake, ocean beach and ski slope-looking for the perfect getaway.

When cottages first became the vogue around the turn of the last century, those getaways were generally charmingly rustic structures designed to give their owners a taste of a simpler way of life for the summer season. But today, recreational property markets are reporting a stunning increase in teardowns and renovations-as rustic simplicity gives way to luxury accommodations. Today's recreational property mix covers the gamut from luxury waterfront homes, resort-style condominiums, ski chalets and timeshare properties. Many of the traditional-style cottages are still standing, of course… and they sell for top dollar on the rare occasions that they actually come on the market.

But more and more average Canadians have cabin fever: they're looking for a recreational property both as an investment and an enhancement to their own lifestyles. And for many, the goal is achievable: we've seen historically low mortgage rates over the last few years-and greater affordability for ordinary Canadians.

But financing a recreational property is more challenging than funding a principal residence. Traditional lending institutions typically find second homes a much less desirable investment. Purchasers are often advised to take out an equity loan or a second mortgage on their principal residence in order to buy the recreation property.

But the lending landscape has been changing in the past few years. We are beginning to see that some lenders have developed flexible new mortgage products and policies that are specifically designed for the recreational property market. The upshot is that Canad ians who are longing for that cottage or condo may now be able to bypass conventional lending criteria-opening the door to ownership much sooner than they imagined. Recreational property mortgages are available for owner-occupied second properties, including winterized and non-winterized, with as little as 15 per cent down for purchasers with good credit. And in some cases, 10 per cent down could get you into the recreational property market if you qualify.

And do your homework. In today's heated recreational property market, some purchasers have an edge in the marketplace because they are cash buyers. To level the playing field, buyers who are financing their purchase may want to consider talking to a professional to determine approximately how much they qualify for before launching their search.

For some, recreational property is an attractive investment, with rentals providing an extra income stream. But the allure is usually more emotional: a cottage or condo often becomes a symbolic centre for family life, where families come together at all ages and stages in their lives to share common activities and traditions.

If you're dreaming of your own beach sunset or the perfect ski slope at your door, begin with a conversation with a mortgage professional. Your own getaway could be closer than yoWhat is a Recreational Vehicle and Its Classifications?

Are you the type of person who likes to travel to different places? Are you fond of camping and other recreational activities? Then, using a recreational vehicle would provide you with almost all the indispensable facilities that you will need on your travels.

In North America, people would rather define recreational vehicle as their second home. This is because they use the equipment as a means of transportation and at the same time a travel quarters.Generally, recreational vehicles are automobiles specially designed to serve as transitory home for people who are on travel, on a camping activity, or just about any activity that would require temporary dwelling at a certain time and place.

Most of the recreational vehicles consist of, but is not restricted to, a travel trailer, camping trailer, truck camper, and a fifth-wheel trailer. Actually, recreational vehicles can be set up like that of the truck campers, they can have their individual motor power like that of the motorhomes or they can be hauled by one more automobile just like the folding camping trailers and the travel trailers. Contrary to most popular belief, the basic description and definition of recreational vehicles do not include the mobile homes or the park trailers that are permanently manufactured to accommodate people for continuing dwelling, off-the-road motor vehicles, and conversion vehicles. To know more about recreational vehicles, here is a list of the different classifications of recreational vehicles:

1. Travel trailer. This refers to the recreational vehicle that has more weight than the other types of recreational vehicle. It is especially made to be hauled by most automobiles through the use of a frame hitch or a bumper.
2. Truck camper. This is one type of recreational vehicle where the component is attached to the bodywork or the cradle of a pick-up truck. It is mainly used for recreational camping purposes.
3. Fifth Wheel Travel Trailer. This is the type of recreational vehicle that is extraordinarily made to be drawn by a pick-up truck furnished with an exceptional frame hitch in the truck cradle.

These are just a few of the many classifications of recreational vehicles. Whatever type you want to use, you can be sure that every recreational vehicle has its own storage areas, beds, food preparation areas, and tables. These facilities may vary depending on the size of the recreational vehicle.

Recreation, Tourism, and Rural Well-Being

While the economies of many rural areas in the United States have been sluggish in recent years, rural communities that have stressed recreation and tourism have experienced significant growth. This has not gone unnoticed by local officials and development organizations, which have increasingly turned to recreation and tourism as a vehicle for development.

However, not all observers are convinced that the benefits of this approach are worth the costs. There are concerns about the quality of the jobs created, rising housing costs, and potential adverse impacts on poverty, crime, and other social conditions. This report assesses the validity of these concerns by analyzing recent data on a wide range of socioeconomic conditions and trends in U.S. rural recreation areas. The purpose is to gain a better understanding of how recreation and tourism development affects rural wellbeing.

Recreation and tourism development has potential advantages and disadvantages for rural communities. Among the advantages, recreation and tourism can add to business growth and profitability. Landowners can benefit from rising land values. Growth can create jobs for those who are unemployed or underemployed, and this can help raise some of them out of poverty. Recreation and tourism can help diversify an economy, making the economy less cyclical and less dependent on the ups and downs of one or two industries.

It also gives underemployed manufacturing workers and farmers a way to supplement their incomes and remain in the community. Benefiting from growing tax revenues and growth-induced economies of scale, local governments may be able to improve public services. In addition, local residents may gain access to a broader array of private sector goods and services, such as medical care, shopping, and entertainment. While other types of growth can have similar benefits, rural recreation and tourism development may provide greater diversification, and, for many places, it may be easier to achieve than other kinds of development—such as high-tech development—because it does not require a highly educated workforce.

Many of the potential disadvantages of recreation-related development are associated with the rapid growth that these counties often experience; on average, "recreation counties" grew by 20 percent during the 1990s, nearly three times as fast as other rural counties. Rapid growth from any cause can erode local natural amenities, for example, by despoiling scenic views.

Cultural amenities, such as historic sites, can also be threatened. Growth can lead to pollution and related health problems, higher housing costs, road congestion, and more crowded schools, and it may strain the capacity of public services. Small businesses can be threatened by growth-induced "bigbox" commercial development, and farms can be burdened by increased property taxes. In addition, newcomers might have different values than existing residents, leading to conflicts over land use and public policies.

Growth can also erode residents' sense of place, which might reduce support for local institutions, schools, and public services. Aside from these general growth-related issues, some specific problems have been linked to tourism and recreation industries. These include the potential for higher poverty rates associated with low-wage, unskilled workers who are attracted to the area to work in hotels, restaurants, and recreation sites. Higher poverty rates could lead to various other social problems, including higher crime rates, lower levels of education, more health problems, and higher costs of providing public services.

With this mix of positive and negative impacts, it is understandable why experts on development policy may be uncertain about the value of rural tourism and recreation development strategies. Hence, it is important that policymakers have access to information about the nature and extent of the socioeconomic impacts of this type of development.

Past research has examined some of the impacts. Much of that research, however, is in the form of case studies, with only a few empirical studies examining nationwide rural impacts, such as the articles by English et al. (2000) and Deller et al. (2001). English et al. examined the impact of tourism on a variety of measures of local socioeconomic conditions (local income, employment, housing, economic structure, and demographic characteristics). Deller and his colleagues examined recreational amenities (including recreational infrastructure), local government finances, labour supply characteristics, and demographic demand characteristics, estimating their effects upon the growth of local population, employment, and income.

Our research used an approach similar to that of English and his colleagues, which identified a group of tourism-dependent counties and then used regression analysis to estimate the effect of tourism on various indicators of local rural conditions. Using the new ERS typology of rural recreation counties developed by Kenneth Johnson and Calvin Beale (2002), we identified differences between rural recreation counties and other nonmetro counties for various indicators of economic and social well-being.3 We also examined socioeconomic variations by type of recreation county. We then used regression analysis to test statistically for the effect that dependence on recreation (including tourism and seasonal resident recreation) has on local socioeconomic conditions.

Details about the regression analysis are provided in the appendix. We hoped to shed light on several important questions about this development strategy. Among these are:

- How does rural recreation development affect residents' ability to find jobs?
- How are local wages and incomes affected?
- How does recreation development affect housing costs and local cost of living?
- What effect does recreation development have on local social problems such as crime, congestion, and poverty?
- How are education and health affected?
- How do various types of recreation areas differ in socioeconomic characteristics?

What is a Recreation County?

In 1998, Beale and Johnson identified 285 nonmetropolitan recreation counties based on empirical measures of recreation activity, including levels of employment and income in tourism-related industries and the presence of seasonal housing. They modified and expanded their typology a few years later. Their 2002 typology identified 329 recreation counties that fell into 11 categories, varying by geographic location, natural amenities, and form of recreation. It is this typology that ERS has adopted as its recreation county typology. We used the 2002 typology, which covered only nonmetropolitan counties. To simplify our analysis, we excluded Alaska and Hawaii.4 This reduced the number of recreation counties in our study to 311.

One of the advantages of this typology is that it includes not only places with significant tourism-related activity but also those with a significant number of seasonal residents. Like tourists, most seasonal residents are attracted by opportunities for recreation, including some who come simply to relax in a scenic rural setting. In theory, seasonal residents should have a bigger economic impact on the local community than tourists because they stimulate the housing industry and their season-long presence significantly increases the demand for a wide range of local goods and services. In addition, seasonal residents often later become permanent residents. Because many seasonal residents first came to the area as tourists, it is difficult, if not impossible, to separate the long-term impact of tourists from seasonal residents. Our use of the ERS typology, which covers both tourism and seasonal recreational/residential development, thus seems ideal for estimating the long-term, overall impacts of tourism and recreation combined.

Another advantage of this typology is that it is derived from a continuous variable—a weighted average of tourism and seasonal housing dependence. In theory, this continuous variable may be used more effectively to estimate impacts than a simple recreation/other nonmetro dichotomous variable because it allows us to examine variations in the extent of recreation. Similarly, the different types of recreation counties in the Johnson/Beale typology can be used to further elucidate and estimate the impacts of recreational activity on local socioeconomic conditions.

General Characteristics of Recreation Counties

The 311 recreation counties in our study are located in 43 States, but tend to be concentrated in the West, the Upper Great Lakes, and the Northeast. In the West, this reflects the ample opportunities for hiking, mountain climbing, fishing, and wintertime sports found in the many national parks and ski resorts there. By contrast, the high concentration of recreation counties in the Upper Great Lakes and Northeast—especially in New England and Upstate New York—is largely due to the popularity of long-established second homes in areas with lakes. Many of these areas also have significant wintertime recreation activities, including snowmobiling and skiing. Not surprisingly, recreation counties score higher (4.25) on ERS' natural amenities index than other nonmetro counties (3.34). Data from the 2000 Census reveal that recreation and other nonmetro counties average similar population sizes. However, during the last decade, the population of recreation counties has grown almost three times as fast (20 percent vs. 7 percent, on average). Recreation counties also have relatively low population densities, and more of their residents tend to live in rural parts of the county (those with less than 2,500 population).

Using the ERS 1993 county economic and policy typologies, we found that the economies in recreational counties were generally more diverse than in other nonmetro counties. For example, only 30 percent of recreation counties were highly dependent on a single major industry (agriculture, mining, or manufacturing), while 58 percent of other nonmetro counties were highly dependent on just one of these industries. Recreation counties also were slightly less dependent on neighbouring counties for employment; only 13 percent of recreation counties were identified as commuting counties (with a high percentage of their resident workforce commuting outside the county for employment), compared with 17 percent of other nonmetro counties. We also found that about a third (32 percent) of recreation counties were retirement-destination places vs. only 4 percent of other nonmetro counties.

How Were Recreation Counties Identified?

The 2002 Johnson/Beale typology covered only nonmetropolitan counties, using the 1993 Office of Management and Budget (OMB) definitions of metropolitan areas. Johnson and Beale began by examining a sample of wellknown recreation areas to determine which economic indicators were most appropriate for identifying other such counties.

They then computed the percentage share of wage and salary employment from the Census Bureau's 1999 County Business Patterns data and personal income from Bureau of Economic Analysis data as these data apply to recreation-related industries, i.e., entertainment and recreation, accommodations, eating and drinking places, and real estate. They also computed a third measure: the percentage share of housing units of seasonal or occasional use, from 2000 Census data.

They then constructed a weighted average of the standardized Z-scores of these three main indicators (0.3 employment + 0.3 income + 0.4 seasonal homes). Counties scoring greater than 0.67 on this recreation dependency measure were considered recreation counties. Next, they added several large nonmetro counties that did not make the cut but had relatively high hotel and motel receipts from 1997 Census of Business data. Additional counties were accepted if the weighted average of the three combined indicators exceeded the mean and at least 25 percent of the county's housing was seasonal, Then Johnson and Beale deleted 14 counties that lacked any known recreational function but appeared to qualify "either because they were very small in population with inadequate and misleading County Business Patterns coverage or because they reflected high travel activity without recreational purpose, i.e., overnight motel and eating place clusters on major highways."

These calculations produced their final set of 329 recreation counties. In 2004, ERS established these recreation counties as one of its county typologies. By 2004, some of these counties had changed their metropolitan status based on the new 2003 OMB definitions of metropolitan areas.

Many recreation counties (38 percent) were Federal land counties, meaning that at least 30 percent of the county's land was federally owned; only 7 percent of other nonmetro counties had that much Federal land. In addition, relatively few recreation counties (10 percent) had experienced persistently high levels of poverty, whereas about a fourth (26 percent) of other nonmetro counties fell into this category. Because recreation counties are not homogeneous with respect to these and other characteristics, the averages we present for all recreation counties mask considerable variation.

Economic Impacts

The conventional wisdom among researchers in recent years has been that recreation and tourism have both positive and negative economic impacts for recreation areas. On the positive side, recreation development helps to diversify the local economy, and it generates economic growth. It achieves this partly by acting as a kind of export industry, attracting money from the outside to spend on goods and services produced locally. It also stimulates the local economy through other means. Infrastructure, such as airports and highways and water systems, often must be upgraded to meet the needs of tourists, and such improvements can help foster the growth of nonrecreation industries in the area by attracting entrepreneurs and labour and by providing direct inputs to these industries.

Recreation development can involve significant economic leakages, however, in that many of the goods and services it requires come from outside the community—for example, temporary foreign workers often are drawn to the area to fill jobs in hotels, ski resorts, etc.—and many of the recreation-related establishments (restaurants, hotels, tour and travel companies) are owned by national or regional companies that export the profits. Thus, part of the money from tourists and seasonal residents ends up leaving the locality. Another economic drawback involves the seasonality of recreation activities, which can create problems for workers and businesses during off-seasons, though this may actually be a plus for places where seasonal recreation jobs are timely, coming when farmers and other workers normally have an off-season.

The greatest economic concern is that recreation development may be less desirable than traditional forms of rural development because it increases the incidence of service employment with relatively low wages. According to Deller et al. (2001), "There is a perception that substituting traditional jobs in resource-extractive industries and manufacturing with more serviceoriented jobs yields inferior earning power, benefits, and advancement potential" and that this may lead to "higher levels of local underemployment, lower income levels, and generally lower overall economic wellbeing."

In addition, many researchers are concerned that recreation may result in a less equitable distribution of income. These problems may be compounded by the higher housing costs in some recreation areas. These concerns reflect findings from individual case studies. Only a few studies have attempted to estimate how rural recreation areas nationwide differ on economic measures. Deller et al. (2001) found that rural tourism and amenity-based development contributed to growth in per capita income and employment, and concluded that as a result of the positive impact on income "the concern expressed about the quality of jobs created … appears to be misplaced." English et al. (2000) also found that rural tourism was associated with higher per capita incomes, and with a higher percent increase in per capita income, although they found no significant relationship for household income. English and his colleagues also found housing costs and the change in housing costs over time to be significantly related to rural tourism. On the other hand, they found no evidence that the distribution of income was less equal due to rural tourism. To address these economic issues, we examined a variety of indicators reflecting employment, earnings, income, and housing costs.

Employment

Two employment measures, the local employment growth rate and the local employment-population ratio (percentage of working-age resident population employed in 2000) are particularly illuminating.

Recreation counties, on average, had more than double the rate of employment growth of other rural areas during the 1990s: 24 percent vs. 10 percent. The regression analysis, moreover, indicated that the extent to which a recreation county was dependent on recreation was positively and significantly related to the rate of local employment growth. Employment growth generally offers residents more job opportunities, enabling some unemployed residents to find jobs and employed residents to find better jobs. However, job growth does not necessarily improve job conditions for current residents. If too many people come into the area seeking employment, and if those newcomers aggressively compete with locally unemployed (or underemployed) residents, the resident job seekers may end up having greater difficulty gaining employment. Thus, we need to look closely at employment data to determine how recreation affects the local ability to find jobs.

Data Sources

The source for most of our data is the Decennial Census (Census Bureau, U.S. Department of Commerce). Other sources include:

- The Bureau of Economic Analysis, U.S. Department of Commerce, for data on earnings per job, and the Bureau of Labour Statistics, U.S. Department of Labour, Local Area Unemployment Statistics, for employment growth.
- The Uniform Crime Reporting Program (an unpublished data source available on an annual basis from the Federal Bureau of Investigation (FBI)), for data on serious crimes. Note: These data have not been adjusted by the FBI to reflect underreporting, which could affect comparability over time or among geographic areas.
- The Area Resource File (a county-specific health resources information system maintained by Quality Resource Systems, under contract to the Health Resources and Services Administration, U.S. Department of Health and Human Services), for the age-adjusted death rate, the number of physicians, and the area (in square miles) used to compute population densities for regression analysis.
- Kenneth Johnson and Calvin Beale for the recreation county types and the measure of recreation dependency used in their 2002 article.

To measure the ability of residents to find jobs, we examined the percentage of the working-age population that was employed. For our study, we broke this into three separate rates covering three groups of the working-age population: ages 18-24, 25-64, and 65 and over. We hypothesized that recreation counties might be particularly advantageous for younger and older populations that may have a harder time competing in places with less job growth.

In addition, younger and older groups may find it more convenient to work in recreation counties, which are thought to provide more part-time and seasonal jobs than most other places. As expected, we found higher employment-population rates in recreation counties for both the younger and older age groups. However, the difference was less than 1 percentage point. The main working-age employment rate (ages 25-64) was roughly the same for both recreation and other nonmetro counties in 2000. However, for each of these age groups, the upward trend in the employment-population rate during the 1990s favoured recreation counties. Our regression analysis indicates that recreation had a positive and statistically significant impact on the employment rates for all three age categories in 2000. Recreation also had a positive and statistically significant impact on the increase in the employment rate during the 1990s, except for the older age group.

Earnings

Conventional wisdom suggests that a main drawback of tourism is that many of the jobs it creates are in restaurants, motels, and other businesses that tend to offer relatively low wages and few fringe benefits. But does this mean that rural recreation development generally leads to low-paying jobs?

To address this question, we examined average annual earnings per job (which include wages and salaries and other labour and proprietor income, but exclude unearned income and fringe benefits). We found that average earnings per job were $22,334 in 2000 for recreation counties—about $450 less than in other rural counties. The difference, though only about 2 percent, is consistent with the low-wage hypothesis. On the other hand, our finding that earnings per job increased faster in recreation counties than in other rural counties in the 1990s was not consistent with the conventional wisdom, but again, the difference was relatively small ($200).

Our regression analysis, however, found no statistically significant relationship between earnings per job and recreation dependency, at least no simple linear relationship. With regard to change in earnings per job during the 1990s, the regression analysis found that recreation had a positive and statistically significant impact on earnings per job. So these findings do not support the conventional wisdom that recreation results in generally lowpaying jobs.

The data on earnings per job covered all jobs in the county, including those filled by nonresidents. A different picture emerges when we look only at earnings per resident worker. Aside from excluding nonresidents employed in the county (who, in theory, might be lowering the average earnings per job in recreation counties), this measure totals the income workers receive from all the jobs they have. This is important because recreation counties often provide numerous part-time and seasonal jobs, potentially allowing more of their residents to have multiple jobs than the residents of other counties. The average worker's earnings from multiple jobs exceeded the average earnings per job. In recreation counties, earnings amounted to $29,593 per resident worker (16 years or older) in 1999—about $2,000 more than in other rural counties—an 8-percent difference. Our regression analysis found recreation had a positive and statistically significant effect on earnings per resident worker. Thus, some residents may work more hours in recreation counties, but on average they end up earning more than residents of other nonmetro counties.

Income

Earnings are only one source of income. Other sources include interest receipts, capital gains, and retirement benefits like social security. Because many recreation areas have attracted wealthy individuals—including retirees, whose earnings are only a small part of their incomes—we expected recreation county income levels to be higher than in other rural areas. Consistent with this expectation, we found average per capita income was 10 percent higher in recreation counties than in other nonmetro counties. Moreover, per capita income levels were growing more rapidly during the 1990s in recreation counties than in other nonmetro counties. These findings were reflected in our regression analysis, which found recreation had a positive and statistically significant effect on both the level of per capita income and the change in per capita income over time. This should also benefit the community as a whole, because higher incomes mean an increase in demand for local goods and services, as well as increased local government tax collections and contributions to local charities and other social organizations. One problem in interpreting per capita incomes is that they average together the incomes of the wealthiest and the poorest individuals. Thus, a small number of extremely wealthy people could make the community seem much better off than with other measures, for instance, the income of the typical (or median) person in the county. If recreation counties had more wealthy individuals than other rural counties, the per capita measure might be a misleading indicator of how the average family or household in each of these counties differed in income. For this reason, we include a second income measure: median household income in the county in 1999.

Using this measure, we found that median household income was 10 percent higher in recreation counties than in other rural counties. The recreation county advantage amounted to $3,185 per year for the median household. The regression analysis reflected this finding, showing a positive and statistically significant relationship between recreation and both the level and change in median family income.

Housing Costs

One of the main complaints about recreation areas is that the cost of living in them is often higher, offsetting much of the advantage that residents might obtain from their higher incomes. Of particular concern is that high living costs could become a significant hardship for people struggling to raise families on minimum-wage jobs. A high cost of living could force some lower paid workers (including some longtime residents) to look for housing outside the area.

The cost of housing is one of the most important contributors to the cost of living. According to Census data in 2000, median monthly rents for housing averaged $474 in recreation counties, 23 percent higher than the $384 median rent in other nonmetro counties. Our regression analysis also found a positive and statistically significant effect of recreation on median rent. Rents also increased faster during the 1990s in recreation counties, with the extent of recreation positively and significantly related to the extent of rent increase.

Though recreation counties had higher rents than other nonmetro counties, over the course of a year this amounted to a difference of only $1,080 per household—about a third of the $3,185 advantage we found in median household income in recreation counties. So after deducting for their higher rents, we found that households in recreation counties still had a significant income advantage over those in other rural counties.

It is difficult to draw conclusions from this kind of information, for several reasons. First, rents show only part of the housing cost picture. Most housing units in the nonmetro counties we studied (in both recreation and other nonmetro counties) are owner-occupied rather than rented. Assuming that higher rents reflect higher home prices and greater equity in homes, higher home prices should increase the wealth of homeowners in recreation counties. In addition, higher rents and home prices may reflect better housing quality in recreation counties, rather than simply higher costs. This might be expected because more of the housing in these rapidly growing places is likely to be relatively new (and hence more valuable), and recreation county residents, having generally higher incomes, may demand better housing than residents of other nonmetro counties. Higher home values also increase the local tax base, which may lead to higher tax collections, enabling local governments to increase public services. Thus, on balance, it is unclear whether these higher housing costs are a plus or minus for the community.

Social Impacts

Various researchers have examined the relationship between nonmetro recreation and social conditions in a community. Page et al. (2001) note that rapid population growth in nonmetro recreation counties has resulted in overcrowded conditions and traffic congestion. Recreation may also affect local poverty rates. Some authors have argued that recreation activity creates new sources of employment, helping to raise the poor from poverty. Others have pointed to the low-wage, seasonal, and part-time nature of many tourism jobs, arguing that tourism may actually add to the number of poor in the community. Recreation affects social conditions in other ways. For example, Page et al. argue that tourism and recreation activity may help to maintain or improve local services, such as health facilities, entertainment, banking, and public transportation, because of the increased demand that tourists generate for these activities. The relationship between recreation and crime has also been explored by a number of researchers, with a popular question being whether casinos increase criminal activity.

To address social impact concerns, we identified eight social indicators. Two involve conditions associated with rapid population growth; one identifies a population subgroup (persons in poverty) that may present special challenges; two relate to education; two deal with health-related concerns; and one measures crime.

Population Growth

The first social variable we examined was the county population growth rate during the 1990s. Population growth can be beneficial for stagnant or declining rural areas looking for new sources of employment and income, but in some places it can bring problems.

This is particularly true if growth occurs rapidly and haphazardly, contributing to sprawl, traffic congestion, environmental degradation, increased housing costs, school overcrowding, a decrease in open land, and loss of a "sense of place" for local residents. Perhaps because of their natural amenities and tourist attractions, recreation counties experienced a 20.2-percent rate of population growth between 1990-2000, nearly triple the 6.9-percent rate for other nonmetro counties during the same period.

These results are consistent with our linear regression analysis, which found a positive and statistically significant relationship between recreation and the county population growth rate. Further analysis revealed an apparent curvilinear relationship, in which recreation counties with moderate recreation dependencies experienced higher growth rates than those with smaller and larger recreation dependencies.

Travel Time to Work

This variable was included to test the hypothesis that growth in recreation counties may lead to increasing traffic congestion. We found that mean commute times for recreation and other rural counties were not significantly different in 2000. Moreover, during the 1990s, commute times increased at roughly the same rate (4.4 percent for recreation counties vs. 4.3 percent for other rural counties). The regression analysis, however, revealed a significant negative relationship between recreation dependence and change in travel time to work during the 1990s. One explanation may be that expanded economic opportunities in recreation counties during the 1990s meant that residents had to travel shorter distances for jobs.

Poverty Rate

Poverty poses a problem for communities by increasing the costs of providing public services and contributing to crime rates, health problems, and neighbourhood blight. Previous research has found that an expanding tourist industry is linked with a decreasing rate of poverty. Given that many recreation counties have attracted well-off retirees and that average income levels have risen in recreation counties, the counties might, on average, be expected to have fewer individuals living in poverty than other nonmetro counties.

However, as noted earlier, some have argued that tourism, by expanding the number of lowpaying, part-time jobs, could increase the number of individuals living in poverty in these counties. We found that the poverty rate was substantially lower in recreation counties than in other rural counties. In 1999, 13.2 percent of all residents in recreation counties were living in poverty, compared with 15.7 percent in other nonmetro counties. Mirroring the national trend of declining poverty rates during the 1990s, the proportion of residents living in poverty during the decade declined (at approximately the same rate) in both recreation and other rural counties. Our regression analysis also found a significantly negative relationship between recreation and the poverty rate. In addition, the regression analysis found a statistically significant negative relationship between recreation and the change in the poverty rate.

Educational Attainment

Previous research has identified the central role that education plays in rural poverty. Education is important, not only because it contributes to the economy, but also because it can affect the quality of life in rural communities and can help raise people out of poverty.

Nonmetro areas with lower levels of education tend to be poorer and offer fewer economic opportunities for their residents. Migration (movement to another area) tends to increase with higher levels of education. Hence, recreation counties, which have had many in-migrants in recent years, may be expected to have higher levels of educational attainment than other nonmetro counties. English et al. (2000) found rural tourism to be associated with higher levels of educational attainment. We examined educational attainment at two levels: high school and college.

Our results show that residents in recreation counties have higher levels of education than other nonmetro residents. Recreation counties have both a smaller share of residents 25 years or older without a high school education, and a higher share of those with at least a bachelor's degree, than residents of other nonmetro counties. In 2000, 18.4 percent of residents age 25 or older in recreation counties did not have a high school diploma, compared with 25 percent in other nonmetro counties. For the same year, 19.2 percent of recreation county residents age 25 or older had a 4-year college degree or higher, compared with 13.6 percent in other nonmetro counties. During the 1990s, educational attainment on both measures improved in recreation as well as other nonmetro counties. These findings are supported by our regression analysis, which found that recreation had a significant negative correlation with the share of residents without a high school diploma and a significant positive correlation with the share of residents with a bachelor's degree or higher. In addition, a statistically significant relationship was found between recreation and an increase in the share of college-educated residents during the 1990s. However, the change in the share of high school graduates during the 1990s, although positive, was not significantly related to recreation.

Health Measures

Health is important for quality of life. In some recreation counties, many individuals moving in are retirees who demand more from health services than younger people; this could result in improved health services in these places. Many recreation counties are in pristine locations with clean air and water, which might also lead to better overall health. In addition, residents in recreation areas are probably more likely to be involved in outdoor activities than individuals in other nonmetro areas, which may also promote better overall health.

Our indicators of local health conditions—the number of physicians available and the age-adjusted mortality rate—support the view that recreation county residents have better health and health services than other nonmetro residents. In 2003, recreation counties had 123 physicians per 100,000 residents, compared with 83.4 per 100,000 residents in other nonmetro counties.

The analysis also shows that the age-adjusted death rate (computed as a 3-year average) was almost 10 percent lower in recreation than in other nonmetro counties. Our regression results show that recreation had a significantly negative correlation with the age-adjusted death rate. However, the relationship between recreation and the number of physicians, although positive, was statistically insignificant.

Crime Rate

Many researchers have looked at the link between recreation activity and crime. Some types of recreation counties attract criminals who prey on tourists inseason and rob unoccupied houses during the off-season. Also, some low income residents of these counties may commit crimes of opportunity, taking advantage of the influx of well-off outsiders. Some researchers have argued that crime may be particularly associated with casinos.

The results of our analysis indicate that recreation counties had nearly a 17-percent higher rate of serious crime (murder and non-negligent manslaughter, forcible rape, robbery, and aggravated assault) than other nonmetro counties. In 1999, the overall rate of serious crime in recreation counties was 2.8 incidents per 100 residents, compared with 2.4 incidents per 100 residents in other nonmetro counties, a statistically significant difference. These results are consistent with our regression analysis, which found that a significantly positive relationship exists between recreation and the crime rate.

However, the meaning of this finding is not clear because the crime rate is a biased measure in recreation areas, due to the fact that crimes committed against tourists and seasonal residents are included in the total number of crimes (the numerator of the crime rate), while tourists and seasonal residents are not included in the base number of residents (the denominator of the crime rate). So the crime rate is expected to be higher in recreation areas, even if residents of these areas are not more likely to be crime victims than residents of other rural areas.

Variations by Type of Recreation County

As noted, Johnson and Beale (2002) categorized each recreation county as belonging to 1 of 11 mutually exclusive recreational groupings, a classification that provides greater insight into the recreational component of each county. The single most common category is the Midwest Lake and Second Home, accounting for 70 counties and overwhelmingly concentrated in central and northern Michigan,

Minnesota, and Wisconsin. The Northeast Mountain, Lake, and Second Home group, a closely related category, is mainly concentrated in northern New England (Maine, New Hampshire, and Vermont) and in portions of New York and Pennsylvania. Together, these two similar categories account for more than a quarter of all recreation counties. Both categories are relatively prosperous: Northeast counties had the highest level of earnings per job among all recreation types, and the Midwest category experienced sharp increases in household income during the 1990s. Both regions had rates of poverty among the lowest of all recreation categories.

Although almost every type of recreation county registered at least doubledigit population growth during the 1990s (the exception being the Northeast Mountain, Lake, and Second Home), Ski Resort counties grew the fastest (increasing 38 percent), continuing a trend from the 1980s. Other recreation categories in the West (West Mountain and Other Mountain) also experienced rapid population growth.

Ski Resort counties stand out in other ways, measuring substantially higher than other recreation counties on a number of economic variables, including ratio of employment to population, earnings per job, earnings per worker, per capita income, and median household income. Ski Resorts also had the lowest poverty rate among all recreation categories, but had substantially higher housing costs—nearly 40 percent higher than the average for other nonmetro counties—which grew rapidly during the 1990s.

Ski Resort counties also stand out in terms of social indicators, having the highest levels of educational attainment, the largest number of doctors, the lowest death rates, and the highest rate of crime among all recreation categories.

In contrast, Reservoir Lake counties and South Appalachian Mountain Resort counties are among the most economically challenged recreation county types. Reservoir Lake counties, which are mainly located in the Midwest and Great Plains regions, and South Appalachian Mountain Resort counties—in the upland areas of Georgia, North Carolina, Virginia, West Virginia, and Maryland—have among the lowest earnings per worker and lowest median household income levels. They also have among the lowest rents. Both of these regions have among the lowest levels of educational attainment. Further, they have higher-than-average age-adjusted death rates, but relatively low crime rates. The South Appalachian Mountain Resort category also has a significantly longer commute than other nonmetro counties, possibly a reflection of its mountainous topography.

Casino counties also have relatively low levels of economic development, with the highest rate of poverty—over 40 percent higher than for all recreation counties—as well as below-average levels of per capita income, median household income, and earnings per worker. Still, during the 1990s, Casino counties, which are mainly located in the Upper Midwest, the Dakotas, the Mississippi Delta region, and Nevada, collectively had sharp employment growth (a third faster than the average for all recreation counties).

Casino counties, which benefited from the establishment of gambling on Native American reservations during the 1990s, had a lower level of educational attainment, fewer physicians, a higher-than-average ageadjusted death rate, and a significantly higher rate of crime than most other recreation counties.

Conclusions

This study provides quantitative information on how tourism and recreation development affects socioeconomic conditions in rural areas. Specifically, we wanted to address economic issues related to employment, income, earnings, and cost of living, and social issues such as poverty, education, health, and crime. A summary follows of our main findings on the socioeconomic impacts of rural recreation and tourism development.

Employment. Our regression analysis found a positive and statistically significant association between recreation dependency and the percentage of working-age population with jobs. We also found that, with the exception of the older (65 and over) population, recreation dependency positively affected the change in this employment measure during the 1990s.

Earnings. We examined earnings per job and earnings per resident to measure the value of the jobs associated with rural recreation development. We found that the average earnings per job in recreation counties were not significantly different than in other nonmetro counties, and we found no direct (linear) relationship between local dependency on recreation and local earnings per job in our recreation counties.

However, our regression analysis found a positive relationship between recreation and growth in earnings per job during the 1990s. Thus, the trend seems to favor the pay levels for jobs in these recreation counties. These findings concern earnings of all who work in the county, including nonresidents. They report earnings per job, not per worker—an important distinction because workers may have more than one job, and the availability of second jobs (part-time and seasonal) may be greater in recreation counties than elsewhere. When we focused on total job earnings for residents of recreation counties, we found these earnings were significantly higher ($2,000 more per worker) than for residents of other rural counties. The regression analysis also found a significant positive relationship between recreation and resident-worker earnings. So the earnings picture for recreation counties appears positive for the average resident.

Cost of living. Our research suggests recreation development leads to higher living costs, at least with respect to housing. We found that the average rent was 23 percent higher in recreation counties, and it was positively and significantly associated with the degree of recreation dependency in our regression analysis. While this may reduce some of the economic advantages for residents of recreation counties, it does so only partially. Median household incomes, on average, were $3,185 higher in recreation counties than in other rural counties. Annual costs associated with rent were $1,080 higher in recreation counties, offsetting only about a third of the recreation county income advantage.

Growth strains. We found recreation led to significantly higher rates of population growth. In theory, this can aggravate social problems, such as school crowding, housing shortages, pollution, and loss of identification with the community. The one growth-related social problem we addressed was road congestion. Examining the time it takes to commute to work, we found little evidence that congestion was presenting undue problems for residents in recreation counties. Moreover, our regression analysis found that recreation was associated with smaller increases in average commute times in the 1990s than in other rural counties.

Poverty. Another social problem that appeared to be reduced in recreation counties was poverty. Our regression analysis found recreation was associated with lower poverty rates and with larger declines in the poverty rate during the 1990s.

Crime. There may be some cause for concern with regard to crime. We found crime rates (for serious crimes) were higher in recreation counties than in other rural counties, and our regression analysis also found a statistically significant positive relationship between crime rates and recreation dependency. However, crime statistics may be biased in recreation areas because crimes against tourists and seasonal residents are counted in the crime rate, while tourists and seasonal residents are not counted as part of the population base upon which the rate is calculated. Thus, even if people in recreation areas do not face a higher chance of becoming victims of crimes, the crime rates of these areas will appear higher than elsewhere. Nonetheless, one may still argue that recreation-related crime adds to the local cost of policing and incarcerating criminals, just as recreation-related traffic—even though it may not create congestion—adds to the cost of maintaining roads.

Education and health. Our analysis found that recreation is associated with a more educated population, particularly with a higher percentage of college-educated people. We also found relatively good health conditions (measured by age-adjusted death rates) in recreation counties. This might be expected from the higher numbers of physicians per 100,000 residents that we found in recreation counties. However, our regression analysis did not find a statistically significant relationship between recreation dependence and the local supply of physicians. So some other explanation must be posited for the general good health in recreation counties, such as greater opportunities for physical exercise or residents who are more health-conscious.

Variations by county type. Conditions vary significantly by recreation county type. For example, Ski Resort counties have among the wealthiest, best educated, and healthiest populations of all recreation county types. Ski Resort counties also have relatively high rates of crime. In contrast, Reservoir Lake counties and South Appalachian Mountain Resort counties have among the poorest and least educated residents of all recreation county types, along with relatively high ageadjusted death rates, but they have relatively low crime rates. Casino counties—which had among the highest rates of job growth and the largest absolute increases in earnings per job during the 1990s—also had among the highest rates of growth in employment per person for seniors, perhaps reflecting the greater need for jobs among those over age 65 in these relatively high-poverty communities.

Ideas for Future Research

We focused mainly on conditions facing residents of mature rural recreation counties, that is, places that already have a substantial amount of recreation. Additional insights may come from expanding the analysis to include emerging recreation areas and neighbouring places that may be affected by spillover impacts from recreation areas. Future research might also address issues related to specific population subgroups, such as low-paid workers, who may face more significant problems related to the high cost of housing in recreation areas. The analysis might also be expanded to examine recreation impacts on other aspects of community wellbeing, such as the environment, public services, institutions like churches and charitable foundations, and small business formation and entrepreneurial activity. Our knowledge of rural recreation impacts might also benefit from different formulations of the regression model. For example, models could be finetuned to focus on individual indicators, or they could be estimated separately for individual regions and types of recreation areas. Feedback effects might be incorporated into the model—for example, recreation can lead to higher housing costs, which in turn can lead to reduced tourism and recreation development. More sophisticated models may be able to separate out these two effects. The models might also be examined over different time periods to test for cyclical effects and robustness over time.

Research might also measure the effects of specific State and local policies, along with other factors thought to affect the level of rural recreation and tourism (such as the availability of natural amenities and proximity and access to nonmetro areas). This might help State and local officials assess their potential for recreation and tourism development and identify strategies to further this development.

4

Second Homes and Coastal Tourism

Coastal Tourism and Recreation and the U.S. Economy

Growth in International Travel and Tourism

Travel and tourism is the world's largest industry. As reported by the World Tourism Organization, travel and tourism involved more than 528 million people internationally and generated $322 billion in receipts in 1994. In 1995, travel and tourism generated an estimated $3.4 trillion in gross output¾ creating employment for 211.7 million people, producing 10.9 percent of world gross domestic product, investing $693.9 billion in new facilities and equipment, and contributing more than $637 billion to global tax revenues.

The mammoth global tourism industry is a "massive consumer of energy and resources", and is expected to continue to grow significantly in the future. In 1995, the World Tourism Organization forecasted international arrivals worldwide to reach 661 million by the year 2000, up from 528 million in 1994, with arrivals predicted to reach 937 million by 2010. By 2005, it is estimated that the industry will have expanded globally, generating employment for 305 million people, producing 11.4 percent of world gross domestic product, investing $1,613 billion in new facilities and equipment, and contributing more than $1,369 billion in tax revenue. This growth in world tourism is related to three main factors: increased personal incomes and leisure time, improvements in transportation systems, and greater public awareness of other areas of the world due to improved communications.

Foreign tourism has been a very important factor for the U.S. economy. In 1994, 45.5 million international visitors came to the United

States, according to the Department of Commerce, and spent $60 billion dollars. The U.S. travel and tourism industry, with 6 million jobs, represents the second-largest employer in the United States after health care.

In 1986, the United States was the world's leading tourism destination. However, since that time, the U.S. leadership position in world tourism has been eroding; in 1996, France became the world's leading tourism destination. In 1995, the Commerce Department projected a 2.5 million dip in the number of international visitors to the United States and a dip in tourism revenues of 2.7 percent. Continuing economic difficulties in Europe and the strengthening of the U.S. dollar could account for some of this decline.

Balance of Payments Contributions of International Travel and Tourism

In 1994, the Wall Street Journal estimated that the United States receives over 45 percent of the developed world's travel and tourism revenues and 60 percent of its profits. While the United States runs a substantial merchandise trade deficit, it has a trade surplus in the service sector, with travel and tourism accounting for the largest and most rapidly growing part of this surplus.

According to Business Week, "foreign visitors spend about $80 billion a year in the United States, producing a $26 billion U.S. trade surplus in travel and tourism". Likewise, this publication reports 1.4 million U.S. jobs are supported by foreign tourism¾ ten times the number of jobs in the U.S. steel industry.

Foreign tourism to the United States in 1995 was expected to generate a trade surplus of $26 billion compared to a surplus of $17 billion in 1992 and a deficit of $7 billion in 1986. U.S. employment due to international tourism has been projected to grow by as much as 18 percent annually during the 1995-2000 period, doubling the number of tourism-related jobs every four years. The Department of Commerce has estimated that foreign tourist spending in the United States will rise to $132 billion dollars in the year 2000.

Tax Revenue Contributions of International Travel and Tourism

It has been estimated that travel and tourism produces tax revenues for all levels of government of about $58 billion annually. Of this total, foreign tourism is responsible for tax revenues of about $7.5 billion, about $4 billion of which goes to the federal government. Houston has observed that federal expenditures for beach re-nourishment have averaged only $34 million a year between 1950 and 1993 (in 1993 dollars), noting that the federal government receives tax revenues from foreign tourism that are 180 times its expenditure on the nation's beaches.

Promotion of International Tourism to the United States

The United States lags far behind other nations on spending on tourism promotion. Ronald Allen, chairman of Delta Air Lines, Inc., notes "...The Republic of Ireland, with a population of less than 4 million people, spends $45 million in public funds annually to promote tourism. This country, with 260 million people, spends less than $17 million in federal money" Wildavsky, 1995, p. 2280). Spain, with its attractive beaches and climate, spends 10 times more than the United States in advertising to attract international tourists. The United States ranks 31st in the world in international tourist market advertising.

Indeed, there has been a debate at the national level in the United States on whether a greater national presence concerning tourism promotion is needed, with industry advocates arguing for a greater role to eliminate "creeping neglect by public policy makers". Opposition to this has been expressed by economists and others who argue that private companies, not taxpayers, should bear the costs of promotional activities that benefit the U.S. tourism industry.

Coastal and Marine Tourism in the United States

The precise magnitude of foreign and domestic tourism in U.S. coastal and marine areas is not clear, since no separate statistics are kept for foreign or domestic tourists to these areas. Figures on foreign tourism receipts are generally based on surveys of departing travellers, generating data which are "imperfect and cannot be compared over time with precision". Data on tourism in coastal areas cannot easily be disaggregated from national-level statistics, but impressionistic evidence as well as a number of recent works on the subject suggest continued growth of tourism in coastal and marine areas in the United States and worldwide. Detailed information on the economic impact of domestic tourism has been difficult to find, but growth in all forms of recreation in coastal areas in which both foreign and domestic tourists partake is readily apparent. Such activities include beach going, recreational boating, cruises, marine mammal watching, recreational fishing, underwater recreation, bird watching, nature appreciation, and the like.

In terms of U.S. tourism, studies have shown that beaches are the leading tourist destination while national parks and historic sites are the second most popular destination. Consistent with these findings, approximately 180 million people visit the coast for recreational purposes, with 85 percent of tourist related revenues generated by coastal states. In addition to growing numbers of visitors, the permanent population of U.S. coastal regions is also increasing at a faster rate than the population as a whole.

The population of coastal counties has increased by approximately 25 percent since 1970. In California, for example, Wilson and Wheeler (1997) provide the following estimates for the annual contribution of various ocean industries to the California economy. Their study shows that tourism (predominantly coastal) is the largest contributor at $9.9 billion, with the next largest contributor being ports at $6.0 billion. Offshore oil accounted for $860 million, and fisheries and mariculture combined contributed $550 million. Similarly, between June 1995 and May 1996, 2.5 million visitors to Monroe County, Florida (in the Florida Keys) spent about $1.2 billion. Recreation and tourism (all coastal) accounted for over 60 percent of output/sales, 45 percent of income, and over 46 percent of all employment.

Recently the Environmental Protection Agency (EPA) undertook a national study on the benefits of water quality improvement in terms of numbers of people involved and the economic value of the activities in which they participate (EPA, 1996). This study provides some valuable quantitative information on the importance of coastal tourism and recreation:

- Saltwater fishing generates expenditures of over $5 billion annually, a total economic output of $15 billion, total earnings (wages) of over $4 billion, and over 200,000 jobs.
- Over 77 million Americans participate in recreational boating (NMMA, 1996). The number of recreational boats in the United States almost doubled from 1970 to 1990 (16.2 million), and is expected to increase by a further four million by the year 2000 (EPA, 1996). In 1996, Americans spent approximately

$17.7 billion on boats and directly related items (NMMA, 1996).

- Over 80 million Americans participate in outdoor (non-pool) swimming, with visitors to beaches and lakes increasing from 18 million in 1981 to 23 million in 1989. In seven states, beachgoers spent $74 billion with the most popular recreational activities being swimming, sunbathing, and walking in coastal areas (EPA, 1996).
- Birdwatching is estimated by the U.S. Fish and Wildlife Service to generate spending of about $18 billion per year by over 24 million "birders" and other wildlife watchers, a generous proportion of which occurs in coastal regions (EPA, 1996).

A number of the estuary programs that make up EPA's National Estuary Program have undertaken studies of the economic activity generated by the coastal and estuaries resources in their region. Some findings related to coastal tourism and recreation are given below (EPA, 1997):

Corpus Christi, Texas. Nature tourism in Corpus Christi is the fastest growing component of a tourism sector that generates $23 billion annually. Recreational fishing provides aggregate net benefits to the area of $83 million, including $37 million per year in state and local taxes, with a regional economic impact of $546 million. Non-fishing coastal recreational activity adds another $23 million in state and local taxes, and $340 million in regional economic impact.

Long Island Sound, New York. The economic impact of water quality-dependent uses in Long Island Sound, including boating, commercial and sport fishing, and swimming, is estimated at more than $5 billion annually. Commercial and recreational fishing contributed more than $1.2 billion to the total, while beachgoing has a direct benefit of more than $800 million annually.

Indian River Lagoon, Florida. The Indian River Lagoon region is a popular resort and vacation destination which received over six million visitors in 1995 and provided economic benefits of approximately $730 million.

Santa Monica Bay, California. Tourism is the Los Angeles region's second largest industry with 392,000 full and part-time jobs contributing $3.6 billion annually to the region's payroll. With nearly four million tourists annually, and over 45 million beach visits per year, Santa Monica Bay contributes significantly to the regional economy.

San Francisco Bay, California. The economy of the 12 counties bordering this estuary exceeds $175 billion and supports more than four million jobs. Many of these jobs are dependent on the estuary's natural resources or are water-related. Revenues from maritime activities exceed $5.4 billion each year, and marinas annually generate some $167 million. Tourism, which generates over $4 billion annually, is likewise strongly tied to the aesthetic values of the estuary.

Policy Frameworks for Coastal Recreation and Tourism: An Assessment

Understanding Tourism

A perusal of the literature on tourism suggests that it is easy to make generalizations: on the positive side, to extol its huge economic development potential; on the negative side, to decry impacts on the environment, overuse of resources and energy, ignorance of local culture, and absence of local benefits. For analytical purposes, it is best, however, to consider tourism in neutral terms as an agent of development and change which may have both positive and negative effects, as the following quote suggests:

> *"As Butler (1990) points out, tourism, like other industries, is an agent of development and change and must be recognized as such. It is consumptive like any other industry and the level of consumption is determined by the scale and style of tourism development. At low levels and with careful design, tourism may be able to operate at a sustainable level. However, controlling the level and style of development over the long term presents challenges which, to this point, have not been successfully met. Because of its potentially high impact, tourism should be considered in the same manner as any other industry and should be subjected to the same environmental and social impact assessment processes during the planning stages".*

Butler suggests the following working definition of sustainable development in the context of tourism: "tourism which is developed and maintained in an area (community, environment) in such a manner and at such a scale that it remains viable over an indefinite period and does not degrade or alter the environment (human and physical) in which it exists to such a degree that it prohibits the successful development and well being of other activities and processes".

Tourism has often been ignored by public sector agencies. Where it has been considered as a specific development feature, it has often been viewed as a "soft" option, which can be pursued relatively easily and which does not require much in terms of specific planning or resources. While this view has changed somewhat in recent years as the magnitude and importance of tourism has begun to be appreciated, ignorance about tourism and many of the processes associated with it is still widespread.

The lack of attention by public agencies to tourism is especially problematic in the case of marine and coastal tourism. In most countries, there usually is no coordination between programs that promote and market tourism and those that manage coastal and marine areas. Integrated coastal management often tends to be done within environmental or planning agencies. On the other hand, agencies dealing with the promotion of tourism are not involved with the evaluation of its effects or with advance planning and management of the adverse impacts of tourism through avoidance, mitigation, and compensation strategies. Hence, one of the greatest challenges facing coastal managers in the United States and elsewhere is how to integrate tourism development within the ambit of integrated coastal management, and thus increase the likelihood of long-term sustainability.

The Role of the Federal Government in Coastal Tourism Management

As an economic activity, tourism is difficult to influence and manage directly. Like most coastal development in market economies, tourism-related development is driven largely by the private sector and its assessment of economic opportunities. Miller and Auyong (1991) point out that tourism involves mainly three sets of actors: tourists, locals (those who reside in the region of tourism destinations but are unconnected to the tourism industry), and two categories of brokers (those in the private sector who are engaged in the business of tourism, and those in the public sector who in one way or another monitor, manage, or govern tourism). Tourism tends to be globally driven by market forces influenced by such factors as advertising (by public or private agents at the tourist destination), the perceptions of the travelling public about security, amenity values, etc., and, in the case of international tourists, by currency factors.

Notwithstanding these difficulties, there is much that the federal government, working with the states and localities, does to ensure that coastal tourism is conducted in a sustainable manner, thereby ensuring long term economic and environmental benefits for coastal communities and the nation. Sustainable development of coastal tourism is dependent on:

1. *good coastal management practices* (particularly regarding proper siting of tourism infrastructure and the provision of public access);
2. *clean water and air, and healthy coastal ecosystems*;
3. *maintaining a safe and secure recreational environment though the management of coastal hazards (such as erosion, storms, floods), and the provision of adequate levels of safety* for boaters, swimmers, and other water users;
4. *beach restoration efforts* that maintain the recreational and amenity values of beaches; and,

Sound Policies for Wildlife and Habitat Protection.

While there are separate federal programs dealing with each of these areas, some more successfully than others, in recent years there has been a growing realization among a number of federal agencies that these factors are interconnected and that all are needed to achieve healthy ecosystems and sustainable economies in coastal communities. To cite just one example, the Sustain Healthy Coasts 5-year Implementation Plan, developed by NOAA's Office of Ocean and Coastal Resource Management, defines the following objective: "Foster well-planned and revitalized coastal communities that are compatible with the natural environment, minimize the risk from natural hazards, and provide access to coastal resources for the public's use and enjoyment."

In the sections that follow, existing efforts by federal agencies the categories outlined above are reviewed and assessed. The small but growing sector of ecotourism, and the need to manage this activity carefully to avoid adverse impacts on protected species and sensitive habitats, is also discussed.

Coastal Management and Planning

The United States has the oldest national coastal management and planning program in the world, initiated under the Coastal Zone Management Act of 1972. The program, administered by NOAA's Office of Ocean and Coastal Resource Management, now includes coastal management programs in 31 U.S. states and territories, covering 97.2 percent of the U.S. shoreline. The program uses incentives (in the form of grants to the states and the "federal consistency" provision) to assist states in the preparation and implementation of coastal management plans. These state efforts have been multifaceted and have addressed, through a variety of means (regulatory, planning, public awareness raising), all uses of coastal areas.

Three management practices under the Coastal Zone Management (CZM) program are especially important for ensuring sustainable tourism development: (1) provisions for the management of coastal development; (2) provisions to improve public access to the shoreline; and (3) provisions to protect (and, where necessary, to restore) coastal environments.

Management of Coastal Development

All CZM programs have elements which, in effect, help manage coastal development. Two of these are especially relevant to tourism development: (1) encouragement of water-dependent uses in the coastal zone and (2) the appropriate siting of new facilities in the coastal zone.

Encouragement of Water-Dependent Uses

State CZM programs actively encourage and facilitate the use of land adjacent to the shoreline for those purposes which require such a location. This policy helps ensure that proposals for tourism and marine recreation projects receive appropriate consideration in the government review process. It also helps ensure that meritorious coastal tourism developments are not crowded out of the coastal zone by uses that do not require a shoreside location.

Appropriate Siting of Facilities

Construction of new facilities in the coastal zone must meet the setback requirements of state CZM programs. While states differ in their requirements, the trend is to relate setback lines to annual erosion rates and, thus, to require the greatest setbacks from the high tidemark in those areas having the largest erosion rates. Facilities siting policies also help ensure that new tourism construction is not located in hazardous areas from the standpoint of coastal storm damage and flooding.

Improvement of Public Access to the Shoreline

A strong emphasis in the federal Coastal Zone Management Act relates to the importance of ensuring adequate public access to the nation's shorelines for recreational pursuits. All 31 state programs are actively pursuing this goal. Recognizing the limitations of simply planning for access, Congress added section 306A to the CZMA in 1980 to allow states to acquire land and fund low cost construction projects to provide public access ways to the beach and coastal waters.

Since 1980, for example, the California Coastal Program has acquired over 2,300 public access ways along the coast while the San Francisco Bay Conservation and Development Commission has increased public access around the perimeter of San Francisco Bay from 4 miles in 1977 to more than 96 miles in 1990. Under the CZM program, states and localities use grant funding and regulatory tools to secure improved public access for recreational purposes.

Protection of Coastal Habitats

The existence of healthy coastal habitats (wetlands, beaches and dunes, sea grass beds, mangroves, coral reefs, estuaries) is important to coastal recreation and tourism.

State CZM programs represent one of the important management avenues in obtaining this protection. Within specified coastal zone boundaries, states and/or their local governments regulate activities which could adversely impact these habitats. Other federal programs, such as those under the Clean Water Act's Section 404 (dredge and fill program) and Section 320 (National Estuary Program), the Marine Protection Research and Sanctuaries Act (which controls ocean dumping), the Coastal Barrier Resources Act, the National Seashore Program, the Endangered Species Act, and the Marine Mammal Protection Act, also serve to protect coastal habitats.

Furthermore, a national system of estuarine research reserves aimed at providing a representative system of natural field laboratories for management-related research and monitoring also exists as an adjunct to the national CZM program.

Management of Clean Water and Healthy Ecosystems

Clean water and healthy coastal ecosystems are essential to the maintenance of coastal tourism and recreation. Foreign tourists and the recreating domestic public stop going to areas where the waters are polluted, beaches are closed, or fish are tainted. For example, it is reported that the State of New Jersey lost $800 million in tourism revenues following reports that medical wastes had washed up on some of its beaches. According to EPA estimates, coastal and marine waters support 28.3 million jobs, generate $54 billion in goods and services, contribute $30 billion to the U.S. economy through recreational fishing, and provide a destination for 180 million Americans to recreate each year.

In the past 25 years, there have been extensive efforts made by federal agencies, especially EPA and NOAA, in association with the coastal states, to improve coastal water quality. Under programs authorized by the Clean Water Act of 1972 (as amended) and administered by EPA, significant improvements in water quality have been realized. Point sources have been largely controlled under the National Pollution Discharge Elimination System (NPDES).

Significant challenges remain regarding the control of non-point sources of water pollution (resulting from such sources as agricultural practices, urban and storm water run-off, and air deposition), especially in coastal areas abutting agricultural lands. EPA's non-point source program (under Section 319 of the Clean Water Act), and NOAA's program under Section 6217 of the CZM Act, have been used in combination in a number of coastal states to begin more effective measures to control non-point sources of pollution.

Protection of the marine environment is one of the critical services provided by the U.S. Coast Guard. This includes prevention of environmentally threatening marine accidents and responses aimed at minimizing adverse effects should accidents occur., This also includes protection of living marine resources and marine sanctuaries. The implementation of the Oil Pollution Act of 1990 is resulting in safer ships entering U.S. ports, safer vessel operators, and hence, cleaner coastal waters. NOAA's National Ocean Service provides safe navigation services, such as nautical charts, and information on water levels and currents, that help prevent marine accidents. It also performs hazardous material spill response activities. NOAA's role in pollution monitoring (National Status and Trends Program) and damage assessment are also important aspects of managing clean water and healthy ecosystems.

In addition, special planning and management efforts, largely directed at improving water quality and habitats, have been made in many of the nation's estuaries under the aegis of EPA's National Estuary Program (NEP). Under the NEP, 28 estuaries, designated as estuaries of national significance, have been the beneficiaries of substantially increased research and management attention. Management conferences convened in each estuarine area are used to oversee the characterization of each estuary, and the preparation and implementation of Comprehensive Conservation and Management Plans (CCMPs).

These include resource and water-quality related goals and the action plans necessary to meet these goals. An enduring commitment from NEP stakeholders at all levels is vital to the successful implementation of the CCMPs and the long-term health and sustainability of these estuarine resources. This commitment must include the acquisition and leveraging of sufficient funds by state and local governments, follow-through on commitments agreed to by the implementors, and the full use of appropriate authorities. The continuing involvement of the federal government, notably the EPA, in the oversight and support of the NEP is also likely to be critical to the long-term success of the program.

The direct contribution to coastal economies made by cleaning up coastal waters is often not fully recognized. A recent report by the EPA indicates that in seven estuaries alone, tourism and beach going activities generate economic benefits of more than $16 billion to their respective regions (EPA, 1997). Clearly, these benefits depend on the maintenance of clean coastal waters and attractive ecosystems. While substantial progress has been made in improving coastal water quality since 1972, much remains to be done. Meanwhile, reauthorization of the Clean Water Act has been stalled for several years, the national policy framework for dealing with non-point source pollution remains somewhat unclear, and funding levels for water quality improvement programs are inadequate. Furthermore, the nation needs to decide if the current largely voluntary approach to non-point source pollution will be sufficient, especially for dealing with agricultural runoff problems.

Management of Coastal Hazards

In siting coastal resorts and other facilities, there is understandably a predilection for locating in beautiful but high-risk zones that are as close as physically possible to the edge of the sea, or otherwise take advantage of scenic views and proximity to beaches and ocean recreation. Of course, it is precisely these areas that are most vulnerable to both long-term and episodic coastal hazards: such as erosion, storms, and floods.

While government cannot be expected to protect individuals from their own recklessness, it does have a responsibility to provide the information necessary to permit informed decisions to be made with regard to the kinds and degrees of risk associated with living in various parts of the coastal zone. Furthermore, coastal areas that are clearly hazardous as building sites should be reserved for other uses. Government also has the responsibility to provide adequate warnings of impending storms or other hazardous conditions, and to develop plans for coping with such emergencies. Several government programs exist to meet these needs as discussed below.

At the federal level, FEMA's National Flood Insurance Program (NFIP) and the Coastal Zone Management Program exist, in part, to address these problems. The NFIP offers flood insurance to coastal landowners in communities that have met government standards for building in coastal areas (elevating structures above a designated flood level, designation of high hazard areas where no building is allowed, etc.). FEMA is also responsible for supporting and facilitating the work of state emergency preparedness offices in the preparation of coastal evacuation plans and plans to deal with disasters such as hurricanes both during the event and during the cleanup and reconstruction phases. NOAA's National Weather Service devotes considerable resources to the job of providing timely "state-of-the-art" forecasts and predictions of hurricanes and other coastal storms.

Through the federal CZM program, coastal states build in their own regulatory approaches such as construction setback lines, storm-resistant building codes, acquisition programs for hazardous areas, and the like. Recognizing the connections that should exist between the planning and management efforts under CZM, and cognizant of the lessons being learned during storm events by the emergency management programs, NOAA and FEMA are initiating a series of workshops to strengthen the coordination between these programs.

Advanced planning and follow-up are required to maintain a safe and secure environment for visitors. Tourists take their safety for granted when they go to the beach or visit a coastal resort or even rent a sailboat for the day. Yet the coast is inherently a place with real risks, even under good weather conditions. Swimmers can drown and boats can collide or go aground, poisonous jellyfish can sting. And, of course, episodic large storms and hurricanes can have devastating consequences in coastal areas heavily populated with visitors.

Increasing numbers of Americans find themselves on the nation's waterways in connection with recreational boating, fishing, travelling to and from coral reefs for snorkelling and diving, and so on. Maintaining an adequate level of safety and accident prevention requires properly marked channels, rescue services, oversight of boating safety requirements (e.g., life jackets and other emergency equipment), and monitoring and enforcement of boating operations, including so-called "thrill craft." While some of these duties can be performed by local and state authorities, the maintenance of safe and well-marked waterways and maritime safety in general has traditionally been a federal government responsibility.

In any event, the federal government is in the best position to ensure than an adequately comprehensive safety program is in place in coastal areas. The U.S. Coast Guard is the primary federal agency with responsibility for coastal search and rescue, enforcement of maritime laws, and maintenance of a national waterway marking system. The Coast Guard is also the coordinator of the national recreational boating safety program aimed at ensuring the safety of boats and associated equipment, and their safe operation by boaters. Through the production of accurate nautical charts and related products, NOAA provides essential information for navigating the nation's coastal waters.

Beach Restoration Programs

The federal government, acting through the U.S. Army Corps of Engineers, has long played an important role in the maintenance and restoration of the nation's beaches and shores. Experience in shore protection efforts has shown that soft solutions involving beach re-nourishment have produced better, more economical results than hard solutions such as seawalls and groins in many circumstances. Seawalls and revetments first developed as the field of coastal engineering emerged., While these measures are often successful at protecting the development and infrastructure behind a beach, they do not address the real cause of beach erosion, which is a lack of sediment in the system. As understanding of coastal systems has grown through research and data collection programs, solutions to such problems has progressed. Today, beach re-nourishment represents a sound engineering solution that is economically feasible and environmentally sensitive. Only in areas with very high erosion rates and substantial shoreside facilities to protect are hard structural solutions considered.

The shift of population to coastal counties and the increased demand for coastal tourism destinations has exacerbated many existing beach erosion problems. Development in areas with high erosion rates and building on or in front of sand dunes, rather than behind them, are major factors contributing to increased beach erosion problems. Relative sea-level rise caused primarily by subsidence is another major factor in some areas. The interruption of sand flowing along the coast by natural or stabilized inlets is also an aggravating factor.

The Corps has conducted assessments of many of the nation's important beaches and has assisted coastal communities in the funding of beach nourishment projects. The bulk of the costs of these projects have been borne by the federal government with the local share generally being about 30 to 35 percent of the total cost. Just as the federal government is reconsidering its policies in this regard, coastal erosion and increasing relative sea-level rise in some parts of the country (notably the middle Atlantic and Gulf coasts) are increasing the need for beach replenishment projects.

As statistics cited earlier show, America's beaches are an important element in this country's attractiveness as an international tourist destination. A case in point concerns Miami Beach which virtually had no beach left by the mid 1970s as a result of erosion. Beach re-nourishment (at the cost of $52 million) in the late 1970s rejuvenated Miami Beach and enabled its beach to be reopened to the public. Beach attendance subsequently increased from 8 million in 1978 to 21 million in 1983. Annual governmental revenue obtained from foreign tourism in Miami Beach alone is about 40 times the cost of the beach re-nourishment project that has lasted over 15 years.

Given the role played by beach tourism in the nation's balance of payments and its impact on government revenues and regional and local economies, it is crucial that these assets be maintained at levels that promote and enhance their recreational use. If budgetary constraints make it necessary to reduce federal assistance for beach restoration and maintenance, a gradual and predictable approach should be adopted and states and coastal communities assisted in developing viable alternative funding arrangements.

Coastal Tourism and the need to Coordinate Federal Policies and Programs

While the issues discussed above are usually considered separately, all are of central importance to sustainable coastal tourism. Any one, be it poorly planned development, poor coastal water quality, unsafe or hazardous conditions, or eroding beaches, could seriously impact the tourism potential of a coastal area. Furthermore, policies and programs in each of these areas need to be developed and implemented in an integrated fashion, each taking account of the others. Failure to do this can result in such undesirable outcomes as erosion control structures that impair the recreational experience, or poorly designed development that causes water pollution or beach erosion.

Management of Ecotourism

Ecotourism or nature tourism is: "Tourism that involves travelling to relatively undisturbed or uncontaminated natural areas with the specific object of studying, admiring, and enjoying the scenery and its wild plants and animals, as well as any existing cultural areas." While still relatively small, ecotourism is one of the fastest growing segments of the tourism industry and presents special management challenges.

Internationally, ecotourism is growing at a moderate rate with the financial impacts greatest in rural areas near important ecotourism activities. In 1988, international ecotourists numbered 236 million worldwide, with an estimated economic impact of $233 billion (U.S.). In 1994, the number of international ecotourists rose to 317 million with direct economic impact of $250 billion (U.S.). Although specific data on coastal ecotourism are difficult to obtain, market surveys in the United States show good prospects for ecotourism growth. In 1992, a U.S. Travel Data Centre survey indicated that 7 percent of U.S. travellers had taken at least one trip that they considered ecotourism and 30 percent claimed they would take one within the next three years.

In the United States, some coastal states have begun promoting ecotourism and nature-based tourism through the preparation of guides to ecotourism attractions and other publications. For example, the Marine Advisory Service of the Delaware Sea Grant College Program produced a guidebook to ecotourism sites in the state. In 1996, the State of South Carolina, with the collaboration of the South Carolina Sea Grant Consortium, produced a handbook entitled *Guidelines and Recommendations for Nature-Based Tourism Planning and Practice in South Carolina.* Yet another example is the California Coastal Conservancy, which devoted its Summer 1997 issue of *California Coast & Ocean* to nature tourism.

Ecotourism in association with marine and estuarine protected areas, especially the National Marine Sanctuary Program and National Estuarine Research Reserve Program, has a great potential. However, for ecotourism activities to be sustainable, they must be managed properly and with special care. Unless properly managed, the impacts of ecotourism (for example, to remote pristine areas) may be worse than those of tourism to clearly defined and confined resorts.

In the United States, for example, concerns have been raised about the impacts of ecotourism on marine mammals, which are protected under the Marine Mammal Protection Act.

Commercial cruises to observe and "feed wild dolphins" operating in such areas as Texas, South Carolina, and Florida, were found to harm dolphins by making them reliant on accepting food from humans and decreasing their ability to survive in the wild. Threats to the marine mammal populations and to humans in these situations include: (1) substantially altering the natural behaviour of marine mammals, including foraging for food and migration, (2) the loss of wariness by humans, which places the animals at increased risk of injury or death from interaction with vessels, (3) animals receiving inappropriate or contaminated food, and (4) increased injuries to humans as the habituated animals become predictably more aggressive when they lose their wariness of humans and compete for handouts.

Management of Coastal Recreation Activities

The last decade has seen a great increase in the nature and magnitude of coastal recreation activities, which as has been shown, generate billions of dollars in economic activity. Recreational uses of a consumptive nature include hunting, fishing, shellfishing, shell collection, and the like, while non-consumptive uses include swimming, surfing, sunbathing, boating, wind-surfing, jet skiing, bird watching, snorkelling, diving, glass-bottom boating, and many more. As coastal recreation activities have proliferated, the need for active management has increased as well.

At least three sets of concerns related to the management of coastal recreation activities must be dealt with, namely, environmental/ resource concerns, amenity concerns, and safety concerns. Environmental/resource constraints include the maintenance of good water quality, and habitats and living resources which are free of health hazards, and which have good air quality, healthy coral reefs, healthy shellfish areas, etc.

Amenity concerns include adequate controls on congestion, noise, landscape degradation, and the like. Safety concerns include adequate lifeguard systems, first aid facilities, telephones, codes of conduct for beach users, and notice systems for beach and water hazards and for weather-related risks.

In most cases, the responsibility for meeting these concerns is divided between the beach "owner" (often a local government or state government, but sometimes federal or private), resort and/or recreation facility operators, and state environmental or health departments. In general, nationwide standards for recreational beach operation do not exist, even with respect to beach closings. This would appear to be an area where additional attention at the national level is needed.

A promising start in this area is a new program recently launched by the EPA and designated the Beaches Environmental Assessment, Closure, and Health (BEACH) Program. This program is designed to encourage government agencies at all levels to strengthen beach water quality standards and testing methods using predictive water pollution models, to better inform the public about beach water quality conditions, and to make information about the risks associated with swimming in contaminated beach water available to the public.

Emerging Tools and Techniques

Although coastal tourism constitutes a strong force (both positive and negative) in shaping coastal communities and local, regional, and national economies, coastal tourism is generally not seen as a specific sector requiring policy, planning, and management attention and resources. This is due, in part, to the fact that data and information tend not be gathered and aggregated under this heading. Hence, the magnitude and importance of leisure and recreationally motivated development in the coastal zone tends to be understated, understudied, and under-managed.

However, certain aspects of this situation may be changing. Since the Earth Summit in Rio de Janeiro in 1992, a number of new initiatives for sustainable tourism practices have appeared. For example, in 1993, a new periodical entitled *Journal of Sustainable Tourism* appeared, focusing on applying the principles of sustainable development to the tourism field. In 1997, on the occasion of the five-year review of the implementation of Earth Summit agreements, three organizations: The World Travel and Tourism Council, the World Tourism Organization, and the Earth Council; jointly published *Agenda 21 for the Travel and Tourism Industry: Towards Environmentally Sustainable Development* (WTTC et al, no date).

This report presents a summary of Agenda 21 (one of the main outputs of the Earth Summit), and the role that travel and tourism can play in achieving the goals of Agenda 21. It also outlines a program of action. Planning for sustainable tourism development is one of the priority areas of the program, which calls for complementarity between tourism and coastal development by adopting suitable policies such as the Global Blue Flag Program (WTTC et al.). The Blue Flag Program is a European campaign started in the 1980s which encourages local authorities to provide clean and safe beaches for local populations and international tourists. Blue Flag awards go to beaches that achieve certain standards in water quality, beach management and safety, and environmental information and education.

A guide for tourism managers has also been developed by the World Tourism Organization (WTO, 1996) on the formulation and use of indicators of sustainable tourism. Indicators signal unacceptable levels of impacts or stress, and these can in turn lead to the development of standards to govern tourism activities. Core indicators developed by the WTO include use intensity (persons per meter of accessible beach), species counts (number of species, change in composition), pollution levels (fecal coliform, heavy metal counts, etc.), and accident rates (WTO, 1996).

New tools are also being developed in connection with coastal tourism and natural disasters, such as hurricanes. The University of Florida, for example, in cooperation with the Florida Hotel and Motel Association, has prepared *The Hurricane Preparedness Handbook for Hotels and Motels.*

In a slightly different direction, Clemson University has prepared a handbook to guide communities and their tourism industries through crises of various types including those associated with natural hazards such as hurricanes. As outlined in its introduction, this guidebook "is intended to serve as a guideline to facilitate tourism recovery by protecting or rebuilding a local area's image of safety and attractiveness; reassuring potential visitors of the safety of the area; reestablishing the area's functionality and attractiveness; and aiding the local travel and tourism industry members in their economic recovery efforts").

Findings

As detailed above, coastal tourism and recreation involve major economic activity in U.S. coastal and ocean areas, and must be planned and managed with special care to insure that the environmental quality on which coastal tourism and recreation depend is maintained and enhanced. Major findings and areas of future work are summarized below:

Economic importance of coastal tourism and recreation. Coastal tourism and recreation provide a huge positive economic benefit in the United States, both in terms of jobs and earnings and in terms of balance of payments and governmental revenues. As discussed, over 90 percent of foreign tourism spending is concentrated in coastal states where beaches are the leading tourism destination. For example, Miami Beach reported more tourist visits (21 million) than were made to any National Park Service property. The federal government, moreover, receives about 6 times as much tax revenues annually from foreign tourism spending at Miami Beach than it spends to restore beaches in the entire nation. Yet, these values often go unrecognized, and are not the subject of concerted attention by federal, state, and local policymakers. There is little information on marine and coastal tourism. There is no systematic collection of data and information on the magnitude, nature, and economic and social impacts of tourism and recreation in the nation's coastal zone. This is, in part, responsible for a general under-appreciation of this set of activities and for the failure to devote adequate planning and management attention to the relevant issues that are raised for coastal tourism and recreation. To properly guide coastal tourism in a sustainable development manner, better data focused on coastal and marine areas will be needed. The types of information needed include:

- Systematic collection and interpretation of coastal tourism data on a coastal county basis;
- Collection and interpretation of data on coastal and marine recreation activities;
- Expansion of existing databases, such as, for example, the Sea Grant Coastal Recreation and Tourism web service (organized by Oregon State University, in collaboration with many other Sea Grant programs);
- Conduct of studies on the dynamics of tourism in coastal and marine areas. For example, what constitutes an optimal type and scale of coastal tourism? Who gets what, when, and where from expanded tourism? What is the distribution of benefits from tourism?.

U.S. promotional efforts to attract foreign tourists to U.S. coastal areas lag significantly behind those of other nations. Foreign tourists use U.S. coastal areas very frequently and contribute significantly to jobs, earnings, and tax revenues in coastal communities. Foreign competition in marketing other world coastal destinations, however, is increasing. In contrast to many other governments, the U.S. government spends very little in tourism promotion.

Federal policies and programs essential for the maintenance of healthy coastal tourism and recreation (coastal planning and management, clean water, beach nourishment, management of coastal hazards and of coastal safety) are interrelated and should be treated as a whole. The economic viability and sustainability of coastal tourism and recreation are directly affected by at least four sets of federal policies and programs:

- Coastal planning and management (CZM) programs, especially in relation to the appropriate siting of tourism development and in ensuring public access, are of central importance in sustainable coastal tourism.
- Clean water and healthy ecosystem programs are vital to sustainable coastal tourism.
- Programs to ensure a safe coastal environment, especially with reference to natural hazards such as hurricanes and storms and to the maintenance of safe marine recreational and boating conditions, are essential for sustainable coastal tourism.
- Programs to maintain recreational beaches, by means of beach re-nourishment to combat erosion and relative sea-level rise, are also of central concern to sustainable coastal tourism.
- Programs to protect wildlife and coastal habitats are also essential to sustainable coastal tourism.

While a variety of federal efforts are focused on different programs of importance to coastal tourism, these have not been successfully coordinated. To remedy this situation, consideration could be given to the creation of an interagency initiative devoted to coastal tourism among the major federal agencies with programs in this area (e.g., NOAA (NOS [OCRM, NMS, NERRS], NMFS, OAR), the Department of Interior, EPA, FEMA, Army Corps of Engineers, Coast Guard, etc.).

Related options could entail the mobilization of a public-private partnership to work in conjunction with the federal inter-agency group (involving such entities as state coastal programs, state tourist offices, aquaria, and waterfront redevelopers), and the development of a public awareness and outreach program focused on the determinants of successful coastal tourism.

Little guidance (in the form of standards, codes of conduct, manuals, etc.) is currently available to states and communities for guiding appropriate tourism development in coastal areas. While individual coastal communities and coastal states have taken initiative in preparing guides and codes of conduct related to coastal tourism and recreation, many others have not yet done so. The federal government can play a useful role here in providing guidance to states and communities in their attempts to manage coastal tourism and recreation appropriately.

Useful activities include the development of standards, guides, and manuals for managing coastal tourism, in cooperation with relevant non-governmental organizations, the private sector, and international entities working on these issues. Also, management standards for recreational beaches, for example, those developed for the European Blue Flag program, could play a valuable role in improving conditions at some U.S. beaches.

Importance of Coastal Tourism

The Welsh Coast is vital to the tourism industry in Wales. In 2006, spending associated with an overnight visit to the coast amounted to around £648million nearly 40% of total tourism spending in Wales. It attracts around 4 million staying trips (16.9 million nights) each year together with an estimated 25 million tourism day trips. The greatest bulk of seaside tourism is for leisure and holiday purposes although cities and resorts such as Cardiff, Swansea and Llandudno also attract business and conference tourism. Visits to the coast account for 41% of all overnight trips in Wales-a much higher proportion than in England and Scotland where visits to the seaside only account for 20% and 13% of trips.

Within the regions, seaside tourism is particularly important for North and South West Wales where it accounts for half of all activity (57% and 48% of tourism spend respectively). Seaside tourism is least important in South East Wales where it accounts for 12% of all tourism spend.

The direct impact of tourism amounts to an estimated 3.2% of whole – economy value added in Wales. The economic impact of tourism is much higher in many rural and coastal areas that, in relative terms, are more dependent on tourism.

Coastal Tourism Employment

Recent research has indicated that just under half of all full time jobs associated with the marine and coastal environment are in tourism related activities. The North Wales marine and coastal economy is predominantly, though not exclusively, tourism based. In West Wales, tourism accounts for over a third of direct coast and marine employment and in South East Wales it accounts for over half of coastal and marine sector direct jobs.

The Coastal Tourism Environment

The coastal environment is a major attraction to visitors who are drawn by the quality of its landscape, wildlife and sea water. The environmental quality of the Welsh coastline is reflected in the wide range and large number of designations and protected sites that cover the coastline of Wales. Some 70% of the coastline has been designated for its environmental quality.

In terms of EU and international designations, many parts of the coastal and marine environment are designated as Special Areas of Conservation and Marine Special Areas of Conservation. These areas are chosen for being the best examples in the UK for containing habitat types and species listed in the EU Habitats Directive. Other parts of the coast are designated as Special Protection Areas to conserve the habitats of certain rare or vulnerable birds and regularly occurring migratory birds. The Dyfi Estuary is the only designated Biosphere Reserve in Wales. The Biosphere reserves are areas nominated by national governments and designated under UNESCO's Man and the Biosphere (MAB) programme. In addition, vast sections of the coastline are designated under UK wide designations including:

- National Parks-Pembrokeshire Coast and Snowdonia.
- Areas of Outstanding Natural Beauty at Anglesey, Lly^n and Gower.
- Heritage Coasts at Great Orme, Anglesey, Lly^ n, Cardigan Bay, Pembrokeshire, Gower and the Vale of Glamorgan.
- National Nature Reserves.
- Marine Nature Reserves.
- Sites of Special Scientific Interest.

Important sites of archaeological and historic interest are also found along the coastline ranging from prehistoric sites to the Edwardian castles of Beaumaris, Caernarfon, Conwy, Harlech and Flint. Registered historic landscapes, parks and gardens make a significant contribution to the distinctiveness of the Welsh coast and to its appeal to residents and visitors.

Current trends in Coastal Tourism

Over the past 15 years, it is apparent that visitors are undertaking less trips to the Welsh seaside, with a decline in the number of trips and nights spent by UK visitors overall on the Welsh coast. The seaside share of the UK holiday market in Wales has fallen from 61% in 1991 to 41% in 2006.

The seaside sector has been particularly affected by the continuing rise in the number of long holidays taken abroad by UK holidaymakers. The number of long holidays taken at the Welsh seaside declined in number from over 2.7 million in 1991 to 1.76m in 2006. This decline, however, has been off set by a growth in short breaks which rose from a low point of less than 1m in 1993 to a high of over 2.2m in 2006.

Visitor Profile

In terms of visitor profile, figures suggest that in 2006, almost 24% of staying trips to the Welsh coastline originated in Wales. The North West (25%) and the West Midlands (23%) were the two main sources of staying visitors from England. Visitors to the North and Mid Wales coast tended to come from the North West of England, while visitors to South West and South East Wales came from a more varied origin base.

Staying visitors to the seaside were more likely than the average holidaymaker to Wales to be travelling in large groups, with accompanying children and to be from lower socioeconomic groups. Caravans and camping, particularly static caravans, were the preferred form of accommodation for tourists staying at coastal locations, accounting for 44% of all trips in 2006. Staying in self catering flats and cottages was also moreprevalent than the average while a smaller proportion of trips stayed with friends and relatives or used serviced accommodation.

The coast attracts a higher proportion of long holidays compared to other types of location, with 45% of seaside trips involving a stay of over 4 nights, compared to 37% of all trips to Wales.

Seasonality

Seaside holidays show a greater seasonal peaking with 49% of trips being taken in the peak season (June, July, Aug) compared with 36% and 42% for small town and countryside trips respectively. The high seasonality reflects the relative importance of family holidays, many of which are governed by school holiday periods, as well as a preference for warmer weather for water based activities Only 19% of spend for coastal tourism occurs in the shoulder season (Oct – Mar) compared to 33% for tourism overall in Wales. In terms of occupancy, the seaside hotel sector has similar occupancy levels (57%) to that of small towns (57%) and country/village (53%) whilst the highest levels of occupancy are found in city/large towns (71%).3 Room occupancy rates in the hotel sector across most locations have remained relatively constant during the 1998 – 2006 timescale with any differences typically only a few percentage points. Levels of occupancy in self catering units at the seaside average at 57% over the year. Static caravan parks at coastal locations have a relatively high level of occupancy at 67% whilst the lowest levels of occupancy are found in touring parks (41%).

Day Visitors

In terms of day visits, the last day visitor survey, undertaken in 2002, showed that family groups with children also accounted for a higher proportion of tourism day visits to the coast than for tourism day trips overall. In addition, a higher proportion than average of people over 55 years undertakes day trips to the coast.

Activities

Whilst the proportion undertaking an activity as the main purpose of their holiday has not increased greatly over the last 15 years, the number taking part in an activity, as part of their visit, has almost doubled with 80% of staying visitors taking part in an activity whilst staying on the coast. The most popular activities are shopping, walking, visiting heritage sites and swimming.

Information on activities undertaken by overseas visitors was collected in a visitor survey undertaken in 2003. The survey suggests that overseas holiday makers undertake a wide range of activities and have a higher propensity to visit heritage sites and museums than UK holidaymakers.

Tourism day visitors were much less likely to be involved in individual activities than staying tourists. For day visitors to the coast, the main activity was beach related including sunbathing and paddle. Future drivers and trends in Coastal Tourism

Drivers

As with general tourism activity, future changes in visitor activity on the coast will be influenced by a number of common factors. These are likely to include:

Available Leisure Time

Holiday entitlement has remained relatively stable over the last decade but the future will see increases in statutory holiday entitlement to 24 days in October 2007 and to 28 days from April 2009. This could lead to an expansion in the number of trips and nights spent away from home. However competition for consumers' free time is becoming more intense with the choice of things consumers can do in their spare time becoming increasingly diverse. There has been an increase in the number of retired people as a proportion of the total population. This sector has therefore experienced a growth in the total volume of available leisure time, but may in the future have fewer resources to significantly increase holiday taking.

Disposable Incomes

Until recently, incomes for those in work have grown faster than inflation although we are now experiencing a reverse in this trend. Expectations about retired incomes are uncertain given the changes in pension schemes in recent years.

Demographic Change

The older age groups will increase both absolutely and as a proportion of the population. Children under 16 will increase in number but the proportion of family households will decrease.

Socioeconomic Change

There is likely to be an increase in the upper socioeconomic groups with some decline in the proportion of DE groups. The proportion of the population benefiting from higher education is also increasing.

Lifestyle Changes

A growth in interest in personal health and fitness and in nature conservation has been apparent over the last decade. These trends are likely to continue, reinforced by concerns about climate change.

Information Technology

The growth and take up of the Internet has had a major impact on customers' ability to research and book tourism trips at home and abroad. It is essential that the tourism industry on the coast maintains a strong presence on the Web to compete with other destinations at home and abroad, although the proliferation of sites will also underpin other forms of marketing activity such as word of mouth. Information technology will also impact on information provision and distribution at the destination, through mobile phones and freestanding interactive panels extending the reach of traditional tourist information networks.

Ethical Consumerism

Consumers are becoming more ethically aware. In 2004, UK consumers spent a total of £25.8 billion on ethical goods, an increase of 15 per cent on the previous year. Over the same period, UK household expenditure increased by only 3.7%.

Market share of ethical consumerism had increased by 40% in the previous Other research indicates a growth in awareness amongst holidaymakers of the environmental dangers of tourism, whilst increasing numbers of people believe that travel companies should do more to protect the environment and support local people.

Climate Change

There is some anecdotal evidence that concerns about climate change may deter people from taking as many short breaks abroad, and that they will switch to taking more breaks in the UK. There is little evidence currently to suggest that UK visitors will be prepared to give up their main holidays abroad in favour of destinations in UK.

Transport Issues

Rising car ownership and use is likely to be reflected in growing road congestion both in destination and origin areas, which could inhibit any growth in tourism day trips in particular. The volume of traffic on roads in the UK has increased by 22% over the past decade according to the Department for Transport.

The continued growth in budget air travel will ensure fierce competition from overseas destinations both for long holidays and short breaks. The potential imposition of a fuel tax to meet climate change considerations could slow or reverse such growth.

Structure of the Industry

Tourism infrastructure provided by the private sector is very fragmented and often disadvantaged by limited resources and/or skill bases. This factor may inhibit the private sector from playing a full role in taking up opportunities unless innovation and business development advice is available.

Future Demand

In terms of future demand for holidays on the coast, our available research indicates that the long term trends that have impacted on coastal tourism over the last fifteen years are likely to be sustained. Long main holidays by UK residents to Wales are likely to be static in volume and are more likely to decline. Being relatively more dependent on the long main holiday, the seaside is likely to be more affected than other locations. Tourism data shows that there have been significant increases in the number of UK residents choosing to take short breaks in the UK. We are therefore likely to see sustained growth in the short breaks and additional holidays market, although the growth may be slower as a result of competition from overseas destinations. Demographic and income changes are likely to stimulate growth in higher value activities which are attractive to older age groups including yachting, motor boating in the sea cruising and golf. The same drivers will raise expectations of standards and quality of accommodation.

Socioeconomic and demographic drivers are likely to increase interest in arts, culture and heritage opportunities, whilst lifestyle and income growth are likely to sustain the growth in food, local products and eating out. Activities appealing to most age groups, such as walking, will continue to dominate in terms of the volume of participants. Adventure sports such as kite surfing, sub aqua diving and similar activities will continue to grow and attract the younger active age groups, although there may be some displacement from older established sports.

Key Challenges for Coastal Tourism

The Tourism Market

One of the main challenges for many parts of the coastline and particularly noticeable in coastal resorts is the continuing need to adapt in line with changing visitor expectations. The traditional two week 'bucket and spade' holiday has changed, visitors' needs and demands are now much more diverse. The tourism industry needs to continuously improve and develop new products to meet the evolving tastes and needs of consumers, in particular the needs of growth markets such as the short break market. In addition, a number of coastal resorts in Wales are suffering from social and economic problems. These stem from a number of sources including:

- seasonality of employment.
- a higher number of elderly residents.
- poor accessibility in some cases.
- out of date and ageing tourism infrastructure.
- imbalances of housing stock.

Accommodation

Many resorts are dominated by caravan accommodation. Much of the caravan stock is used by individual families and their friends rather than being available for holiday letting. The larger sites often provide shopping and recreational facilities on site, which reduces local spend, although owners of caravans tend to spend more in the locality.

A broader range of serviced accommodation would allow more choice for the visitor and appeal to the growing short break market Similarly, high quality accommodation, in all sectors, will attract visitors with a higher purchasing power. Consumer expectations are rising, making it imperative to invest in the quality of accommodation in order to attract and retain visitors to the coast.

Lower occupancy rates within the seaside accommodation sector overall have a detrimental affect in terms of attracting private investment. Any public sector support should not only be directed towards investing in the quality of accommodation itself, but in stimulating demand during the quieter off peak season.

Skills and Labour Resources

The seasonal nature of the tourism industry on the coast, together with the small scale nature of most tourism businesses poses challenges in retaining and equipping staff with the appropriate skills. In the short term, labour gaps, particularly in low paid jobs are being filled up by workers from other countries with lower wage levels.

However, as these countries develop, the source of labour is likely to decrease, increasing the importance of recruiting and retaining staff locally through improved working conditions and career prospects. Local people sometimes feel excluded from new establishments set up by entrepreneurs from outside the area. There is a continuing need to stimulate entrepreneurship within the local population and to adopt an integrated approach to stimulating and supporting business start ups and business growth.

Access

The strategic access via the M4 and A55 has significantly improved journey times to many parts of the Welsh coast. However, there are still many areas of the West Wales coast perceived as difficult to access due to journey times and the nature of the road network. Public transport access by rail to the coast is also relatively good with regular services along the North Wales and South Wales coast. However, services become less frequent further west and throughout Mid Wales. Many coastal locations are accessed by narrow country lanes which can suffer from congestion during the summer and cause safety issues for walkers and cyclists.

While the private car is likely to remain the main mode of travel for staying and day visits, the challenge is to develop innovative forms of public transport, to move people around local 'hot spots', and to make it easier for visitors to walk and cycle around destinations. There are a number of good examples already in Wales. In considering forms of public transport, consideration needs to be given to the specific needs of people undertaking outdoor activities both in terms of the equipment that will need to be transported and in relation to the frequency and times of transport.

Coastal Erosion

All coastlines are subject to change over time due to tidal and wind effects which can result in coastal erosion. Coastal erosion and falling sand levels have become an increasing concern around some parts of Wales. If such erosion continues, it could have a major impact on both the environment and the economy and on tourism in particular. Coastal erosion takes place over many years, so it can often be perceived as stable on a human timescale. However, how we deal with the consequences of coastal erosion will be an important consideration in taking forward the Coastal Tourism Strategy.

Climate Change

Climate change is likely to have significant impacts on the coast. Figures from the UK Climate Impacts Programme (UKCIP) and the Met Office indicate that:

- Globally temperatures could rise anywhere between 1.5 and 5.8 by 2080 –between 2 and 8 times the rise already seen since 1990. In the UK, an average rise of 2 – 3.5c is anticipated.

- Winters will become wetter (20-30% wetter by 2080) and summers may become drier (35-50% drier by 2080). Heavier rainfalls will become more frequent.
- Relative sea level will continue to rise around most of the UK.

The potential impacts of climate change are likely to be various. An example is the possible increase in extreme weather events such as storminess which may have the effect of increasing flooding in low-lying areas, and increase erosion rates that could lead to a less of beaches. A rise in sea level would have implications for low lying lands and coastal infrastructure. Tourism is also a contributor to climate change. The tourism industry and visitors alike are becoming more aware of the need to reduce their carbon footprints-this may well lead to an increase in demand for domestic holidays.

Managing and Developing the Coastline

There is increasing pressure on the coastal resource, and a growing recognition that the coastline should be managed in a more strategic and coordinated way. The impact of visitors on sites around the coast result in additional management costs to land owners and local authorities in terms of sustaining the quality of the environment and providing facilities for visitors to enjoy a safe experience. While some revenue costs can be recovered through car parking and other charges, much of the management costs arise in respect of public goods and spaces, with the costs having to be borne by the host authority. Resources required to cover the management costs arising from visitor activity are often under pressure from other spending priorities. Without appropriate management, there is potential for activities to spoil the peace, tranquillity and quality of the environment that many visitors to the coast are seeking.

Conflict Between Activities

The potential conflict between specific activities is another challenge facing the coastline. The beach can be used for a variety of different activities ranging from sun bathing to physically demanding sports such as parakiting. The challenge is to manage the coastal area to the maximum benefit of all potential users. Conflicts between activities exist not only on land but also at sea. Activities such as bathing, windsurfing, surfing, sailing, angling, and the use of powerboats and personal watercrafts need to be properly managed.

The pursuit of such activities will undoubtedly have an effect on the natural environment. The challenge is to instil a sense of responsibility for the coastline Analysis amongst stakeholders.

Second Home Ownership

There is continued concern in some areas as to the degree to which second home ownership within coastal communities is adversely affecting capacity in terms of visitor accommodation and the affordability and availability of housing to the local workforce. In terms of absolute numbers, higher concentrations of second homes and holiday homes are found along the coast at Penarth, St. Brides Major, Gower, the Pembrokeshire coast, along Cardigan Bay, the Lly^n peninsula and Anglesey.

The Assembly Government recognises that in-migration and the purchase of second homes has influenced community structures in some rural and coastal tourist areas of Wales. The issue of the Welsh language being lost from rural communities is also one that has taken on increasing importance owing to the increase in net in-migration and pressures that this has placed on local housing markets in Wales.

Partnership and Integration

The challenge for the Coastal Tourism Strategy will be to achieve a consensus on the way forward and to foster a collaborative approach to delivering the strategy. A range of organisations and interested parties have different responsibilities for the coast. Within Local Authorities alone, coastal related responsibilities are carried out by a wide range of departments including beach cleaning, coastal defence, licensing, tourism, countryside and recreation and some local authorities are also Harbour Authorities.

Initiatives such as the Green Sea Partnership involving the public, private and voluntary sectors are already achieving coordinated action to improve the quality of Welsh beaches. The Partnership has finalised a Green Sea Development Strategy to cover the period 2006 to 2015 which aims to achieve a target of 100 blue flag/green coast award beaches and 9 blue flag marinas by 2015, the year of the introduction of the new Bathing Water Directive. This is an example of successful partnership working on the coast which has involved the pooling of resources to deliver a set of agreed outcomes.

Developing the Strategy

In this chapter, we set out the strategic context and outline the key policy objectives that the strategy will need to address. We outline a vision for the strategy and establish the aims and key outcomes that the strategy will seek to achieve.

Policy Objectives

The One Wales document agreed by the Welsh Assembly Government presents the Assembly Government's priorities and programme for the next four years. It sets out a vision for a prosperous Wales where there is a strong an enterprising economy and full employment based on quality jobs. Tourism is regarded as being vital to economic prosperity and job creation in all regions of Wales.

The priorities for tourism are:

- Promote Wales actively in external markets, drawing on our unique markets, culture, history and environment.
- Strategic investment in facilities and employee skills.
- Support for the tourism industry as the market moves increasingly towards shorter and activity based breaks.

The Coastal Tourism Strategy will also help to deliver the following key One Wales commitments:

A Sustainable Environment

Tourism is an activity that can have a truly major impact on sustainable development, due to the unique relationship that tourism, compared with other economic activity, has with the environment and society.

Tourism is highly dependent on a quality environment and cultural distinctiveness-qualities which can be destroyed if badly planned or managed. However, tourism can be a driving force for the preservation and promotion of these qualities through raising awareness and income to support them, and indirectly by providing an economic justification for the provision of such support by others.

There is strong emphasis in One Wales on protecting the environment including commitments to support local authorities and voluntary action to improve the quality of the local environment and the creation of an all Wales Coastal Footpath.

Creating Jobs

The tourism industry is well-placed to provide important employment opportunities throughout Wales, even in the most sparsely populated and peripheral regions. The industry needs to increase profitability and productivity so that earnings and the quality of jobs supported by the industry can improve. Initiatives that contribute to extending the tourism season will help to support more year round jobs within the industry and increase productivity.

Improving Health and Activity Levels

Clear advantages can be gained from linking the tourism and recreation agendas. It is therefore highly appropriate to link planning for leisure and tourism together and to develop approaches that ensure that local people are also able to benefit from facilities which visitors come to enjoy. Tourism businesses can also promote health and wellbeing amongst their own employees. There is a specific commitment in One Wales to fostering a public sense of ownership in relation to the countryside, urban green spaces and our coastline, recognising that many socially excluded groups do not currently enjoy their social, cultural and health benefits.

Regenerating Communities

Tourism is often a catalyst for wider economic and local regeneration activity. Spending by tourists can help support local services, shops and community amenities that would not otherwise be viable thereby enhancing quality of life and creating a greater range of opportunities for all sectors of the community. The tourism industry can provide entry-level jobs and offers employment opportunities for economically inactive people or other returners to work, with the right support and training. Community based initiatives that support tourism can also act as an entry point for people into the paid workforce.

Equality

The Assembly Government has a statutory duty to promote equality and is committed to promoting gender equality, good race relations and tackling discrimination on the grounds of age and disability. Tourism is a major employer of women in Wales – with women representing nearly 60% of the workforce within the tourism, hospitality and leisure sector. This raises specific issues in relation to providing suitable training and working arrangements for women working in the industry. In addition women and men will undertake different activities on holiday and catering for women, men and families will be increasingly important for tourism providers. It is also essential that the tourism industry in Wales meets the needs of disabled visitors and other disadvantaged groups in society.

Strategic Context

We have reviewed in the technical report all the key documents at national, regional and local level that will affect to some degree the development, use and management of the coast of Wales. The following have been identified as being of particular relevance to the development of coastal tourism.

Achieving our Potential – mid Term Review

The mid term review of *Achieving our Potential*, the national tourism strategy for Wales has set five strategic challenges for developing tourism in Wales. These are:

- Distinctive branding.
- Higher quality.
- Easier Access.
- Better skills.
- Stronger Partnerships.

A series of priorities and individual actions have been identified for each of these challenges to describe what needs to happen differently to ensure that sustainable growth is achieved within the industry. While all of the five challenges outlined above are important, arguably it will be the achievement of higher quality that will be the most critical and crucial. Tourism businesses which are most likely to succeed will be those that deliver a high quality experience to visitors, understand their markets and communicate effectively with them, invest in their products and staff and attract and retain a motivated and skilled workforce.

Catching the Wave

Catching the Wave (2004) is the Welsh Assembly Government's tourism watersports activities and facility development strategy. The strategy states that few UK destinations can match the diversity and all inclusive nature of the Welsh coastal offer in the watersports market. The strategy is underpinned by a number of targets for 2010 including:

- to grow the number of UK watersports trips and nights by 20% to just over one million trips representing around 5 million bed nights.
- to grow the value of UK watersports tourist spending by 40% to over £200 million
- to grow the numbers of trips taken by the higher spend overseas market by 50% and to increase overseas visitor spend by 40% to £15 million.

To support the 'Catching the Wave' initiative the Welsh Assembly Government, in partnership with local authorities and other organisations, have prepared local maritime studies. To date, two studies have been prepared to investigate opportunities for investment in coastal regeneration and watersports in Cardigan Bay (St. David's to Trefor) and an action plan for increasing the economic benefit of the Mon a Menai coast. A similar study is currently underway in Conwy and Denbighshire and a Waterfront Masterplan has also been prepared in the Swansea Bay Spatial Plan area. The Coastal Tourism Strategy will build on this work, and will link the opportunities that have been identified for watersport development with the wider tourism product on the coastline.

Assembly Government has produced a strategy for Integrated Coastal Zone Management *Making the most of Wales' Coast* 10 which aims to provide a management framework to facilitate integrated working on the coast by the different interests involved in managing our coastal assets. It also sets out the links that must be made between diverse national and local policies and strategies so that people involved in managing and using the coast can do so in a way that takes into account the needs of others. A key objective of the ICZM process is to help ensure that all sectors and organisations successfully integrate ICZM management principles into the development of relevant policies.

Transport Strategy

The Welsh Assembly Government has recently published a Wales Transport Strategy *Connecting Wales*. The Transport Strategy will have a key role in improving accessibility to and within Wales and in helping to achieve a more sustainable tourism industry. The tourism sector will need to work closely with the four Regional Transport Consortia to ensure that tourism related solutions and innovative ideas are properly identified and prioritised. It will be important to consider the role of public transport and non vehicle modes in reducing the reliance on the private car.

Marine Bill

The proposed Marine Bill is likely to have a major influence on coastal tourism. The aim of the Bill will be to help develop the UK Government's vision for clean, healthy, safe, productive and biologically diverse oceans and seas. Proposals include developing a more integrated management regime for the marine environment through introducing the concept of marine planning. Marine Planning would develop a much wider strategic approach to considering the needs, aims and possible locations of sectoral activities for the marine area as a whole. It would also look at the potential of cumulative effects of many different activities together, and the compatibility or conflict between activities, or between activities and environmental protection. In addition, the Marine Bill White Paper outlined several proposals to protect Marine Biodiversity in UK Waters. These include a proposal to set up Marine Conservation Zones to provide protection for species and habitats considered of national value that cannot currently be protected by EU habitats designations. The Bill is also likely to introduce powers to manage unregulated activities (such as tourism and recreation) where these might have an impact on a Marine Conservation Zone or on important marine wildlife outside protected areas. The Welsh Assembly Government will be responsible for deciding how the Bill's proposals are implemented in Wales.

Health Challenge Wales

The Welsh Assembly Government's approach to improving health recognises that the way forward lies in adopting an integrated approach in which different policies and programmes add value to each other. The Health Challenge Wales programme has been developed to provide a new national focus and a way to drive forward all efforts to improve health. It means that government at all levels, organisations in all sectors and individuals can be challenged to do more to take action to improve people's health. The Assembly Government has outlined its aim of increasing the numbers of Welsh people using the Welsh natural environment for outdoor activities in its Sports and Physical Strategy Climbing Higher.

Better Place to Play

The Environment Agency-Wales published a Strategic Plan for Water Related Recreation in Wales that provides a set of priorities and opportunities for the development of water-related recreation. The plan is aimed at encouraging more people in Wales to take part in water related recreation and identifies new opportunities for water recreation at the coast and inland.

Vision, Aims and Outcomes

This strategy sets out the following vision for coastal tourism:

> *'An integrated year round coastal tourism industry, based on an outstanding natural environment and a quality tourism product that exceeds visitor expectations, whilst bringing economic, social, cultural and environmental benefits to coastal communities'.*

The Strategy

The following strategy has been developed to meet the vision, strategic aims, policy objectives and challenges identified in previous chapters.

It has been presented under five themes. The final theme, Coastal Management, covers areas relating to the whole coastline while the other themes concentrate on particular locations or activities. Inevitably, there is some overlap between the themes, which reflects the integrated nature of activities and responsibilities along the coast.

The themes covered are:

- Coastal Towns and Resorts.
- The Rural Coast.
- Coastal Activities.
- Coastal Culture.
- Coastal Management.

Coastal Towns and Resorts

Towns and cities around the coast of Wales vary greatly in size and character from the capital city to small resorts and fishing ports. Tourism's contribution to local economies will vary with seaside resorts being particularly dependent on visitor spending.

Cities and Towns on the Coast

Larger cities and towns on the coast such as Cardiff, Swansea and Newport have a tourist offer that embraces a wide range of shopping, eating out, cultural, recreational and leisure attractions, as well as specific opportunities related to the coast for water and land based informal recreation. They also have a range of serviced accommodation to support business tourism and the short break leisure market. In Swansea and Cardiff (45%) and (60%) respectively of accommodation demand comes from business travel. Smaller towns such as Aberystwyth and Bangor also benefit from local economies which include a university sector as well as other services. The wider local economy provides a stronger base to support shopping and catering activity than those towns dependent primarily on tourism. As a result, they provide a focus for day visitor activity from home and holiday accommodation in the surrounding areas. In addition, Aberystwyth, due to its location between North and South Wales, its increasing importance as a national centre and the new location of the Welsh Assembly Government regional office, has the potential to strengthen its accommodation base. Initiatives to regenerate the town and to develop its tourism role are emerging from the masterplanning work that has been undertaken which will enhance Aberystwyth's role as a coastal tourism town.

There are other coastal towns which have a distinctive appeal relating to their history, townscape and setting, such as Caernarfon and Conwy. Some other coastal towns such as Llanelli and Burry Port have not traditionally attracted much tourism activity, but the development of their coastal resources such as the Burry Port Harbour Development, Pembrey and the Millennium Coastal Parks provide opportunities for attracting a wider day visitor market as well as stayingtourists.

Holyhead, Swansea, Pembroke and Fishguard provide points of entry for visitors using the ferry services from Ireland, as well as catering for UK visitors to Ireland. Apart from regular ferry services, there is potential to develop cruise ship facilities particularly at Holyhead and Swansea to meet the growing market for this form of tourism. Milford Haven also has potential in relation to the cruise market.

Coastal Resorts

Coastal resorts are those towns on the coast where the local economy is dominated by tourism. They include Prestatyn, Rhyl,

Llandudno, Beaumaris, Pwllheli, Porthmadog, Barmouth, Tenby, Saundersfoot and Porthcawl. They vary greatly in terms of their size, character and accommodation base. Apart from staying tourists, many of the resorts attract substantial numbers of day visitors from home, particularly those located on the South East and North East parts of the Welsh coast. While coastal towns such as Colwyn Bay, Aberavon and Barry may have a wider economic base, tourism is still important.

Resorts will continue to be a major focus for visitor activity at the seaside. However, there will continue to be competition, not only from other seaside destinations at home and abroad, but also from city and countryside destinations in Wales and elsewhere. Moreover, many resorts have been adversely affected by changes in tourism activity, remaining over dependent on long family holidays and having limited appeal to the younger generation and overseas markets.

As a result, the tourism season in most resorts is short, with a high proportion of employment being seasonal and often poorly paid. Coupled with other economic difficulties, this has led to some of the most deprived economic and social wards in Wales being found in coastal resorts. While leading resorts such as Llandudno and Tenby provide an attractive living environment for residents and visitors, others suffer from a poor or run down appearance reflecting low levels of investment and confidence by the private sector.

The future prosperity of resort communities will depend not only on tourism activity but also on strengthening the local economy to provide additional employment and income opportunities for residents. This will best be achieved by diversifying the local economy to provide a greater choice and range of employment opportunities, and by adding value from tourism activity. Successful regeneration schemes will depend on the public, private and voluntary sectors delivering a concerted package of projects tailored to meeting the needs and opportunities of individual resorts. They will need to build on the Assembly

Government's approach to regenerating disadvantaged communities which focuses on building capacity within communities and engaging with all groups of residents to help understand the root causes of the problems that face individuals and households within the community. This process will help ensure that communities within resorts are empowered to take up the economic and social opportunities that are created. Some resorts have already benefited from regeneration programmes, which can provide lessons for future initiatives.

In supporting regeneration initiatives, priority at national level should be given to those areas where:

- the local economy is particularly dependent on tourism activity.
- existing tourism infrastructure is not well adapted to changing market needs.
- there are opportunities for new development to meet emerging market demand.

Deprivation in Coastal Communities

The prosperity of the different settlements varies widely depending on local circumstance, as do the levels of multiple deprivation in local communities. In some cases, such as Cardiff, areas of relative prosperity can be found in close proximity to areas of multiple deprivation.

Coastal settlements with communities falling within the top 10% of communities suffering from multiple deprivation include:

- Major settlements with a varied economy including Cardiff, Swansea, Newport, Aberavon Llanelli and Barry.
- Resort towns, including Barmouth and Rhyl.
- Smaller towns where tourism contributes to the local economy, including Holyhead, Amlwch, Conwy, Caernarfon, Pwllheli, Aberystwyth, Pembroke Dock.

These wards are included in the Assembly Government's Communities First Programme which supports the establishment of Communities First Partnerships and helps to deliver capacity building projects.

It will be important to engage with the Community First Partnerships that have been set up within these areas when undertaking regeneration initiatives and other projects outlined in the implementation plan to ensure that local communities are involved in identifying local needs and solutions for regenerating their areas. The Community First model may also be appropriate for other areas where significant regeneration programmes are undertaken. The Welsh Assembly Government is committed to developing Communities First into Communities Next from 2009.

Providing an Attractive Environment

A crucial objective for resorts will be to improve and maintain the public the natural and historic environment to ensure that they are attractive to residents, investors and visitors. The appearance of the approaches to the resort, the sea front and the town centre are crucial in forming the visitor's initial impressions of the resort. An environment which is shabby, ill kept with ugly and poorly sited street furniture will detract from the visitor's enjoyment of the resort.

Resorts therefore need to ensure that they set high standards of design and landscaping for their public areas, including the provision of street furniture on the beach and adjoining areas. High standards of design, including innovatory architectural approaches should be encouraged for new development and redevelopment schemes while conserving the best of the resort's heritage, which contributes to the unique character of the place.

The private sector can also play an active part in maintaining public frontages in good order, and contributing towards the costs of landscaping and planting in the town centres and promenades. The existing public and partnership initiatives already being undertaken to improve the urban seaside environment need to be strengthened and expanded. The objective is to provide an attractive urban and seaside environment for the enjoyment of residents and visitors alike, which contributes to the unique character of each resort.

Beaches and Seaside

The beach and adjoining sea areas provide the unique attraction of seaside resorts. The Blue Flag and Resort Seaside Award schemes set standards for beaches used by the public including criteria relating to water quality, management of land and water recreation to avoid conflict between incompatible activities, safety and first aid provision, toilets, fresh water, litter and refuse disposal and environmental and safety information. A high proportion of resort beaches have attained these awards. However, a number of beaches continue to be affected by diffuse pollution and there are also indications that average beach litter density in Wales is increasing year on year.11 The beach and sea provide opportunities for a wide range of informal and active pastimes including swimming and sun bathing, sailing and beach games and more adventurous water based activities such as personal water craft and water skiing. The enjoyment of the beach experience can be enhanced by good management and provision of facilities such as launch points, fresh water showers and organised children's play provision during the peak periods for family holidays. Good design and landscaping of beach facilities, promenades and street furniture can also add to the experience. The management of intensively used resort beaches is a complex task involving health, safety and environment issues, conflict resolution between different beach and water users, and coordination and liaison with private operators on an adjoining the beach.

The use of innovative management approaches could assist in enhancing the beach and seafront as a primary focus of visitor enjoyment. City and Town centre managers provide a possible exemplar. Beach masters or resort managers could be appointed with similar responsibilities and powers to manage and enhance the visitor enjoyment of the beach and immediate onshore and offshore areas, whilst involving the private, public and voluntary sector stakeholders in a coordinated approach to facility provision and maintenance.

Accommodation

The quality, scale and type of tourist accommodation varies greatly from resort to resort. Many establishments were first developed over 50 years ago and struggle to match customer expectations and aspirations in the 21st Century. If resorts are to continue to attract staying tourists in competition with other destinations, then it is essential that the accommodation provided meets or surpasses their expectations. No accurate figures currently exist for the coastal accommodation stock in Wales although a national audit of all bedstock is currently underway. It is possible to obtain some proxy indication of the quantity of accommodation by type, by relating tourism nights to occupancy data. On this basis, there are over 100,000 bedspaces in commercial accommodation located around the Welsh coast, of which half are in static caravans, either owned or available for holiday letting.

Serviced accommodation capacity is estimated to account for around 12% of the stock and self catering around 8%. There are, however, concentrations that mask the real picture. Llandudno has a substantial stock of serviced accommodation whereas the lack of similar facilities on the Lly^n Peninsula can cause problems when the area is hosting national and international events. Similarly, there are a number of high density caravan/camping sites along the North Wales coast, but a lack of quality camping on certain stretches of Cardigan Bay. In order to adapt provision to the changing needs, a multi-pronged approach will be needed including:

- investing in existing establishments to develop higher quality standards appropriate to their category and type, including serviced accommodation, caravan and camping sites and hostels.
- the redevelopment or conversion of existing establishments which are not physically capable of being improved to appropriate standards to more viable uses.
- the development of new establishments particularly where new opportunities and activities generate additional demand.

Visit Wales has commissioned several serviced sector accommodation supply and demand studies to identify any shortfalls in the range and quality of accommodation provision in specific areas of Wales. These studies, in particular, identify whether deficiencies can be met by the extension/improvement of existing operations or through the provision of new facilities. A number of coastal locations are covered by these studies.

In terms of accommodation trends, a definite growth sector within the accommodation sector has been the rise in importance of 'boutique', 'designer' or 'townhouse' hotels. Key characteristics of this type of accommodation include high quality design fittings, central locations and limited size, targeting the upper end of the market at high room rates.

Many four star commercial hotels and country house hotels in the UK have now developed health/beauty/relaxation spas of varying size and quality. Such spas are emerging as a 'must have' facility to meet the demands of the short break market at the upper end of the market, though these also need local demand.

In terms of static caravan stock, a high proportion is individually owned with only a quarter available for commercial letting. While there are individual sites of high quality, many sites have standard layouts with varying quality of central facilities.

In some cases, it may be appropriate to allow expansion of existing sites in order to encourage operators to reduce density and to provide more imaginative and landscaped surroundings without incurring a potential loss of income. Towns and resorts should also encourage active networking between accommodation establishments to provide exchange of experience, mentoring, general business support and referrals.

Visitor Attractions

In addition to the beach, resorts need to provide a wide range of activities and attractions for the visitor if they are to continue to attract and increase the volume of staying and day visitors. The coast already has a range of visitor attractions including the world heritage listed Edwardian castles in North Wales, the National Waterfront Museum in Swansea, steam railways, local museums and other sites.

However, resorts offer opportunities for developing additional activities and specialist attractions drawing on the concentration of visitors to resorts without displacing visitors from existing attractions. In particular, there should be opportunities to:

- increase the number of opportunities for visitors to try new water and land based activities ranging from boat trips for wildlife watching to sports such as water skiing, dinghy sailing, paragliding and other activities.
- provide additional wet weather facilities such as indoor play areas, climbing walls, bowling greens and alleys and other recreational and leisure facilities.

There may also be opportunities to develop new attractions related to the heritage, culture or physical characteristics of the coast. However such developments will need a robust business plan including a consideration of the impact on existing attractions.

Retail and Catering

Two thirds of visitors enjoy shopping, and even more enjoy eating out while at the seaside but the retail and catering offer in many seaside resorts is limited, reducing the potential level of expenditure by visitors. The development of a wider range of specialist shops offering local arts and craft products together with high quality local produce could widen the retail offer and attract greater visitor spending.

While there are individual restaurants which offer high quality cuisine in some resorts, there are no comparable concentrations of eating out opportunities in any of the Welsh resorts. Visitors (including day visitors) are looking for a quality food experience in a variety of hospitality establishments. There are opportunities to raise the quality and choice of all types of catering establishments, using local Welsh produce particularly fish and shellfish and traditional Welsh recipes. Resorts should make special efforts to encourage a wider range of shops, particularly specialist shops selling local arts and crafts.

Visitor Access

Most visitors to resorts come by car. While staying visitors can be accommodated within the resorts, day visitors from holiday accommodation outside the resort or from home can cause congestion and pressure on parking facilities within the resort, particularly during the peak holiday season. Pressure within the resorts can be eased by promoting alternative methods of travel such as cycle routes and public transport, or by establishing seasonal park and ride systems. The provision of dedicated land trains or bus services connecting car parks and the main attractions within the resort can also assist in reducing car movements while helping to distribute visitors to the range of destinations.

Traffic management schemes can help to reduce congestion particularly at 'hot spots'. Advanced variable electronics signing on key approach routes can assist in directing traffic, as well as 'in car' traffic information or information from the Traffic Wales web site. Development in real time traffic information will be particularly relevant in dealing with peak seasonal traffic demands. Similarly pubic transport users (rail/bus/sea) require an integrated timetable and customer information system to provide them with 'real' information. There is a need to extend interactive tourism information points to include public transport hubs and tourist locations remote from TIC's.

The Rural Coast

The rural coast of Wales is a magnificent resource for residents and visitors to enjoy, offering spectacular coastal scenery, attractive small towns and villages, opportunities for informal land and water based recreation and a wildlife environment of exceptional diversity and interest. The coast is also valued for its unspoilt scenery, peace and quiet. A balance needs to be struck on the rural coast between tranquil areas and areas supporting a large number of people and a range of activity.

Coastal Settlements

Coastal towns and villages were often established as fishing ports or commercial harbours. Inshore fisheries remain an important function in some settlements and can add interest for the holiday visitor. While the commercial use of many harbours has declined, they often offer potential as safe havens for visiting boats, as well as bases for leisure activities such as sea angling, diving and leisure boat trips to watch wildlife as at Aberdovey, Aberaeron and New Quay. Other small coastal resorts include Tywyn and Borth. Tourism is an important contributor to the local economy, with villages attracting both staying and day visitors, as well as acting as service points for the surrounding rural areas. Most have an attractive environment and ambience for the visitor as well as specific heritage attractions, cultural or historic associations such as Conwy, Caernarfon, Beaumaris, Criccieth, Harlech, St. Davids, Pembroke, Laugharne and Llansteffan. The establishment of the Wales Coastal Path, as well as rural cycle and riding routes, should help to underpin and develop existing tourism activity, while the combination of coast and countryside coupled with specific leisure or cultural activities should provide opportunities to attract niche and short break tourism markets.

Rural Accommodation

There is already a substantial amount of holiday accommodation along the rural coast. Much of the rural accommodation is in self catering cottages and static caravan sites, together with individual owned and managed hotel and guesthouse accommodation.

The development of the Wales Coastal Path, as well as water and land based activities along the coast, will provide opportunities to expand the accommodation base to cater for the changes in demand. In particular, there should be potential for camping sites, bed and breakfast and hostel accommodation serving younger and more active visitors.

Rural Beaches and the Rural Environment

The Welsh Coast is blessed with many attractive coves and beaches outside the main resort areas including: Red Wharf Bay, Newborough, Black Rock, Morfa Harlech, Morfa Dyffryn, Aberdovey, Newgate, Broad Haven, Barafundle, Freshwater East, Rhossilli, Oxwich, Pendine, Pembrey. Many of these sites attract substantial informal use for both passive and active recreation and leisure uses, but their management poses problems and costs for local authorities, the National Trust and local communities. Charging for car parking, voluntary donation schemes and other initiatives can help to offset such costs.

The high quality of the coastal environment is recognised by the large number of environmental designations covering the bulk of the coastline. The quality is a major attraction for visitors to the coast, and it is vital therefore that development and visitor pressures are controlled to ensure that the resource is not inadvertently damaged or degraded. Where damage is occurring as a result of overuse, then positive management measures should be taken to match the capacity of the site to the user pressure, and restoration measures taken to make good damaged areas. Because of their rural character, the criteria for Blue Flag designation are not always appropriate for rural beaches. In order to provide a quality standard for such beaches, the Green Coast Award has been developed by Keep Wales Tidy, setting out a set of criteria designed to sustain the conservation value as well as visitor enjoyment of these areas. Wales is unique in developing the Green Coast award, thereby reinforcing the strong image of an unspoilt coastline for visitors to enjoy

In addition to meeting the provisions set out in the criteria with regard to management, safety, information and conservation measures, local communities are also encouraged to set up local support groups to monitor and assist in the management of the beaches. The principle of involving the local community in the management and conservation of the local coastal environment should be encouraged through support for a range of possible organisations from voluntary associations to local trusts and companies. The Keep Wales Tidy Clean Coasts initiative encourages community participation through the establishment and operational management of voluntary Coastcare Groups. There are currently 98 voluntary Coastcare groups. Tourism businesses can also play their part, through encouraging their employees to participate in volunteering schemes on the coast.

Access

While access to the rural coast in many parts of North and South Wales is afforded by the M4 and A55 as well as the main rail routes, local access to individual rural sites is often reliant on narrow lanes and minor roads. As a result, congestion often occurs on routes providing access to popular sites during peak visitor periods. The heavy use of cars to reach those sites adds to pollution levels, as well as detracting from the visitor's experience of the visit.

There are a number of innovative public transport initiatives around the coast which provide visitors with alternative ways to enjoy the coastal experience. These include dedicated coastal bus services linking sites along the coast, and boat excursions along the coast and to islands off the coast. Such alternatives can help to reduce traffic pressures as well as adding interest and opportunities for the visitor.

The proposed development of the Wales Coastal Path will provide enhanced opportunities for walking along the coast, while the extension of existing cycle and riding trails, including the National Cycle Trail will also provide additional facilities to enjoy the coast in an environmentally friendly way.

Coastal Activities

There is considerable variation in volumes of participation, demand trends and spending for outdoor activities around the coast of Wales. By far the largest demand is for walking, (69% participating whilst on holiday). Adventure (8%) sailing (5%), sea angling (6%) and (wildlife watching (5%) have 'medium' levels of participation. Other activities include golf (3%) and cycling (4%).

The spatial distribution of activities along the Welsh coast is a function of the physical geography, the distribution of suitable terrain and attractive landscapes, and the location of infrastructure, transport networks, accommodation and other facilities.

It will be important to consider the needs and requirements of disabled people when developing and promoting coastal activities. Wales is establishing a good track record in encouraging equal opportunities for all participants. Where such facilities are provided, they need to be adequately publicised via, for example, the Disability Wales or the Visit Wales website. Whilst information on the types of activities undertaken by men and women on holiday is currently unavailable, it will be important for the strategy to strike a balance between developing activities that appeal primarily to men such as golf or fishing and activities that have more appeal to women.

In relation to the provision of opportunities for coastal activities, both land and water based, consideration needs to be given to strategic planning through the use of appropriate methodology, such as the Recreation Opportunity approach. This will enable consideration to be given to providing for the full range of desired activities in the most appropriate locations whilst retaining more tranquil areas.

Coastal Footpath

Of all the activities undertaken at the coast, walking is by far the most popular. Walking, for the vast majority of visitors to the coast, will be one amongst many activities undertaken during their holiday. There is also a smaller niche market for walkers who undertake specific walking holidays. Growth in niche walking holidays is likely to be strongest for independent centre-based walking breaks. Such holidays already account for the bulk of walking holidays in Wales, and are likely to continue to do so in the future.

There are already a number of coastal paths, including the Isle of Anglesey Coastal Path, the North Wales Path, the Llyn Coastal Path, Ceredigion Coastal Path, Carmarthen Bay Coastal and Estuaries Way, Glamorgan Heritage Coast Path, as well as the Pembrokeshire Coast Path, providing around 1000kms of footpath around the coast. 60% of the coast currently has public access. Some areas will always be inaccessible, for example, ports, industrial sites and areas of nature conservation.

The Welsh Assembly Government has announced a new coastal access programme to increase public access to Wales' coast. A key aim of the programme will be to eventually link all existing coastal paths to form an All Wales Coastal Path. As part of the programme, there will be opportunities to provide links and loops from the spine path and to improve access to cyclists and horse riders in the coastal zone. The creation of circular routes from the spine route will enable local attractions and local communities near the coast to benefit from the Coastal Path, maximising the economic benefits from the investment. It is envisaged that the coastal access improvement programme will last four to five years. The programme will aim to deliver enhanced public access by maximising existing path infrastructure. A number of key interests will be involved including the coastal local authorities, the National Trust, Countryside Council for Wales, Farming Unions, RSPB and the Ramblers Association. It will be important to develop appropriate accommodation linked to the walking and cycling opportunities, including quality accommodation across all types from bunkhouses and Bed and Breakfasts to three and four star serviced accommodation. The Visit Wales Walkers and Cyclist Welcome scheme provides guidance and accreditation to accommodation providers that specifically cater for walkers and cyclists and provides information on the additional facilities that are required, including drying areas and secure cycle storage.

Wildlife Tourism

The coast of Wales has some of Europe's best landscapes and an abundance of maritime habitats, making it an attractive destination for visitors wanting to explore the natural environment and its human imprint. The dramatic cliffscapes and stacks of Holy Island and Pembrokeshire are prime bird nesting areas, the mudflats of the Dee and the Severn hold massive invertebrate populations; the estuaries of the Conwy, Mawddach, Dyfi and Tywi harbour a variety of saltmarsh dwellers, while the unique unglaciated via landscape of Milford Haven offers further marine and freshwater sanctuary.

All the above invite wildlife and coastline exploration, and while it is difficult to assess the potential scale of the market, the Scottish Executive in 2002 estimated that the wildlife tourism market in Scotland was worth £57m and employed some 2000 people. The number of wildlife tourism operators in Scotland grew by 37% between 1997 and 2002. It is also estimated that wildlife watching is growing by some 10% a year across the world. The 'Wildlife Economy Wales' 13 study highlights the considerable potential of developing wildlife tourism in Wales in terms of:

- Extending the tourism season in specific locations where there is an opportunity to do so.
- Securing an increase in visitor spend at sites which are currently popular, where appropriate.
- Improving the links between wildlife activities/interests and other activities such as general outdoor visits, tourism and agriculture.
- Developing new attractions and attracting new people to new and existing sites. A coastal wildlife tourism development programme could include elements of the following:

- wildlife and birdwatching events with wildlife organisations such as CCW, RSPB and the Wildlife Trusts in Wales.
- Seawatching from the shore and from a series of specially designed and constructed coastal hides and viewpoints, with information on different species.
- A programme of coastal boat trips – seal and dolphin watching (although it will be important to observe Codes of Conduct).
- Island explorations – e.g. Anglesey, Bardsey, Skomer and Skokholm, subject to environmental carrying capacity of the Islands.
- A series of seashore safaris – exploratory events for children, using interpretation techniques developed at Ynyslas and Oxwich NNRs.

It is critical, however, that any further wildlife related tourism development is appropriately managed to ensure that the wildlife resource is protected and wherever possible enhanced. Visitor management, particularly at the more sensitive locations, will be an important consideration as will consideration of the degree to which there is capacity for expansion in certain locations.

Other Coastal Land Activities

In addition to the walking and cycling activities mentioned, some parts of the coast are particularly renowned for certain land-based activities, namely golf, climbing and kite sports. Participation in climbing is growing steadily whilst participation in kite sports is growing rapidly from a small base. There would appear to be limited opportunity to further promote climbing or to provide additional facilities.

Kite sports on the other hand are an opportunity to attract a new, younger market to traditional resorts, though management will be needed to avoid conflicts with other beach users.

Golf is already being promoted by Visit Wales as a niche activity. However, to take full advantage of the interest in golf which will be generated by the Ryder Cup in 2010, there is a need to increase the amount of high grade accommodation located close to premier golf courses and to consider the case for additional golf course provision.

Coastal Activities-Water

Levels of participation in water–based activities are relatively low in comparison to land-based activities such as walking. However, water-based activities have significant localised economic impacts where there are harbours or marinas or natural conditions suitable for specific activities such as surf beaches, dive sites or angling locations.

Angling in particular is an important contributor to a number of local coastal economies. Fishing Wales has demonstrated the high value of recreational fishing to the Welsh economy. The 2004/05 marketing campaign generated an additional £27m into the economy, contributing to the estimated £100m+ of angling tourism revenue. Coastal fishing pays an important element with 48% of angling visits being to the coast. Of these 69% are shore based anglers and 31% boat anglers. There are some 70 charter boat skippers operating from Welsh ports. Boating and sailing generates significant economic impacts and helps to create a distinctive atmosphere. The economic impacts of boating tourism can be increased by building new marinas or improving the facilities at existing harbours and marinas to meet the growing demand for berths.

In other locations, new slipways or all-state-of-the tide landing stages could facilitate access to the water for sport use, nature cruises, coastal kayaking and angling boats. Other relatively minor improvements such as the provision of trailer parking and showers would bring additional use and the potential for local economic benefits. It should be borne in mind that facilities require maintenance and use can be very seasonal. It is, however, feasible to provide some facilities from May to September (temporary pontoons) and remove them for the winter.

While there are locations where new slipways or pontoons are required, there is also a need to improve and increase the use of existing slipways. There is a need to review the capacity, condition and current management of the entire coastal network of launching and landing facilities to identify whether investment is warranted. Much work has already been done in some areas with the preparation of coastal recreation audits.

There are water activities that are particular to parts of the Welsh coast. Not only does this generate significant economic impact, sports such as surfing and wakeboarding provide a distinctive atmosphere. It is important to safeguard those markets by providing good quality facilities at key locations and increase numbers and spending where there is the opportunity to do so. There is also potential to initiate 'try it' opportunities to develop an interest, in particular, in watersports.

Various visitor surveys conducted around the coast have all highlighted that one of the main attractions of the Welsh coastline is its unspoilt scenery, peace and quiet. While boating and watersports are important, there should be a focus on activities that are less intrusive.

Enjoyment of coastal or offshore waters for recreational boating need not conflict with conservation initiatives or lead to environmental degradation. Initiatives such as the Green Blue Project set up jointly by the British Marine Foundation and the Royal Yachting Association aim to provide information to the marine industry and users about potential environmental impacts of recreational boating and promote effective mitigation measures.

Most complaints arise from the use of personal watercraft (PWC's) – including noise and safety concerns. However, the use of PWC's is a legitimate leisure activity if appropriately managed.

Local authorities in Gwynedd, Conwy, Denbighshire and Anglesey have already instigated a registration scheme for PWC users. The registration scheme is valid for all four areas and requires users to register with one of the councils with proof of identify and insurance before being able to use any of the beaches/slipways in the area. This offers the advantage of an ultimate sanction against those who do not comply with bylaws and local regulations by withdrawing their registration for the whole region of North Wales. There is a need to explore whether a regional zoning and management system for the use of PWC's could be introduced and implemented on a Wales wide basis. With regard to developing watersports, the following have been identified as opportunities:

- Provide access to water-based activities for new participants within harbours.
- Safeguard the markets in specific water activities and in the following activities increase numbers and spending: Pembrokeshire (improve slipway access and management) and develop the potential for Gelliswick as a Dive Centre – Surfing– Llyn, Pembrokeshire, Porthcawl, Gower (provide better beach facilities, including showers and changing).

Climbing – Holyhead, South Pembrokeshire (continue to manage noclimbing agreements to ensure continued participation at important nature conservation sites), Conwy;

- Kite sports.
- Anglesey, Llyn, Conwy.
- Sea angling.
- Coast-steering.
- Sea kayaking.
- Windsurfing.

There may also be additional longer-term opportunities to develop or increase existing activities by the provision of artificial reefs to improve surfing, diving or sea angling activity. In addition, the Environment Agency's water recreation action plan identifies the following areas as possible hubs for general coastal watersport activity– Swansea, Cardiff, Milford Haven, Anglesey, Colwyn Bay, Cardigan and the Teifi Estuary, Aberdyfi, and Barmouth.

Marinas and Harbours

Catching the Wave identified eleven marinas around the coast of Wales and some twenty three harbours (plus six commercial harbours and fifteen yacht stations). In addition to the above, the Swansea SA1 marina is now a commitment. An audit undertaken in 2003/4 by the British Marina Federation identified over 7500 moorings along the Welsh coastline with active proposals at different stages of development for a further 3500 permanent new berths.

The technical report has identified some 16 schemes relating to potential marina/harbour developments which are at various of stages of consideration, including new marina developments and improvements to existing marinas. A key objective within *Catching the Wave* is to increase the supply of long stay and visitor berths and moorings. The need for this is strongly supported by waiting lists for berths at a number of locations. For example, Pwllheli has a waiting list of some 450 names.

In the past, in the UK and other European countries, most notably Spain and Portugal, marina developments have been supported by residential development in order to fund the cost of the infrastructure e.g seawalls, pontoons and onshore facilities. Without such provisions, marina development is rarely financially viable without public sector support. In many of the potential marina locations in Wales, significant marina related housing would not be appropriate and therefore public sector support towards the capital costs could be required. The scale and type of marinas most appropriate to the majority of the Welsh Coast is more on the lines of the Brittany experience in France i.e. marinas of a scale that do not require major residential development, but development that is restricted to marine related commercial development, some commercial leisure and limited ancillary housing.

The size of the marinas will need to be sufficiently large to be able to generate sufficient income from mooring and related fees to cover the ongoing revenue costs arising from the management of the marina. This is thought to be in the order of 350-400 berths. Smaller harbour schemes, including the use of temporary berths or smaller scale summer moorings can also provide an alternative to larger marinas. Various fact finding missions to Brittany have been undertaken where the following main lessons learnt have been:

- that any marina strategy is a long term strategy.
- that marinas and other watersports can be developed in tandem.
- that there are definite benefits to rural hinterlands from marina developments.
- marina and watersports should be linked to other tourism opportunities – such as heritage and golf.
- there needs to be local support from the outset.
- the incorporation of visiting berths are important e.g. Kernaval marina at Lorient has 680 berths with 100 reserved for visitors and generated 12000 yacht night visitors per year.
- events play an important part of establishing profile and reputation.
- getting children onto water for fun and experience as early as possible is important. 9000 Breton children per year receive boat lessons through schools.
- Innovative building methods and materials used in marina construction.
- facilities for boat waste disposal and drainage systems are important as are proper shower and toilets. EU regulations are increasingly setting higher standards.

- dual use of space – winter storage areas used as food markets in the summer.

Experience has shown that marinas and ancillary facilities can provide significant local economic benefits both in terms of jobs and spend. A recent study by the University of Glamorgan on the economic impact of Pwllheli Marina indicated that the direct income generated by the development in 2005 was £19m with a further £8.9m spent by berth owners outside the immediate area. With regard to jobs, the study estimated some 260 direct and indirect jobs were supported by the income generated. While the demand for berths currently exceeds supply, it would not be practical or desirable to build or improve all the marina opportunities that have been identified especially as many would require sizeable public funding. Therefore, it is necessary to evaluate schemes in order to determine best value for money, local benefits and fit with the wider environmental, economic and social policies of the Welsh Assembly Government and other national organisations.

It is recommended that possible new marinas and existing marinas and harbours that would benefit from improvement works are assessed by the Area Spatial Plan Groups to determine the most appropriate location for investment within their region. The location and development of marinas will also need to be considered from a marine planning point of view as well as from a terrestrial and spatial point of view.

Assessment Criteria

The assessment should consider the following:

Policy and Strategic

- Compatibility with the Wales Spatial Plan and other national environment and economic strategies.
- Compatibility with regional, local and marine planning policies.
- Demonstrate strategic approach in relation to other coastal initiatives (including other marinas).
- Environmental and Wider Conservation Interests.
- Compatibility with the environmental policies of national organisations (CCW, EA etc.).
- Subject to satisfactory geophysical, sediment movement, wave/wind analysis and coastal/estuarial survey and modelling.

- Subject to a comprehensive Environmental Impact Assessment.
- Commitment to attaining Blue Flag accreditation.
- Subject to compliance with WAG flood risk policies.
- Consideration of impact and relationship to environmental designated areas (including the need to screen for potential impact on SAC and SPA sites under the EU Habitats Directive.
- That sufficient land is available for initial operation and potential future development (including winter boat and trailer storage).

– Consideration with regard to access – both in terms of vehicle and pedestrian access and navigable boat access during much of the tidal period.

– Safety of operation.

– Where appropriate, should compliment existing harbour and shoreside facilities.

– Consideration of visual impact on the character of the wider built and natural environment and

– Consideration of impact on water quality (in accordance with provisions of the Water Framework Directive).

Economic and Business

- A robust business case should be prepared including a cost plan, outputs/outcomes and a marketing strategy.
- Must demonstrate proven user demand, proximity and accessibility to markets.
- Should have a local employment policy and demonstrate level of local commitment.
- Should identify appropriate training and skills development and local business support.
- Should not be in direct and immediate competition with existing facilities, thus avoiding economic displacement.
- Should demonstrate added economic value including direct and indirect tourism multiplier effects.
- Should enhance or maintain land and water opportunities where feasible.

Social and Community

- Demonstrate significant local support.

- Provide a consultation strategy that addresses a community engagement plan.
- Should be able to demonstrate local community benefits.

Marina Development

Whilst it has not been possible to undertake a detailed financial viability or market demand assessment of the proposals to build new marinas or extend existing marinas within the context of developing the strategy, a review has been undertaken of existing reports. Taking into account locational considerations, local support and a preliminary view of the criteria above, the following locations have been identified as having a number of attributes that merit further consideration by the Area Spatial Plan Groups.

* Rhyl (new) Pwllheli (extension).
* Swansea SA1 marina (new).
* Beaumaris (new) Fishguard (new).
* Holyhead (extension) Burry Port (extension).

Some of the above are well advanced with regard to obtaining planning permission and the required maritime approvals, but have certain land or dredging issues to resolve, while others are at the feasibility/business planning stage. The development of the above marinas would provide the Welsh coastline with 18 purpose built marinas in addition to a number of other mooring locations (ports/harbours and yacht stations). Where funding is not already committed, Welsh Assembly Government funding will be dependent on them meeting the criteria outlined above. Other potential sites, which are longer term opportunities for new marina or extended marinas include:

* Pont Penrhyn Porthcawl.
* Pembroke Dock Cardiff.
* Newport Barry.
* Colwyn Bay/Llandudno.

The development of these sites will need to be considered against the criteria established, the capital cost, the balance between public/private sector involvement, any impact from new marinas (on both side of the Bristol Channel) and the wider regeneration benefits. Locations where major works may not be appropriate, but certain limited improvements to increase the number of moorings and/or facilities which could bring significant local benefits include:

* Caernarfon Aberaeron.
* Porthmadog Cardigan.
* Barmouth New Quay.
* Aberdyfi Milford Haven.

The types of improvements envisaged include improved public space e.g promenade enhancements, improved parking, identified trailer parking areas, improved slipways, additional fixed shoreside moorings, pontoons to give 24 hour shore access from drying out harbours, toilet and shower facilities. A full list of marina/harbour related facilities are included in the technical report.

It will be important that any new provision or upgrading of existing facilities are made to a high quality and standard. This also applies to any ancillary activities related to accommodation, eating and drinking. Improved facilities will enable Wales to further develop its high profile with regard to international and interregional sailing and watersports events.

Visiting Berths

It will be important to ensure that any new mooring facility includes the capacity to provide an adequate supply of visiting berths, to encourage visits to other areas around the Welsh coast. Visiting berths are also very important for events, competitions and regattas. It is appreciated that visiting berths which are only used occasionally (but frequently during the peak season) do not generate the same income levels as the annual renting of berths and that they require additional management.

However, there are examples around the coast of Wales where pro-active management of berths has made regular berths available to visiting boats whilst the regular user is away. It is important that there are opportunities for sailors to sail around the coast in the knowledge that visiting berths are available. These facilities would also provide 'safe haven berths' for any boats requiring refuge due to the weather, tide or mechanical failure. Marina operators and harbour master have however emphasised that boats would never be turned away. Over time, the interest in travelling around the coast of Wales could become as popular as the current cross Irish Sea ventures.

Cruising

Cruising is one of the growth sectors in international tourism. Passenger departures from British Ports rose from 50,000 in 1990 to over 270,000 in 2003. While the bulk of the cruises were to the Mediterranean, Atlantic Islands or Scandinavia, an increasing number of operators cruise around the British Isles, with the Irish Sea increasing in popularity particularly Dublin and Belfast. The east coast Irish ports are receiving up to 70 cruise liner visits per year. In Wales, there were 15 calls in 2005 and 12 in 2006. Any liner calling at an Irish port could also call at a Welsh port.

There are a number of sub markets within the cruising market, including:

* Capitals of Europe – which could include Cardiff, Dublin and Belfast plus ports en route.
* The four Country Round Britain cruise.
* Short Irish sea cruises.
* The Celtic Fringe – taking in northern Iberia Bay of Biscay, the Irish and North seas.

The size of the vessel also varies-from ships accommodating 600/700 passengers to the typical 2600 passenger liner. The trend is for larger vessels, with the largest liner (new liner for Royal Caribbean) having a capacity of 6400 passengers. The new larger liners will be for the international market, in particular America and the Caribbean, but it will mean that existing cruise liners will be cascaded down to other market areas. The four ports in Wales with potential for developing the cruise liner market are Holyhead, Milford Haven, Swansea and Cardiff. Proposals are at an advanced stage, particularly at Holyhead and Milford Haven. In order to maximise potential, shore side disembarkation is generally required, as this is preferred by cruise liner operators and passengers. Supporting facilities, including covered walkways, coach/taxi areas, information points and general reception areas are also desirable. The importance of alongside facilities and the provision of a cruise liner terminal cannot be overstated. The Port of Seattle, a major port for the Alaska cruise market, is an example of where providing these facilities has had a significant impact on passenger numbers. In 1999, 6,615 passengers sailed from the Port. Since the opening of a cruise terminal in 2000, passenger numbers have increased to 686,000.

Spending from cruise passengers and crew can benefit the port and immediate area, in addition to the income generated from port fees. There are various estimates for average spend by passengers and crew. Assuming that each passenger spends £50 and each crew member £30, a 600 capacity vessel would typically result in £25,000-£30,000 spend per docking.

The Cruise Wales partnership was established in 2004 and involves the Welsh Assembly Government, the ports, local authorities and tourism operators. The partnership has achieved some success in attracting new cruise calls to Wales and in identifying the potential that is presented by the cruise liner market. A Wales Cruise Action Plan for 2006 – 2013 has been prepared. Due regard will need to be given to environmental considerations (such as dredging) when choosing locations for potential new facilities. Coastal Culture The coast has been the muse of writers and poets from the mediaeval story telling of the Mabinogion to Dylan Thomas's *heron priested shore*. Today the coast is home to many different settlements and communities, each with its own distinctive historical and contemporary cultural identity. The Welsh language is still the living, working language in many of these areas and events and festivals such as those held at Aberdaron and Fishguard present a vibrant modern cultural life.

Cultural tourism can attract visitors at all times of the year to established and new places of interest. It can help address seasonality and extend the offer beyond the usual destinations and is attractive to the short break market. It can also enhance the more established types of tourism, by adding an extra dimension to beach and resort holidays. It will be important to ensure that the coast makes the most of its cultural offer and that this is linked to activity and other coastal products in order to broaden visitor appeal and stimulate demand in the off peak season. A review of the cultural tourism strategy has been undertaken and its recommendations will need to be taken into account when developing projects that support the delivery of this strategy.

Food

Food is an essential part of the tourism offer for Wales. In recent years, we have seen significant improvements and additions to the food offer, both in terms of local produce and its preparation and presentation in cafes, restaurants and other eating establishments around the coast.

Restaurants such as those at Portmeirion in Gwynedd, the Harbourmaster in Aberaeron and St. Brides in Saundersfoot are showing a modern confidence in local and regional cuisine.

There are a number of ways that support for regional and local food can be achieved, including:

- Awareness campaigns using television, radio and website media, joint marketing with local supermarkets, production of recipe books and other publications.
- Working with local growers, suppliers and others to develop local supply chains.
- Promoting particularly distinctive Welsh coastal foods, e.g. salt marsh lamb, Llyn and Pembrokeshire lobster, local shellfish.
- Working with hotels, restaurants and cafes to develop quality seafood menus.

The Development of Sea Food Trails

There is also potential to develop the 'slow food' concept-building on the idea originally developed in Italy of quality ingredients cooked with love. Wales could develop a series of coastal town 'Convivia' which run courses, tastings, dinners, food and drink events, and local campaigns.

Food and seafood festivals also have an important role in celebrating and raising the profile of food from the sea and local area. There is scope to develop a high profile Seafood Festival that could attract visitors from further afield and which could also play a useful role in raising the profile of Wales as a quality seafood destination.

It could be held at different coastal locations each year or build on existing seafood festivals such as Pembrokeshire Fish Week, Cardigan Bay, Anglesey and Llyˆn Seafood festivals. Care needs to be undertaken to avoid the over exploitation of food and fisheries and to foster an understanding of limits and capacity – the Assembly Government's fisheries strategy provides guidance on these issues.

Events

Activities are an important part of the coastal tourism experience in Wales and special events and festivals can add an extra dimension and provide an incentive for visitors to visit and importantly participate. Hosting special events during quieter times of the year is another successful measure that destinations can adopt in order to ensure more uniform flow of demand across the year, in particular where an event would generate an overnight stay.

An events programme could have a number of distinct advantages:

- It is an attractive way of presenting an active and dynamic destination to visitors who are looking for participatory holiday opportunities.
- It can provide interesting contact opportunities between residents and visitors.
- It can help to test and develop thematic ideas best suited to the interests of residents and visitors.
- It is a flexible way of market testing, if effective monitoring and feedback mechanisms are included.
- It can assist an area to develop a strongly themed identity.

In order to be viable and offer consistently high quality of information and provision, a degree of coordination and management would be required. It would also have to demonstrate an element of financial independence. Welsh Ministers have decided that a major events unit will be set up within the Welsh Assembly Government that will develop an events strategy in support of wider Assembly Government strategic objectives.

This unit will develop an overseeing/coordinating role, working closely with the Regional Tourism Partnerships. In order to develop an events programme the following will need to be addressed:-

- Collecting and collating relevant events information.
- Developing and introducing a suitable vetting scheme.
- Providing minimal standards and guidance to event providers.
- Developing and maintaining an events database.
- Liaising with participating organisations on effective marketing and promotional activities.
- Seeking, wherever possible, areas for joint working and synergy between events.
- Providing meaningful feedback to organisers and main sponsors.
- Securing longer term financial support, especially from the private sector.

An audit of current provision indicates a patchy and sporadic spread of events along the Welsh coast. The most obvious are those run by local sailing clubs, such as regattas and competitive races. Other coastal events may or may not reflect a marine or maritime theme. In order to address this, a coastal events programme should be developed, which would:

- Place events into a common accessible database which could be the basis for a coastal events website, or a dedicated page on a wider coastal tourism website for Wales, linked to an accommodation offer.
- Filling the gaps (in space and time)-a strategic look at what's missing and the opportunities presented for new activities in different places at certain times of years.
- Local celebrations of related themes – developing events based on maritime history, trade, food, culture, possibly under the banner of Sense of Place.
- A coastal cultural dimension, featuring literature, music, theatre and language.
- Develop events celebrating the link between art and the sea, featuring traditional and contemporary work, involving public and private galleries and public art spaces.
- A series of high profile local or regional maritime festivals, combining the best of local activities such as sailing, watersports, food and drink and related entertainment.
- A coastal ecotourism or green tourism activities programme.
- Introductory and non-competitive events on all aspects of watersports, from primary school level to lifelong learning.
- National and international level competitive sailing and watersports.
- Build on Cadw's events programme at coastal properties and educational interpretation of sites especially World Heritage sites.

The logistics, time and costs of coordinating an events programme should not be under estimated. It will be important that the following criteria is taken into account in developing an events programme. Events also require appropriate infrastructure to effectively cater for them.

- Will the tourism season be extended?
- Is there potential for generating additional bed nights?
- Will there be wider tourism benefits?
- Is the tourism infrastructure adequate to cope with the event?
- Is there potential media interest?
- Are there local benefits?
- Is the event of strategic importance?
- Is there appropriate infrastructure in place to cater for transportation to and from events?

Coastal Heritage and the Arts

Visiting a heritage site is amongst one of the most popular activities undertaken by visitors to the Welsh seaside. Virtually every mile of the coast of Wales bears the traces of Welsh history from prehistoric burials and forts to the coastal defences of the Napoleonic Wars and World War II. Some of the most enduring and iconic coastal images owe their drama and magic to the historic environment – from prehistoric Carreg Samson in Pembrokeshire, to Harlech Castle and Llandudno Pier. The castles of Edward I in North Wales are one of only two World Heritage Sites in Wales and are visited by half a million people a year. The Victorian period brought engineering such as the Telford and Stephenson bridges and the distinctive architecture, piers and promenades of many seaside towns.

The traces of prehistoric settlements and burials are part of what can be discovered when walking the various Coastal Paths (for example in Anglesey). National and local museums hold many of the physical artefacts of Wales' seafaring tradition – fish traps and shipwrecks are monuments to fortune and misfortune.

Opportunities for promoting coastal heritage include marketing Wales' coastal history and heritage as part of the coastal tourism offer and improving the availability of information to visitors about coastal heritage in publications and websites, including website links to Cadw and other historical bodies.

High quality interpretation at coastal and heritage sites is also key in terms of attracting visitors. The setting out of overarching themes that can link together different properties by type, period, activity and locations can help encourage people to visit other sites in the area. It is also important to offer a choice of interpretation, depending on the audience and character of the site. Both traditional and more innovative technological techniques can be used to communicate a site's significance, sense of place and welcome.

The historic environment can, however, be vulnerable to damage from inappropriate leisure activities – the grass banks of a prehistoric settlement may be a new challenge for BMX or trail bikes and a coastal fort may seem an attractive location for a summer evening bonfire or drinking session. Interpretation, information and local interests need to be aware of these dangers and be a positive force for considerate enjoyment.

Arts, Museums and Galleries

There have been key developments over recent years at the coast that provide an important platform upon which to build. These developments include:

- The National Waterfront Museum in Swansea.
- Oriel Mostyn, Llandudno.
- Visitor and conference facilities at the National Library, Aberystwyth.
- Venue Cymru, Llandudno.
- Galeri, Caernarfon.
- Theatr Mwldan, Cardigan.

Museums and Galleries, including local museums, provide a valuable contribution to interpreting the sense of place and history of an area. There are opportunities for museums to develop a more integrated approach through the development of themes and through signposting to other associated museums and attractions. Museums should also be encouraged to schedule key exhibitions outside the peak season that will attract visitors at times of the year that would otherwise see modest customer flows.

The arts, including the visual and performing arts also provide a stimulus for tourism. A new landscape gallery for Wales is currently being built at St. David's that will provide opportunities for tourists to appreciate the artistic interpretation of the Welsh landscape across the centuries. Public Art schemes can help to create a Sense of Place, reinforcing the character of our towns and villages, whilst individual businesses can display the work of local artists helping to create a distinctive, local environment.

Welsh Language

The Welsh language remains the everyday language of most communities along the western seaboard of Wales. It can be encountered in shops, on signposts and in many other day-to-day situations. It can add a real sense of local identity to a place or a situation. *Iaith Pawb*, a national action plan for a bilingual Wales, outlines the Assembly Government's aim of promoting Wales' modern bilingual nature. This work should be further supported in order to make the Welsh coast a truly bilingual holiday destination, helping to give it its unique selling proposition.

Bodies such as the Welsh Language Board and Mentrau Iaith (county-based language bodies) are actively promoting the use of Welsh in tourism, through introducing initiatives that encourage tourism businesses to make more use of Welsh, adding a valuable dimension to the coastal tourism experience.

Tourism and other relevant economic activity can help to maintain the viability and sustainability of many of our traditional Welsh speaking communities. The Assembly Government recognises, however, that large scale developments can affect the linguistic balance within communities. Planning Policy Wales and the accompanying Technical Advice Note 20 on the Welsh Language affirm that policies for the location of such development should take into account which areas could best accommodate them to secure economic benefits whilst not eroding the position of the Welsh language. The One Wales agreement includes a commitment to review and reissue TAN with a view to allowing authorities to use Language Impact Assessment for planning purposes in areas of housing pressure.

Coastal Management

The Welsh coastline is diverse in character ranging from urban seaside resorts, working harbours and ferry ports, to small rural communities and isolated stretches of coast. There are a number of landowners, including local authorities, the National Trust, Ministry of Defence, private owners and the Crown Estate together with a number of bodies with management or regulation responsibilities. These include the Local Authorities (various departments), Harbour Authorities, Sea Fisheries Committees, Crown Estate, Environment Agency, Countryside Council for Wales, Welsh Assembly Government and various UK Government Departments. Coastal Management needs to consider issues surrounding the management of coastal destinations/resorts, environmental management, visitor management and people management.

The ICZM strategy advocates a broad holistic approach to coastal management that will enable coastal planning and management to look at the big picture and view coastal issues in the wider context. Partnership working that involves agreeing and delivering common goals for coastal areas is key to effective management.

There are many examples of partnership working at national and local levels in Wales, including the Wales Coastal and Maritime Partnership, the Green Sea Partnership and local forums such as the Pembrokeshire Coastal Forum and the Severn Estuary Partnership. In North Wales, CCW is taking forward the 'Straight to Head' initiative which is considering how the economic, social and environmental assets of the Menai Straits can be maximised through better coordination of activity. It is imperative that tourism and regeneration interests are fully engaged in such partnerships where they exist. The ICZM strategy also advocates the need to explore opportunities for similar coordinated action elsewhere on the coast.

Visitor Management

Much of the natural coast already benefits from positive countryside management through the efforts of the National Park Authorities, Areas of Outstanding Natural Beauty organisations, Countryside Council for Wales, local authorities, and voluntary organisations such as the National Trust, the Wildlife Trusts and the RSPB.

Whilst it is recognised that a strong policy framework is in place for the development and protection of the Welsh coastline, there is a need to strengthen visitor management at the coast to meet rising visitor expectations. Studies for DEFRA by the Institute of Estuarine and Coastal studies of Hull University have identified that in coastal areas, unregulated activities – such as recreation and tourism-have the potential to cause adverse impacts on conservation in terms of the risk they present for the marine environment.

At some sites, there may be conflict between a group of activity users and wildlife interests in particular areas or at particular times, for instance, climbing on the sea cliffs at Holyhead during the breeding season, or the harassment of dolphins and seals by overenthusiastic pursuit by visitor boats.

Disturbance to wildlife as a result of coastal tourism activity is not solely restricted to water-based recreation. Larger numbers of visitors to rural coastal areas could potentially damage coastal habitats and wildlife such as sand dunes, salt marshes, coastal heath and rocky shores. The provision of better coastal access could result in disturbance to previously untouched areas.

In some areas, voluntary agreements and codes of conduct have been agreed between user groups and operators to limit any environmental disturbance.

These initiatives have value in raising awareness of the potential damage/disturbance that certain activities can cause. There is scope to seek to agree other similar arrangements at other sites with existing or potential conflict. Accreditation schemes have also been developed for operators that have signed up to follow various codes of conduct. The WiSe (Wildlife Safe) scheme for example has been set up to deliver training and accreditation for operators of registered passenger and charter vessels who wish to view marine wildlife. All WiSe operators have agreed to abide by appropriate Codes of Conduct for the animals that they view, created to ensure that their operations are safe and sustainable.

Coastal Recreation Areas

There are a number of locations around the Welsh coast which because of their character, the recreational opportunities they offer or their location, attract substantial numbers of visitors. They range from popular resort beaches to country parks areas with wildlife and archaeological interest.

These sites are a vital resource for coastal tourism, absorbing pressures which might otherwise fall on more sensitive areas, and have a major impact on visitors' experience and enjoyment of the Welsh coastline. However, the popularity of these areas generates additional management costs over and above those which would otherwise be incurred by the land manager in meeting local demand.

While some organisations such as the National Parks and AONBs receive support from the Welsh Assembly Government, resources for visitor management in other cases have to compete with other revenue expenditure priorities. Some areas are able to recover management costs through car parking or launch fees, or the provision of catering and retail facilities on a franchise or self operated basis.

However, the ability to recover costs is often limited by the costs of collection or the commonality of facilities such as beaches and open countryside where public access is freely available. The consultation highlighted the fact that many coastal managers are struggling to find the resources to maintain existing facilities and sites, let alone consider exploiting potential opportunities to provide improved facilities and new recreational facilities within a safe and well managed environment.

These costs arise from the need to:

- Provide visitor facilities such as toilets, freshwater showers at beaches and car parking for visitors. These involve capital costs as well as on-going revenue costs in maintenance, cleaning and supervision.
- Increased land management costs in providing and maintaining footpaths, styles and other access, which because of the heavy use require stronger provision and increased maintenance to avoid damage, erosion and other adverse effects.
- Water management costs including buoys and signage to separate different water use areas as well as enforcement costs of safety regulations and by laws.
- Cleaning and litter clearance from beaches and countryside areas.
- Safety provision ranging from lifebelts and first aid facilities to lifeguards and safety boats for water activities.
- Information and interpretive provision to increase visitor enjoyment of the site.
- Preparation of activity management policies.

To address the issues outlined above, it is proposed that consideration is given to identifying coastal recreation areas that provide informal recreation opportunities for a substantial number of visitors. The management of these areas would be given a high priority with regard to a beach/coastal warden or, if appropriate, lifeguards. They would also be areas where minimum standards with regard to the range and quality of facilities would be set.

In the first instance, it is proposed that two pilot areas are identified. The pilot coastal recreation area's principal aims would be the integration of resource planning and visitor management and the consideration of innovative but practical and fair ways of raising revenue from visitors.

One pilot area would be chosen to reflect visitor pressure from a range of beach/water sport users, and another where the main issue is visitor pressure and environmental capacity. The pilot areas could consider whether the income from car parking, use of slipways or franchising of refreshment facilities could be directly used to improve general facilities, cleaning, life guard or beach wardens provision.

There is also potential for the pilot recreation areas to explore in more detail issues surrounding the carrying capacity of the area. The results could then be used to develop a methodology that management bodies could apply in their particular circumstances. Capacity should be considered to encompass the environment, the effects on users, the needs of local communities and the limits of existing infrastructure. They could also take into consideration how different management approaches could limit or extend the capacity of an area. Potential pilot areas will be decided by the Welsh Assembly Government and funds identified for a 2/3 year pilot study.

Environmental Management

Water Quality

Bathing water quality and beach cleanliness is fundamental when looking to maintain or achieve standards. Substantial investment has been made over recent years to improve water quality around Wales, resulting in 98.8% compliance of Mandatory, and 88.8% of Guideline Bathing Water Standards being achieved at EU designated bathing waters around Wales in 2006. At non-EU identified bathing waters 92.6% complied with the mandatory standard whilst 45.3% complied with Guideline standards. In 2006, 43 beaches were awarded a Blue Flag, 4 marinas were awarded a blue flag and 50 beaches were awarded the Green Coast Award. Such quality standard compliance and presentation of awards enhance the offering and attract tourists, particularly for family beach holidays, water sports and other water related activities. There are challenges ahead with tighter bathing water standards coming into place by 2015, together with the introduction of the Water Framework Directive requiring nearly all inland and coastal waters to achieve 'good status' by 2015.

Climate Change

Climate change is likely to have a huge impact on tourism and on coastal tourism in particular. Climate is an essential resource for tourism, especially for beach, activity and nature tourism segments. Changes in our climate are likely to present opportunities for the Visitor Economy in Wales, as well as posing potential threats that will require adaptation measures to manage their impacts. Our understanding of these threats and opportunities are at present limited, and it is therefore proposed that further research is undertaken in this field. Some of the key issues that will need to be addressed include:

Rising Sea Levels and Coastal Erosion

UKCIP predicts that sea levels around the UK will have risen another 26 to 86 centimeters by 2089. Extreme high tides and severe storms will occur more frequently. Shoreline Management Plans, prepared by Coastal Defence groups, comprising representatives of maritime local authorities, the Environment Agency, Countryside Council for Wales and other interested bodies, set out a strategy for sustainable coastal defences. These are currently being revised to take account of the latest evidence available and will map areas at risk of coastal erosion in greater detail. Planning policies identify areas on the coast at risk of flooding. Any tourism developments will need to take account of these plans.

The Welsh Assembly Government is currently refreshing its policy with regard to flood and coastal risk management and moving away from the traditional approach of building sea defences to one which focuses on the overall management of the flood risk. This approach could include adopting measures such as:

- allowing areas to flood to create saltmarshes for wildlife or restoring sand dunes that can provide natural coastal defences.
- relocating buildings/ facilities.
- refurbishing buildings to accommodate flooding.

This new approach, while placing much greater emphasis on managing the consequences of flooding will nonetheless continue to rely on the effective maintenance and improvement of the sea defence infrastructure. This will inevitably require significant investment in existing infrastructure in the future in a climate where funds will be in short supply. The Welsh Assembly Government will need to maximise benefits from such investment through, for example considering the potential of incorporating tourism and regeneration considerations into coastal defence schemes. Tourism considerations could cover visual aspects, effects on access, the current use of the coastal area and importantly whether there can be additional 'new' benefits/uses for the local community and the visitor economy. This may require innovative approaches with regard to evaluation and cost/benefit analysis.

In addition, rising sea levels may well alter the wave configuration around the coastline, thus impacting on water sport activities.

Environmental Capacity

The natural landscape is a key attraction for most visitors to the Welsh coast. Climate Change is likely to put pressure on vulnerable landscapes and is likely to further impair their ability to accommodate visitors. Responding to this challenge will require measures that sustain the environmental capacity of these landscapes whilst developing new opportunities in less vulnerable locations.

Visitor Trends

Climate change is likely to lead to a significant change in visitor patterns to Wales. Drier summers could attract more visitors to Wales, while an increase in temperatures and shortage of water could displace tourism from established destinations in southern Europe. A recent study by the Hadley Centre has suggested a major revival of the British seaside holiday as a result of destinations such as Greece and Spain becoming too uncomfortable in the summer. Other research has claimed that there is little evidence to suggest that we would automatically give up our holiday abroad to become domestic tourists, rather than switching to other foreign destinations. Conversely, wetter and stormier winters could reduce tourist volume and value outside of the peak season. The increased seasonality of tourism could place a strain on business profitability and lead to full time jobs being replaced by seasonal jobs thereby reducing the quality of jobs in tourism.

If the mitigation of climate change leads to a reduction in air travel as a result of taxes on aviation fuel, international visits to Wales may suffer but visits to Wales from within the UK are likely to increase. Forward planning for an increase in visitor numbers to Wales would be necessary to ensure that capacity is in line with summer demand. There will also be pressures from other mitigation measures such as renewable energy developments adjacent to coastal resorts.

Managing Coastal Destinations

The visitor experience is made up of a wide range of individual elements provided by many different businesses, public organisations and individuals. It only requires a weakness in one or two of these elements to undermine the whole experience.

If a destination can meet and even exceed the expectations of its visitors then it will have an advantage over prospective competitor destinations.

In order to do this, destination stakeholders need to understand their market and its needs. They also need to understand and meet – even exceed – the expectations and needs of local residents. This can only be achieved through partnership working with tourism businesses, the voluntary sector and the community to ensure an integrated approach.

One technique that can help deliver an integrated approach to destination management is Integrated Quality Management (IQM) which the European Commission's Tourism Unit has sought to encourage destinations to adopt.

Integrated Quality Management is an approach to managing a tourism destination which focuses on an ongoing process of improving visitor satisfaction, while seeking to improve the local economy, the environment and the quality of life of the local community.

It is a tool which can be used by destination stakeholders to understand their markets and the communities living within the destination. It can help them identify needs and expectations, assess how the destination is performing against these needs and expectations and identify ways in which they can be met. An important part of the process is the monitoring of the impacts of tourism on the local economy, community and the environment.

Managing Coastal Facilities

Resource Management

The Welsh Assembly Government's Environment Strategy outlines the importance of achieving a more sustainable pattern of consumption and production in order to reduce the impact that economic activity has on the environment. Tourism businesses have a key role to play through improving the way they manage their resources, through for example, reducing waste and water use. It is recognised that smaller and medium sized businesses have limited technical and managerial capacity to improve resource management and a range of environmental management schemes have been developed to assist these businesses. One such scheme is the Green Dragon Environmental Standard, which is an environmental management system designed to meet the specific needs of Welsh organisations. It has, in recent years, been applied to the tourism sector and has been a condition of Visit Wales tourism grant support. Better environmental management can increase profits, improve efficiency, mitigate carbon footprints, reduce waste, improve local supply chains and provide a key marketing edge.

Some of the main future challenges are:

- ensuring greater sign-up to environmental management schemes by tourism businesses.
- ensuring a high retention and progression rate through schemes.
- further adaptation of the Green Dragon scheme to meet the specific needs and characteristics of the tourism sector.
- championing exemplary projects and businesses, illustrating clear actions and benefits.
- appropriate siting of tourism facilities that takes account of the availability of water resources.

Quality Assurance

Accommodation standards are another consideration with regard to enhancing the visitor's experience. Customers demand high standards in tourism accommodation, and their expectations are continuously rising as their own standard of living rise at home and abroad. It is essential that operators provide high quality accommodation if coastal tourism in Wales is to compete successfully with other destinations. Visit Wales, together with other national partner bodies, operate quality assurance schemes for different types of accommodation, attractions and activity provision. Only accredited accommodation is promoted nationally and internationally by Visit Wales.

In compliance with the Disability Discrimination Act 1995, tourism businesses are required to make reasonable provisions to meet the needs of disabled people in terms of equality of access and employment. The UK population is ageing and this will have further implications for facility provision and employment structures. The industry must be prepared therefore to invest in new facilities and promotional tools to cater for the needs of all visitors. Specialist advice and financial assistance is made available to tourism businesses to prepare accessibility statements and to provide adequate facilities for people with special needs.

Managing People

Tourism like other industries needs a skilled and experienced workforce and it is therefore crucial that the tourism industry in Wales invests in its people to ensure profitable businesses are developed and a high level of service is provided. Training and skills development will offer more rewarding and clearer career development opportunities, which are essential for retaining staff. Developing an appropriate qualifications structure for the industry will also help to professionalise the industry. The majority of tourism businesses in Wales are self employed operations or small businesses employing less than five people, which means that training and skills development is often difficult to fund and accommodate within working practices. Innovative training opportunities therefore need to be supported and developed that fit business needs. To support the successful development of tourism at the coast, appropriate skills will be required not only in the hospitality sector but in other related areas including:

- Marine Environment and Conservation Management.
- Management of coastal public sector resources.
- Ecotourism development and delivery.
- Watersports management and marketing.
- Management, Customer Service and communication skills.
- Craft Skills Development (particularly chefs).
- Interpretation and information provision, including Web-based services and wireless technology.

- Marine engineering relating to the maintenance and repair of boats.
- Coastal Heritage interpretation and promotion.

It is also important to ensure that opportunities are provided for local people to gain relevant skills and knowledge, in particular, to undertake specialist roles such as watersports instructors or to undertake management roles. Providing opportunities for local people, especially young people, to experience activities that visitors come to enjoy will increase employment opportunities for local people in coastal tourism related jobs and will provide associated economic development opportunities in the longer term.

The skills required to support the effective delivery of the strategy identified above fall under the remit of the following Sector Skills Councils:

* SkillsActive: Active Leisure and Learning-sport and recreation, health and fitness, outdoors, playwork and caravan industries.
* Lantra: land management and production; animal health and welfare; environmental industries.
* People 1st: hospitality, leisure, travel and tourism.

Skillsmart Retail Retail

* Creative and Cultural Skills advertising, crafts, cultural heritage, design, music, performing, literacy and visual arts.
* Semta: Science, engineering and manufacturing technologies sector (including marine sector, covering shipbuilding and repair, boat building and marine equipment manufacturers).

These Sector Skills Councils (SSCs) are part of a network of 25 Uk-wide employer-led bodies that have been established by Government to ensure that the needs of employers form the starting point for future education and training.

The SSCs, as part of the Sector Skills Agreement (SSA) process, have analysed each sector's skills needs and provision and have mapped out the skills needed by employers in these sectors. Action plans have been agreed within the SSA between the SSCs and the Welsh Assembly Government, JobCentre Plus, Careers Wales, the Higher Education Funding Council for Wales (HEFCW) and Wales TUC that will seek to fill any skill gaps and shortages through influencing the Assembly

Government's mainstream learning policies and programmes. Details on how the Assembly Government is addressing skills development in these areas are contained in these action plans.

The new school curriculum, published in October 2007, also places a greater emphasis on outdoor learning.

The new Physical Education curriculum will encourage schools to offer pupils the opportunity to acquire skills in adventurous activities such as watersports, which may be pursued in curriculum time, after school, or as part of an out-of-hours residential experience in new and challenging environments 60% of the workforce employed in the tourism, hospitality and leisure sector in Wales is female. Many women are attracted by the part time opportunities offered by the industry, but part time working can have certain draw backs, including fewer advancement opportunities, lower pay per hour and less formal training. There are also implications for tourism employers in terms of providing flexible training and working arrangements and addressing childcare and elder care issues.

Unemployment in Wales is at a 30 year low. However the Welsh Assembly Government's, Skills and Employment Strategy, *Skills that Work for Wales* demonstrates that the employment rate is still lower that in many other parts of the UK, due to higher levels of economic inactivity in Wales. Latest figures indicate that 24.5% of the working age population is economically inactive compared with an unemployment rate of just above 5%. There is therefore a potential pool of indigenous labour which, with appropriate support and targeted training, could benefit the tourism industry.

Jobcentre plus is currently looking to roll-out the successful Pathways to Work pilot – an initiative aimed at helping claimants moving onto Incapacity Benefit to find work. A partnership between the Welsh Assembly Government and Job Centre plus is now extending the Pathways to Work pilot to other parts of Wales through a wider Want2Work initiative. The initiative involves providing financial incentives and flexible trial periods to encourage the economically inactive and employers to work together to their mutual advantage. There are opportunities for the scheme to be tailored to the needs of tourism and leisure employers. Businesses also have a role in tackling the root causes of inactivity through promoting employee health. The two most common causes of sickness absence are stress and back pain. Much of this is preventable and can be addressed by workplace health promotion programmes, such as the Corporate Health Standard which is being promoted by the Assembly Government as part Health Challenge Wales. Tourism businesses should be encouraged to adopt this Corporate Health Standard.

Delivering the Strategy

The strategy has identified a wide range of opportunities that need to be considered and acted upon in order to realise the full tourism potential of the Welsh Coastline.

A three year action plan has been prepared which presents the recommendations and identifies a series of actions necessary to implement or move forward the recommendations. It also identifies the most appropriate lead authority/organisation and other possible partners.

The action plan will be available in electronic format only to allow for regular updating. In developing the delivery strategy and proposed actions, we have been mindful of the vision set out in Chapter 2. As well as considering the vision, account has been taken of the strategic aims of the strategy, the practicality of the proposals, and possible sources of funding.

Delivery of the framework will depend upon cooperation and developing a partnership approach between a number of authorities/organisations. The resources required to implement the strategy are significant but reflect the importance and opportunities presented by the coast of Wales. The availability of funds cannot be guaranteed at this stage in the process, but will need to be considered by the various stakeholders. It is likely that many of the coastal economic and regeneration projects will be eligible for EU Convergence funding under the Spatial Regeneration Frameworks. There are also a number of other budgets that could be involved for different elements of the strategy.

The implementation of the strategy will only be achieved by the key players working together. We will seek to engage all groups involved in developing the economic, social and environmental aspects of the coast in the private, public and voluntary sectors, using existing structures and partnerships wherever possible. Visit Wales, within the Department of Heritage, will chair a steering group within the Welsh Assembly Government that will coordinate the implementation of the strategy at the national level.

Other divisions and departments within the Welsh Assembly Government will also have a crucial role to play, in particular, the Department of Environment, Sustainability and Housing and the regeneration teams based in the regional offices of the Department for the Economy and Transport.

There are also a number of external partners who will have an active role in the delivery of the strategy including the local authorities, the Countryside Council for Wales, the Environment Agency, the National Trust and the RSPB. In particular, Local Authority Local Development Plans, which will form the basis for future planning consents, will have a key role in providing the statutory framework to guide development to implement the strategy.

The role and potential of the coastline of Wales will feature in all six Spatial Plan Areas and detailed below are some of the elements that will need to be considered. In addition, the regional collaborative boards announced as part the Making the Connections proposals for improving public services in Wales could have an important role to play in implementing the strategy, in particular for areas that call for collaborative activity between authorities.

Geographical Considerations

The action plan includes actions that are relevant to all areas. The following actions have a specific geographical dimension that will need to be considered in future funding proposals, regeneration plans and spatial plan area documents.

North East Wales – Border and Coast

The coast includes a number of traditional seaside resorts which have suffered from a changing market and rising visitor expectations. There is a need to diversify their local economies and to improve their image and tourism offer as they still provide quality beaches.

Elements to Consider in North East Spatial Plan Area

- to continue regeneration of the coastal resort of Rhyl and Colwyn Bay to diversify and strengthen the local economy.

- improvements to the coastal defences and the enhancement of the physical links between the town and the promenade at Colwyn Bay.
- to ascertain the financial and market viability of developing further berths at Rhyl (Foryd Harbour).
- to consider further redevelopment of conference tourism facilities at Llandudno based on the enhanced facilities at the North Wales Conference centre and physical improvements to support the development of conference hotels and business tourism.

North West Wales – Eryri a Môn

North West Wales has a strong sense of identity and an outstanding coastline. The quality of the coastline is recognised by its various environmental designations. The coastline provides quality beaches, popular marinas, potential for increasing nature tourism and a backdrop of Snowdonia National Park. There are a number of coastal towns where the local economy is dominated by tourism and service towns, some with heritage attributes, such as Bangor and Caernarfon.

Elements to Consider in the North West Spatial Plan Area

- to consider the potential for developing nature tourism and heritage within the environmental capacity of sensitive sites e.g. Newborough Warren, Holyhead Mountain.
- to implement coastal resort and town centre physical improvement programmes to diversify and strengthen local economies at Holyhead, Caernarfon and Bangor.
- to consider how the accommodation stock in the Llyn Peninsula and Bangor area could be improved.
- to improve the facilities for watersport participants on Anglesey and on the Llyn Peninsula (for diving, surfing and kite sports).
- the creation of a sailing academy and events facility at Pwllheli.
- to explore sustainable forms of visitor transport across the Menai Strait and to consider opportunities to enhance the summer bus service on the Llyn peninsula.
- the provision of visiting berths at marinas, harbours and yacht stations around the north west coast.

- to consider the benefits (for users and the local economy) of improving boating facilities and access at Caernarfon and Porthmadog and the development of further facilities at Bangor.
- to consider the improvement of facilities for cruise liners (including alongside berthing) and for passengers in Holyhead.
- to work with Nant Gwrtheryn to invest in cultural/business tourism on the Llyn Peninsula.
- to continue to develop the tourism potential of the heritage of Caernarfon and Conwy, in particular their Castles and Town Walls.
- to develop the heritage tourism potential of Anglesey.

Central Wales

Central Wales has an extensive coastline from south of Porthmadog to south of Cardigan. There are a number of coastal settlements, Aberystwyth and Cardigan being the main service centres, with smaller settlements with a tourism role such as Barmouth, Aberdyfi, Aberaeron and New Quay. The coastline has a number of environmental designations including the Dyfi Valley which is a designated Biosphere Reserve. While there are perceptions with regard to accessibility of the area, the area does have significant potential with regard to nature tourism.

5

Review of Coastal Degradation

This Section provides an overview of coastal degradation, a three-dimensional framework for analyzing the environmental effects of coastal tourism, and a summary of the topical focus of references used in this report in terms of the analytical framework for coastal tourism.

The principal conclusions of this section are:

- tourism impacts in the Wider Caribbean are extremely diverse, depending on differences among state economies, the relative and absolute size of the tourism sector, the rate of growth of tourism, and the nature of the tourism facilities involved;
- environmental degradation effects from tourism facilities in the coastal area are generally small, often dispersed, critically placed, and multifaceted. Resolution of these effects are addressed by marshaling information and expertise from a wide range of technical resources in both the private and public sector.

Overview of Condition of Coastal and Marine Resources

Coastal and marine resources throughout the Wider Caribbean Region have suffered major impacts by human actions since early colonial days. A synthesis of major impacts conveys a picture in which virtually every state of the Wider Caribbean suffers from sewage pollution of coastal waters, most suffer some contamination from oil spills and production leakages, a majority of states report coastal pollution from mining and industrial activity, and most of the low income states of the region report solid waste contamination of coastal areas. In addition, many states report inadequate monitoring and assessment systems to understand the causes, dimensions, and impacts of coastal pollution. Of these impairments of coastal and marine environments, tourism is a major direct contributor to sewage and solid waste pollution in virtually every country. In tourism-dependent states it is the prime contributor to coastal erosion and sedimentation from construction activities.

Tourism is also a major indirect contributor to much of the oil and fertilizer/pesticide pollution of coastal waters. For example, in the US Virgin Islands most reportable oil spills stem from yacht, ferry and cruiseship fueling activities. In both the Sarasota Bay and the Corpus Christy National Estuary Program assessments, lawn care practices on golf courses and second-homes and condominium resorts were found to be major sources of nitrate and phosphate contamination of the bay from storm water runoff.

For countries in the top quintile (20%) of those dependent on tourism (*i.e.,* those states with more than 50 rooms per 1000 inhabitants: Cayman Islands, Northern Netherlands Antilles, Anguilla, Turks & Caicos, Aruba, Montserrat, British Virgin Islands, Antigua and Barbuda, US Virgin Islands), the environmental costs of tourism are even more evident when examining the named sources of "damage to reefs, mangroves and associated coastal ecosystems:" anchor damage (3 countries), litter (4 countries), spearfishing, mangrove clearing, diver damage, dredging, dynamiting, sand removal, trampling, and boat groundings

toxic chemical management. Poor runoff control during construction and afterwards can also lead to high sediment concentrations and nitrification in fresh waterways, seagrass beds, and eventually on coral reefs.

High levels of natural resource consumption can also be problematic. As tourists and new residents consume local resources, the water table can be drawn down and this can have negative effects on nearby communications, agriculture, protected areas, and other ecosystems. Water use by resorts for swimming pools, laundry, golf courses, showers, gardens, toilets and kitchens can be staggering. Inefficient small hotels in Belize were found by the Caribbean Alliance for Sustainable Tourism (CAST) to consume 265 gallons per guest per night. An average 18-hole golf course, for example, requires over 130 million gallons of water per year – about the same amount of water as 3200 people in the U.S. or up to 7,000 in Costa Rica. Additionally, visitors from diverse parts of the globe can also mean the introduction of invasive species – frequently posing a serious threat to endemic flora and fauna, particularly to fragile ecosystems like the Galapagos Islands.

Finally, as tourists flock to coastal areas for their holidays, they tend to demand that local seafood be present on the menu, and this is leading to over fishing of already-strained fisheries in Zanzibar and other resort destinations.

There is also a loss of by-catch species that are not usually consumed, and reduced numbers of coral grazers can result in algal invasion and lowered coral productivity, as well as increased vulnerability to disease. Local governments are often poorly equipped to monitor and enforce fishing guidelines – especially when demand by tourists for prized varieties of fin fish and shellfish can generate relatively high amounts of foreign currency. Persistent demand makes regulator's jobs even more challenging – and seasonal bans even harder to enforce.

The diagram below, first published in the 1980's, and today appearing in *The Tourism Development Handbook,* illustrates the multiple impacts tourism activities have on the environment, with the outer ring depicting the ultimate impacts.

Characteristics of States in the Caribbean

Politically, socially, and economically, the Wider Caribbean is a large and diverse region; ecologically, the area is a large marine ecosystem. Some of the diversity of the region is demonstrable in terms of the different impacts of tourism. Selected Tourism Characteristics of States of the Wider Caribbean lists the countries of the Wider Caribbean, with several economic indicators and broad measures of tourism impact.

The table is sorted by the relative impact of tourism on the national economies of the Wider Caribbean states, as measured by the number of tourist rooms per thousand local inhabitants. This measure is chosen, rather than the more conventional measures of tourists per capita, or tourism percent of gross domestic product, because it is more reliable (major investments in physical plant are more visible than estimates of expenditures for intangibles) and less variable (capital investments take years to plan and execute) than other measures.

Geographic Zones of Environmental Impact:

- Near Coastal Waters and Fringing Reefs.
- Beach and Shoreline.
- Estuaries, Back Bays, Salt Ponds and Lagoons.
- Coastal Plain.
- Uplands.
- Offshore Waters.

The purpose of the framework is to illustrate *where* in the coastal zone specific types of *tourist activity* or facility are likely to have *what kinds* of environmental effect. The framework identifies seven different *effects* which can occur under thirty-six different combinations of facility type and geographic zone. Each of these 252 potential tourism impacts are then assessed in terms of major, direct or indirect effects, giving a total analytical matrix of 756 elements. Overview of Environmental Degradation from Tourism Facilities in the Coastal Zone then summarizes the 112 *priority tourism impacts* which are judged to be major problems in the six-by-six matrix of geographic zones and tourism facilities.

The analytical model is derived from a wealth of real world experience—its usefulness lies in our ability to use the model for a variety of planning and management processes, but two stand out:

- to look for expected but so far unreported effects, such as "if most entertainment facilities in the beach lead to solid waste problems, why does the beach at Cane Garden Bay remain relatively clean?" or
- to place impacts in a larger framework. For example, a government faced with a number of large coastal resort proposals *must* anticipate making a major investment in *controlling and monitoring construction impacts* because these are known consequences of large resorts in shoreline areas.

Details of the Analytical Framework, including detailed definitions of the elements of each of the three dimensions (Tourism Impacts, Geographic Zones of Environmental Impact and Tourism Facilities), as well as the detailed matrix of tourism impacts are presented in Appendix A.

This section of the report highlights the occurrence of patterns of tourism impact within the Wider Caribbean.

Tourism Impacts

This first dimension of the analytical framework encompasses the direct and indirect effects of tourism facilities. These effects are dynamic and often interactive. At its most basic, if tourism facilities and activities result in a high degree of environmental impact, it is likely that tourism will be reduced. This can become a "development death spiral" if the reduction in tourists causes loss in income which results in curtailment of essential services which further alienates tourists.

Available evidence for the Caribbean indicates that the environmental effects of tourism activities in the coastal area occur within national boundaries. The MARPOL study (UNEP, 1994a) indicated little international transport of land-based sources of marine pollution in the Wider Caribbean, and the contribution of tourism to that problem is undoubtedly small. Marine debris aside, the major "international" environmental effect of coastal tourism in the Caribbean may be the impact of yachts, charter boats, or cruiseships in near-coastal and marine environments, especially anchoring in sea grass beds or on coral reefs.

The major tourism impacts used in this study include:

Including "major" earth changes, bulkheading, construction and maintenance of jetties, groins, piers and wharves, dredging and spoil disposal. "Minor" physical alteration impacts—many of which are very widespread—include sand removal, destruction of mangroves and salt ponds, anchoring damage to corals and sea grass beds, and other coral destruction. The cumulative effects of minor alterations can obviously be extreme. Physical alterations are generally thought to increase susceptibility to natural hazards, as discussed in the section on benefits and costs.

This is the most widespread environmental effect of tourism in the Caribbean, since it results from many different kinds of tourism facility in all of the geographic zones. Spectacularly wrong-headed tourism constructions, such as the Pigeon Island causeway in St. Lucia, or the causeways providing access to the new hotels on the north coast of Cuba receive most attention. Even minor actions, however can have unanticipated effects, such as the installation of a seawall at a guest house in Long Bay Tortola, which changes local wave and transport dynamics and scours a major recreational beach.

Tourism-related physical changes are also common for a wide range of tourism infrastructure projects, such as the much-debated cruiseship pier proposed for Cozumel, or the obligatory 10,000 foot runway required on every Caribbean island to accommodate intercontinental jets. In some of the land-scarce islands, building any kind of runway is difficult—the 7,000 foot runway in St. Thomas includes 88 feet of vertical fill at the end of its seaward extension, the second-deepest fill project in the world at the time of its construction in the early 1980's.

Although distressingly common, impacts from inappropriate physical changes can be "solved" by *known* improvements in construction practice, engineering, architecture, and design processes, and by *known* improvements in public sector planning, control and monitoring. Examples include the Barbados Coastal Zone Management Unit, or the St. Lucia Northwest Coastal Zone Project, which were designed to correct physical changes from decades-old tourism development projects.

Greed and opportunism, of course, describe why such projects continue to happen, such as the rash of new gambling casinos and associated resort developments being built on the Gulf Coast barrier islands of Alabama. Habitat restoration, especially for critical mangrove systems, is being investigated as a coastal management policy by a number of the National Estuaries Programs on the US Gulf Coast. As this technology is refined around the world, it offers promise for coastal tourism impact mitigation. For example, new marinas in the US and British Virgin Islands are being built with some attention to preserving existing mangrove stands—it would be a small step to seeking offsets for mangrove destruction in some areas, with restoration of equivalent resources in other areas. In addition to the migration of chemical pollutants through surface and groundwater resources, as described below, tourism generates direct and indirect solid waste impacts. This problem has received special attention in the smaller islands of the Eastern Caribbean which face difficulties siting solid waste disposal facilities, and which are too small to be able to support economically viable re-cycling programs.

In part because of its high density, high energy-consumption tourism styles, the highly tourism-dependent US Virgin Islands has solid waste problems which have reached extreme levels in recent years, with a number of crises:

- A prolonged "dump" fire on the island of St. John (the least populated of the three Virgin Islands, where 60% of the island is reserved for the Virgin Islands National Park) costs hundreds of thousands of dollars to extinguish.
- Community pressure and the lack of viable alternatives have caused the Government of the Virgin Islands to close *all* public dumps on St. John.
- Trash is now collected in St. John and *trucked daily* via inter-island ferry to St. Thomas (five miles away), where it is deposited in the overfilled Bovoni landfill, the only such site in St. Thomas.
- In St. Thomas, the Bovoni dump has been burning underground for more than a year, with occasional surface "breakthroughs" which spew noxious smoke, fumes and clouds of flies over nearby government-supported housing, a junior high school, and resort and second home communities. The US Environmental Protection Agency is studying both health effects of the burning, and engineering processes required to extinguish the fires.
- Both the Bovoni landfill on St. Thomas, and the Anguilla dump on St. Croix are estimated to be near or above their total capacity.
- To add environmental insult to environmental injury, the Bovoni landfill, much of which is not lined or sealed, is also adjacent to the last surviving mangrove forest in St. Thomas.

Most continental coastal areas and many islands in the Wider Caribbean are forced to site solid waste disposal areas in highly porous soils which are hard to seal, leading to groundwater contamination.

Solid waste problems are also problems of waste that is NOT disposed of in dumps—in many cases the environmental effects of abandoned materials and equipment is very significant. In a scoping study in Tortola, Island Resources Foundation estimates that one five-acre shoreline and mangrove area holds *50 tons* of abandoned and discarded barges, vehicles, boats, and heavy construction equipment—and this is in an area generally believed to be in good environmental condition. Solid waste impacts include the land disposal of ship-generated waste which can no longer be disposed at sea, as a result of the designation of the Caribbean Sea as a special area under the Law of the Sea. The World Bank and the Global Environment Facility have projects to address this problem in many of the Eastern Caribbean states.

Recent hurricanes have also provided a reminder that disasters in tourist facilities have major solid waste impacts both on land (which can include the abandonment of entire resort and hotel complexes) and also from the grounding and loss of boats on shorelines and in lagoons and estuaries.

Toxic Chemicals and Nitrification from Surface Waters Includes herbicides, pesticides, and fertilizers from agriculture and resort landscaping. Sewage discharges are generally believed to be the most serious and widespread pollutant associated with land-based sources of pollution in the Wider Caribbean. Surveys by PAHO (1993) and other organizational have indicated that nonexistent or improperly operated sewerage systems at hotels, resorts, and vacation condominiums are major contributors to this problem.

Groundwater Depletion and Contamination This category includes the introduction of toxic chemicals, pesticides, herbicides, and nutrients to groundwater by both direct injection and percolation from surface waters and irrigation systems. Groundwater depletion and contamination affect both the availability of groundwater for other human uses (or re-use) and the natural systems which use the water in freshwater springs on land and in the sea. Groundwater contamination is also a significant by-product of the region's well-known solid waste management problems.

Groundwater impacts are a major environmental impact of tourism in the Wider Caribbean because they are widespread, and because they are extremely intractable for both assessment and remediation. In a case study of the environmental impact of tourism in Jamaica, Eleanor Jones of Environmental Solutions identified water quality issues as the second impact of tourism:

In questioning the announcement of a major new resort complex to be constructed next to the Beef Island Airport in Tortola, British Virgin Islands, environmentalists cited concerns about impacts on groundwater, wetlands, and surface water quality as a result of a planned golf course as major reasons for opposing the project.

Studies of contamination by the common fungicide Benamyl, used in the banana industry in Dominica, but also common in golf course management, indicated no significant persistent contamination of ground or surface waters under normal farming practices, but a possibility of interference with freshwater crustacean and soil fungi when applied in heavy concentrations, or when washed into streams shortly after application. Change in Sediment Loads Sediment loads are increased by coastal and upland development, construction, roads (especially dirt roads in resorts and subdivisions) and deforestation. *Decreases* in sediment loads from dams and canals can also be damaging to some large estuarine and deltaic ecosystems, such as those found in major river mouths.

Tourism in the coastal zone contributes to increases in sediment loads for both back bay and shore areas, from construction, access and transport systems (especially dirt roads and some ferry activities), facility operations, and run off. Upland tourism facilities, which are not the direct focus of this report, contribute to sediment loads from rivers and other upland surface run off conditions. The Caribbean is especially susceptible to heavy sediment pulses because of the probability of heavy rains. A recent "shower" dropped eight inches of rain (a typical rainfall amount for an entire hurricane) on St. Thomas in three hours, resulting in severe sediment plumes from all developed areas along the coastline, threatening reefs and seagrass beds and forcing the closing of swimming beaches.

In addition to the beach profiling conducted by the UNESCO-supported COSALC I program, researchers are also starting to gather information on coastal stability which includes some effects related to sediment loading for 11 countries of the Lesser Antilles.

Visual Impacts Visual impacts have a high esthetic component which can be culturally biased, but they also derive from poor design, inattention, and large-scale physical alterations to land. "Scenic landscapes and other natural attractions provide the basis for tourism in the [Caribbean] and their value in the region to the tourism industry must be fully appreciated."

Tourism Facilities in the Coastal Zone

This section identifies six categories of tourism facility and the relative extent to which they can cause environmental degradation.

These categories are designed to capture the bulk of tourism activity, but they are not meant to be totally comprehensive or exclusive. That is, for example, a tourism complex could include large and small hotels, restaurants and beach recreational facilities. These categories refer to the activities of tourists, services provided to tourists, and the necessary infrastructure to support those services.

Tourism Complexes and Large Resorts Tourism complexes are large areas of intensive tourist development, generally larger than any single resort, which are almost totally dependent on tourism for economic activity. Complexes include large and small hotels and a variety of ancillary services usually offered by individual operators. Examples include Negril, Ocho Rios, or Montego Bay in Jamaica, La Romana in the Dominican Republic, and areas such as St. Lawrence Gap in Barbados, the Lagoon in St. Martin/St. Maarten, and Rodney Bay in St. Lucia. This category also includes large hotels, condominiums, and timesharing accommodations, which may have very different management structures, but which will have similar environmental effects.

All-inclusive tourist resorts in the coastal zone can exhibit most of the negative environmental effects discussed previously, but they are especially likely to contribute to displacement, physical changes especially related to coastal filling and elimination of mangroves and salt ponds. Groundwater depletion and contamination is another common impact of large resorts.

The size and complexity of large resorts requires a high level of technical expertise for review of permits and on-going monitoring of both construction and routine operations. For example, Jamaica is able to attain a relatively high level of operational compliance with hotel wastewater treatment standards by providing special training to government health inspectors.

Marine Recreational Facilities Includes boat charters, sport fishing and SCUBA diving, as well as marinas, piers, and cruiseship docks (and specialized cruise shopping services such as Pointe Seraphine in Castries, St. Lucia, or Havensite Mall in St. Thomas). Marine recreational facilities create impacts at two different levels:

- One is similar to other mass tourism concerns, based on cruiseships which now carry as many as 3,600 passengers—the equivalent of a floating 1,500 room hotel.

- Two is the effect of scores/hundreds/thousands of individual actions, such as anchoring in sea grass or snorklers touching the edge of a coral patch. These individual insults are not very damaging, but the gradual increase in the number of divers or sailors and the cumulative effect of their actions result in gradual deterioration of the affected ecosystems.

Small Hotels and Resorts In this study, small hotels and resorts are facilities under 100 rooms. There are dozens of ways to characterize hotels and resorts—a simple strategy being the following:

Small hotels and resorts may have relatively smaller negative environmental impacts, but they are also significantly less viable economically. Hoteliers and tourism officials generally believe that a threshold effective size in the Caribbean is approximately 250 rooms, which permits international advertising at a sufficient scale to recruit new guests each year. This rule-of-thumb suggests that governments need to understand the level of subsidy that is required to promote small-scale tourism—a factor that is generally understood. The point that is not understood, however, is that *less* impact does not mean that the facility is totally benign, and in some cases small hotels and resorts need added environmental support. For example, the PAHO study of hotel-based wastewater treatment plants indicated clearly that larger hotel treatment plants were more reliable than smaller plants (PAHO, 1994).

The Grand Anse beach in Grenada is an example of a tourist area where small hotels contaminated the beach because none of them could afford adequate sewage treatment, and because the growth of the tourist area stimulated hillside development of housing (with no sewage treatment facilities) for hotel staff and ancillary service personnel, all of which resulted in severe water quality problems for the near shore areas and eventual destruction of the fronting reefs.

Entertainment Facilities Entertainment facilities include bars and restaurants and similar facilities. The scale of these services can range from the simplest beach bar to large restaurants with acres of macadam parking lots. Food and beverage service facilities are singled out because they imply a number of special costs and benefits such as the disposal of fats and pesticides, and low impact use of shorelines. As indicated in the discussion of small hotel and resort facilities, above, enlightened public policy in support of low impact entertainment facilities also needs to plan for the extra public infrastructure costs which would otherwise be born by larger scale developments.

This category includes beach and shore services such as sunbathing, snorkelling, day sailing, glass bottom boats, submarines, pools, jet skis, and activities such as harbour cruises and reef tours. The use of the term "recreational" facilities is an important reminder that the domestic service component of these services (and their potential environmental impacts) are indistinguishable from the tourist service component. The same overlap occurs for entertainment facilities. Anchoring and mooring systems are features of both shoreside recreational and marine facilities with special environmental implications.

Although often thought of as areas protected *from* tourism and other intrusions, it is clear that throughout the Wider Caribbean, parks and protected areas are major factors in attracting and managing tourists and tourism. Throughout the Eastern Caribbean, for example, cruiseship visitor surveys indicate that 30% of cruiseship passengers who go ashore want to visit the natural areas and parks (OAS and CTRC, 1988). Negative environmental effects of tourism in parks and

Geographic Zones of Environmental Impact

The "coastal zone" is not a homogeneous, easily demarcated area. It is a variety of geomorphological and environmental complexes which are impacted and react differently to stress caused by coastal tourism activities and associated support systems.

For this study there are three general areas of impact: 1) mainland, 2) coast, and 3) ocean; and three directions to look for environmental effects: 1) inland, 2) along the coast, and 3) seaward. These classes are similar to the "coastal environments" used by Pearce and Kirk in their 1986 paper on "Carrying Capacities for Coastal Tourism," UNEP *Industry and Environment*, March 1986. We have used the following six classes for this framework, approximating a transect through the watershed—from the heights through the limits of a country's exclusive economic zone. For this analytical framework there are no hard edges to most geographic zones of environmental impact, but it should be understood that environmental impacts from tourism in upland areas are generally excluded from this study, which concentrates on coastal tourism impacts.

Impacts are most acute in the immediate area of the shoreline, with two-thirds of the identified impacts occurring between the back bays and the fronting reefs. These areas of impact coincide with areas of greatest human use conflict (tourism, housing, agriculture, ports and transportation, urban settlements), and with the most productive and critical habitats and coastal nurseries for reef, coastal and pelagic marine species. The outer limits of these near coastal and fringing reef areas is a broad band, possibly out to 20-fathom depths. Most offshore islets and cays—which are an entire topic for protection unto themselves—are in this area. Impacts result from:

- the construction and operation of docks, piers, wharves, groins, breakwaters and other physical structures;
- sediments stirred up by sea traffic;
- new current and wave regimes created by other changes,;
- anchoring and diving insults;
- the direct introduction of toxics and other pollutants from anti-fouling paints, ship operations and waste discharges;
- the visual impact of anchorages, piers and ports;
- the displacement of fishers and other traditional water users, and
- the irritation caused by loud and boisterous parties on harbour and coastal day-trip boats and barges.

The geographic zone describing the actual intersection of sea and land, which in this framework includes barrier islands.

Numerous human and natural factors contribute to the character of a beach, including ocean currents, presence of reefs, long shore currents, the state of rivers emptying into the sea, and adjacent wetlands. Construction activity, sand mining, effluent discharges, wetland reclamation, sewage and solid waste disposal practices are tourism-related activities which affect beach quality.

Estuaries, Back Bays, Salt Ponds and Lagoons These are the buffers between the land mass and the sea—usually thought of as sinks for sediments and pollutants from the land, these areas also buffer the coastal plain and shorelines from offshore storms and waves. These areas are easily accessible for development and are difficult to protect. This is the site of the bulk of coastal tourism facilities. In general, this is the area which sees most of the use conflicts in the coastal zone as facilities are moved back from the shore and as population growth and migration from the hinterlands leads to higher residential densities.

This area is impacted indirectly by coastal tourism activity, usually resulting from either the displacement of traditional users to upland areas, or the immigration of workers for the tourism services who are excluded from living in the coastal plain or shore areas by high costs of land or land ownership. *Direct* tourism effects in upland areas can occur by visual intrusions on the viewshed of upland properties, especially from high-rise coastal development.

Offshore Waters Isolated offshore reefs, islets and cays, and the open sea, to the limits of the exclusive economic zone. Because these areas are so dispersed, there is not much direct tourism impact on the zone—but again, there is a big difference between "not much" and "acceptable." The problem of marine debris, including beach-fouling tar balls remains acute.

Documentation of Coastal Degradation of Environmental Resources

Research for this project has identified more than 100 publications about environmental degradation from coastal tourism. These references summarize the content of the information available most immediately to the best informed coastal managers.

Documents Related to Environmental Degradation, at the end of Section 5, displays an analysis of these references in relation to our analytical framework. This analysis leads to three conclusions:

- Information resources for environmental degradation from tourism facilities and services in coastal areas are not evenly distributed.
- Environmental degradation effects can be mitigated by known actions from a number of disciplines *outside of* the coastal environment and tourism planning sector.
- Mitigation of environmental degradation effects can best be supported by broad involvement *and information sharing* with several sectors, including for example, agriculture, forestry, hydrology, and environmental health.

At one level, this merely demonstrates the often-repeated statement that coastal environmental planning is multi-sectoral and multi-disciplinary. It also confirms the need for coastal planners to seek information from sources outside of planning. For example, our references have few works which deal with the visual impacts of upland-stimulated developments arising from coastal tourism facilities. But clearly there are regional planning, landscape planning and architectural resources which could be mustered to address the problem, *if* broad-ranging information sharing for environmental impact mitigation is a priority for planners.

Benefits of Tourism in Coastal Areas

Income Direct and indirect income effects of tourism in the coastal zone are large throughout the Caribbean, where tourism is both the largest single industry, and also the fastest growing industrial sector. In the small island developing states of the Caribbean tourism accounts for up to 88% of gross domestic product

Jobs Tourism has a major employment impact both because of the size of the tourism industry, and also because tourism is a labour-intensive industry (0.9 to 1.8 jobs per room in the Caribbean, according to the Caribbean Tourism Organisation, CTO, 1994). Although tourist industry jobs are generally thought of as low paying, in the United States wages are equivalent to or slightly above manufacturing jobs.

Foreign Investment Construction of tourism facilities in the developing countries of the Wider Caribbean is generally financed by foreign investment, and is itself a major source of income and employment for the developing countries of the region.

Infrastructure Development Tourism, and especially the development of mass tourism, frequently brings with it the improved airports, roads, docks and seaports, and commercial distribution systems which improve the quality of life for all of the inhabitants of an island or region. These infrastructure improvements can include sewerage systems, solid waste management facilities, potable water systems, and other infrastructure with direct impacts on environmental conditions and the public health.

Examples of infrastructural improvements from tourism include the World Bank-and Global Environmental Facility-funded programs for solid waste management and disposal of ship-generated solid waste, which are designed specifically to enable governments in the Eastern Caribbean to cope with solid waste impacts from tourism, especially waste resulting from cruise ship tourism. Surveys on all of the islands associated with these projects indicate that the predominant source of solid waste and marine debris in these islands is local, domestic users. Other projects include public power generating facilities and submarine cables paid for by resorts, cruiseship docks and airports throughout the region, and expansion of potable water systems.

Increased Local Support for Environmental Amenities Many of the most tourist-dependent areas of the Wider Caribbean have environmental NGOs or initiatives which are supported by tourists, and which have gradually created new awareness of environmental issues and problems in the region. For example, financial support of some conservation groups, particularly those with an historic preservation focus, relies heavily on contributions from winter residents of the Caribbean. Conversion to Less Stressful Use In some areas of the Caribbean tourism facilities in the coastal zone replace activities which have demonstrably or presumably greater impacts on the environment, such as intensive agriculture with pollutant effects from herbicides and pesticides.

The following box illustrates the ambiguity over the costs and benefits of tourism in the coastal zone. In this excerpt from an article by Gilberto Romero about environmental conditions in Cuba, damages to the country's beaches are enumerated critically, both as direct and indirect effects of tourism, and also because they implicitly prevent the country from exploiting more tourist opportunities. Conditions cited for the Cuban beaches could be identified with numerous other countries in the Wider Caribbean.

Costs of Tourism in Coastal Areas

Water Quality and Quantity Groundwater and surface water supplies throughout the Wider Caribbean are being impacted by overuse and contamination. Loss of this critical resource may be one of the major long-term development problems facing the Wider Caribbean, and tourism facilities have contributed to the problem for many years. Water quality problems may result in the need to invest in alternative potable water supplies, to develop more complex treatment systems with increased operating costs, and to incur extra investments in water distribution systems. Degraded water quality may also result in extra costs for water supplies during droughts and other emergencies, and increased costs from lost work and medical treatment caused by polluted drinking water and contaminated beaches. In direct impacts on tourism, poor water quality effects can range from simply compromising tourist expectations, to major public relations disasters if tourists have to be warned to stay out of the sea in front of their hotels. The Coastal Zone Management program in Barbados grew out of public health and public relations concerns.

Sewage and Solid Waste Disposal Tourists generate greater amounts of solid and liquid waste *per capita* than domestic users. The upside of this cost is that the impacts are generally concentrated in small geographic areas which makes it more economic to collect and treat these pollutants than those generated by the more widely dispersed local users. The downside, as shown in the PAHO study cited previously (PAHO, 1994), is that these small waste treatment plants and landfills are seldom managed to the level of performance that modern standards require. Even the best monitoring of hotel waste treatment plants, for example (in Jamaica) achieved only a 43% compliance with regional standards.

Loss of Non-renewable Resources Sand mining from beaches is a major negative impact related to tourism development in the Wider Caribbean. Beach sand is a non-renewable resource used by tourism for construction and beach replenishment. Sand mining in combination with regional sea level rise and erosion caused by a variety of man-made and natural factors can destroy beaches. The 1995 Annual Report for COSALC I describes and illustrates the loss of the beach in front of Pinney's Beach resort (Nevis) over the past 30 years, with the resort now occupying a peninsula protected by rock revetments, where it once nestled in the midst of the coconut plantation which fringed the old beach.

Overharvesting of Renewable Resources Some tourists are aware that grouper, conch and lobster are becoming scarce throughout the Caribbean. Fewer are aware that mangroves, for example, are renewable resources which are becoming severely stressed throughout the region by overharvesting for fuel and construction materials and by coastal development that diminishes or destroys mangrove habitat. The list of degraded coastal and marine resources is getting longer, and includes the region's critical coral reefs.

The Death of Reefs

Conditions affecting reef communities are familiar to planners and environmentalists throughout the Caribbean:

- sediment-laden runoff from upslope erosion and fertilization causes corals to die or to grow much slower;
- major physical damage, such as boat anchoring, ship groundings, trawlers, and repetitive minor insults, such as boat wakes, fish traps and diver contacts increase the rate of "normal" coral attrition;
- sediment pulses from storm runoff, either stimulated by construction disturbances or permitted by the destruction of fringing mangroves, salt ponds and other shoreside buffers, smother and further weaken or eventually kill corals;
- warm ocean waters, caused by natural factors or as an affect of global climate change, seem to reduce the resistance of corals to disease and other stresses;
- diseases (such as white band disease) caused by natural or unknown sources, and abetted by systemic stresses such as those listed above, wreak havoc on major elements of the coral community, destroying vast proportions of the elk horn corals in fringing and patch reefs throughout the Caribbean;
- major storms—again, possibly caused by global climate change—destroy large areas of weakened reef and totally obliterate large areas of reef rubble which had served as reef and shore protection barriers (Dr. Barry Blake, former director of environmental programs for the British Development Division in the Caribbean, personal communication).

Increased Social Tensions Large number of tourists, especially foreign, richer tourists, tend to stimulate social friction among different classes and racial groups. It is worth noting that the recent review of tourism for the Small Island Developing States Unit of the UN Commission on Sustainable Development recommends three measures for coping with the adverse social and cultural impacts of tourism, including studies of a social carrying capacity for tourism, public education programs, and improved security measures to address increased crime and drug problems.

Stimulation of Imports of Foods and Other Consumables Many tourist destinations, especially in the most tourist-dependent small island states of the Wider Caribbean, are unable to meet the needs of tourists for basic food and other consumables. This economic reality, in combination with the preferences of tourists for goods from the metropolitan countries, contributes to the weak economic benefits of tourism in many countries. This is not an unmixed negative impact, since it provides a scale of import demand which helps to reduce costs for local residents. Foreign consumption patterns also dramatically increase the volume of trash produced from packaging.

Costs of Damage from Natural Hazards Increased density of development, higher unit investments in the precarious coastal zone, and more fanciful architectural styles increase the risks and costs from natural hazards. The 1995 hurricane season heightened awareness of the vulnerability of coastal areas in the Wider Caribbean to natural disasters, and has made securing insurance much more difficult. Coastal damages from the hurricanes have also raised questions throughout the region about the adequacy of shoreline setback policies.

Increased Densities and Conversion to More Stressful Uses High density tourist developments in the coastal zone, plus the displacement effect of such developments on other sectors of the local community, increase the overall density of coastal areas, with negative consequences for most natural systems and overall sustainability. Increased coastal land use from tourism-related activities, in already stressed coastal areas, usually generates adverse cumulative effects over time, unless countermeasures are taken to maintain a productive host environment. Development planning therefore needs to adopt a no-net-loss principle for the support of coastal ecosystems.

The Tourism Death Spiral

The analytical framework devised for this study discussed the possibility that tourism-dependent economies could suffer such environmental degradation that tourism would decline, reducing national income and government revenues which would worsen conditions, leading to more tourist flight and so forth. (This negative feedback loop is discussed in McEachern and Towle, 1974, and in several newer works by McElroy and de Albuquerque) In effect, this death spiral scenario contradicts the more general hypothesis that investors and the local community can cooperate to ensure the maintenance of environmental amenities in order to preserve tourism income.

In the real world it is seldom possible to separate causes and effects so neatly, but development planners and travel agents would probably agree that small areas, such as Miami Beach from the 1960s to the early 1980s, the Condado Beach area in San Juan, and possibly other mass tourism destinations in the Caribbean have suffered from or passed through such cycles. continued...The case of the US Virgin Islands in recent years leads to the hypothesis that the tourism death spiral may be affecting the entire Territory after several decades of tourism-fuelled growth. The US Virgin Islands have suffered substantial environmental degradation in addition to damages from storms and hurricanes in recent years. There are no studies which definitively link the cumulative environmental degradation of the islands to tourism, but in a teritory characterized by both mass tourism and high dependency on the tourism industry (59% of GDP), touism certainly accounts for a significant portion of the wear and tear experienced by the environment over the past 30 or 40 years.

According to the local Department of Tourism (June, 1996), from 1988 (the year before Hurricane Hugo) to 1994 (the year before Hurricane Marilyn), the number of tourists (omitting day tripping excursionists and cruiseship passengers) decreased from 555 thousand to 540 thousand. During the same period (CTO, 1995) Caribbean tourism increased at an average annual rate of 3.1%.

If the Virgin Islands had kept up with the Caribbean, tourists for 1996 would have been 666 thousand, (23% higher than actual) and government revenues would have been $21.7 million higher, based on estimates of the 1994 economic and fiscal impact of tourism on the Territory.

The government revenue figures are especially significant, since the government currently has a recurring annual deficit of over a hundred million dollars, it owes $140 million in back pay to employees; it is two years late in paying $60 million in tax refunds; and vendor payments are months in arrears.

It should be noted that tourism officials and many Virgin Islands residents deny the implications of this analysis, citing short-term economic fluctuations, hurricane-induced reductions in tourism, and bad luck as the sources of business losses. In a front page article in the *Virgin Islands Daily News* for December 2, 1996, however, the president of the St. Croix Chamber of Commerce is quoted as saying that long-terms changes in tourism growth reflected fundamental changes in the Virgin Islands attractiveness to tourists.

Valuation of Beaches

Valuation of beaches is a key element for developing costs of environmental impacts of tourism. Appendix C presents a mid-1996 list of beach valuation resources from worldwide sources as posted on the Internet.

Mitigating Tourism Degradation of Coastal Areas

This Section outlines the principal tools or processes needed by regional and national planners and policy managers to determine specific impacts (plus and minus) of current and proposed tourism activities. These are tools to support *planning* to mitigate coastal degradation from tourism. The broad categories of these tools are:

- An analytical framework for addressing tourism facilities, areas of impact, and types of environmental effect;
- A win-win model for negotiating tourism development among government, the tourism industry, workers, landowners, local residents, non-governmental organizations, and other special interests;
- Adequate technical expertise;
- Improved knowledge of programs and natural resources;
- Five specific mitigation strategies.

The final part of this section, Related Programs of International Groups, page 38 below, discusses some of the international policy and strategic recommendations addressing tourism or coastal environmental policies which may provide guidance to national and regional planners.

A Framework for Analyzing Tourism and the Environment

This report has presented a broad analytical framework for assessing specific elements of environmental degradation from coastal tourism, based on the type of tourism facility and the area being impacted. Planners and managers need a refinement of this [or similar] framework to apply at the local level.

Economic Studies

As discussed in the Section on the Analytical Framework, page 8, and Section 3, immediately above, detailed economic studies (such as those suggested in the 1993 Organization of American States *Compendium of Recent Studies on Tourism Development)* are needed to identify the economic benefits that actually accrue to the host country from investments in and expenditures for specific types of tourism facilities.

At the regional level such studies of economic returns could at least provide the range of probable returns from such investments for various sub-categories of the Wider Caribbean economy. Because of the wide variation in key factors such as land values, wage rates and construction costs, a Caribbean-wide analysis, however, would be less useful than smaller studies of sub-regional economic factors. Priorities should be set for studies of economic conditions in sub-regions or countries with high investments in and growth of tourism.

Win-Win Coastal Planning

Tourism developments are really a subset of the general problems associated with planning and coordinating development in the coastal zone of Caribbean states. The coastal zone management model which is commonly used in the Wider Caribbean is based on an outmoded and frequently damaging assumption that development is a "zero sum game," in which developers and government are locked in combat to win the development game. In the abstract it is now generally conceded that developers *and* government, private *and* public sectors, *must* win in order for the people to benefit from new investments. Win-win negotiating systems are especially important for sectors like tourism which depend on natural resources and high environmental amenity values (UNEP, 1996). Unfortunately, win-win concepts have not yet been widely applied to the actual processes of planning, coordinating and permitting tourism development.

Some recent experiments embodying win-win planning processes, worth studying for both their successes and their failures include:

- Major, long-term tourism development planning processes for the Soufriere area of St. Lucia, involving local residents, fishermen, hotel owners and planners, and a variety of government agencies. This project has been heavily supported by outside interests, including the USAID/ENCORE program implemented by the Natural Resources Management Unit of the Organisation of Eastern Caribbean States.

- Preliminary planning for coastal impact mitigation in the further development of the Bay Islands of Honduras.
- Organization of American States-supported planning for a marine sanctuary and wildlife reserve as part of a larger Parham Harbour Development scheme for the northeast coastal area of Antigua.

All of these planning processes attempt to provide effective participatory avenues for the stakeholders in the development process, including local residents, investors, workers, government, environmental interests, and even future consumers. It is also notable that all of the examples noted above have significant technical or management roles for non-commercial, non-governmental organizations, sometimes as formal groups of cross-sectoral interests, sometimes as representatives of specific interests, such as fishermen's associations or environmentalists.

Adequate Technical Expertise

Tourism development planning and administration involve highly technical issues. In small developing states, such as those found in the Caribbean, it is difficult, often impossible to muster the staff talent to evaluate projections of economic and environmental effects in development proposals, or even to knowledgeably review and react to monitoring and assessment reporting conducted for construction or operation of large facilities. To address these problems in a realistic cost and political environment requires openness and innovative use of outside resources.

The Coastal Zone Management Unit of the Ministry of Tourism, International Transport and the Environment in Barbados has developed a model for getting needed technical skills which is instructive for both national and sub-national jurisdictions throughout the region. As a matter of routine practice (and agency policy in the case of major projects), the Unit seeks a contract or memorandum of understanding with a qualified third-party institution to provide independent consultation and advice (often referred to as "peer review") on technical matters involving the project, as they arise. In the event of encountering special technical problems, the third party (in Barbados, often one of several special institutes affiliated with the University of the West

Indies) is free to seek other detailed advice and support from outside the country (Leonard Nurse, Director of the Coastal Zone Management Unit, personal communication).

In addition to being an excellent solution to the technical problem, the use of the third-party peer review organization frequently has the effect, especially in small states, of building wider knowledge and understanding of the issues surrounding large complex projects among a broader strata of local leadership. This in turn generally enhances the quality of the dialogue and the policy instruments which can be applied to the project.

Knowledge of Program and Natural Resources

Governments, investors, citizens and scientists all need to know about existing and future *programs* that can be used or adapted to support coastal tourism development in the Wider Caribbean. Similarly, there is a vast wealth of *environmental data* and information which could be better used to manage current coastal zone programs or to analyse plans for future developments. Each of these subjects is discussed separately below. In spite of the great differences in subject matter, both of these important information needs require a catalogue of information that can be assembled from existing data sources. This "re-packaging" holds the promise of substantial benefits from relatively modest investments in modern Internet and data management technologies.

This need, however, is purposely characterized as a need for increased *knowledge* of program and natural resources. In the hierarchy of knowledge, one proceeds from data to information to knowledge. The long-term goal is to build knowledge systems for both programs and natural resources which will serve as decision-support tools for private and public policy managers throughout the region. This means that while the first step in this process is to build databases and data access systems from existing information, the next steps should include the institution of specialized World Wide Web search engines, geographic information systems, other decision support and data visualization systems.

Program Resources

There is a recognized need to provide more efficient access to information about program resources which can support planning or investments to mitigate coastal degradation from tourism (and other development pressures). Listed below are four recent attempts to catalogue some of these resources:

The World Bank's 1994 report on *Initiatives for Regional Action on Caribbean Environmental Issues;*

The "Tropical Americas Regional Report on the Issues and Activities Associated with Coral Reefs and Related Ecosystems," prepared by Jeremy Woodley, Centre for Marine Sciences, University of the West Indies, Jamaica, for the *1995 International Coral Reef Initiative Workshop*;

Notes from the "Environmental Interagency Coordinating Committee, Special Meeting on Coastal Management Activities," held at the Caribbean Development Bank, Barbados, March 5, 1996,

The environmental project database for the Wider Caribbean, being assembled by Erik Blommestein of the UNESCO Economic Commission for Latin America and the Caribbean sub-regional office for the Caribbean.

These *ad hoc* efforts need to be systematized in improved, consolidated reporting of program resources so that developers and planners in the Wider Caribbean can assess the environmental supports which they can apply to local development planning and program implementation. The scope of such information systems should be expanded to include a *directory* of regional experts and *NGO and private industry activities*, such as the Blue Flag beach certification program in Europe, or alternative energy systems.

Natural Resources

Environmental conditions in the islands and coastal areas of continental countries of the Wider Caribbean are highly variable, which complicates planning and permitting processes for both natural resource management and development planning. Resource managers and development planners both need improved information about environmental conditions.

Metadata

Paradoxically, while environmental conditions throughout the Caribbean have been studied extensively, there is no organized process for cataloguing or providing access to these studies which may be anywhere in any of a dozen local archives, or in a large number of overseas libraries or historical files. Environmental information specialists (and consultants) have begun to recognize local decision-making needs, at the same time that international organizations are building tools which permit the cataloguing of such studies in a systematic way that can be accessed, in part, by sophisticated search tools over the Internet.

Monitoring and Assessment

Secondary to the need to catalogue existing information resources is the need to collect new information on environmental conditions using standardized or comparable monitoring and

assessment tools that accurately capture major information. Tools such as the coral reef monitoring manuals written by the United States National Park Service in the US Virgin Islands and the UNEP Regional Coordinating Unit in Kingston, Jamaica, are basic to this process.

The CARICOMP marine monitoring program is beginning to amass a wealth of standardized environmental data useful to regional planners from 25 sites around the Caribbean. The COSALC I project is accumulating a similar volume of information on the physical conformation of a number of beaches in the Eastern Caribbean. Both the data *and the methods* applied to collect this data should be widely available to potential users—for example, over the Internet or by some other open, accessible format.

Environmental Information Access Tools

Governments and developers have mutual needs for good, comprehensive access to information about environmental conditions for tourism planning. Cataloguing tools (metadata systems) are becoming widely available in forms that permit the information to be widely accessed by local and international investigators, whether these are scientific researchers, resource planners and managers, or development planners and investors.

The Conservation Data Centre of the Eastern Caribbean Centre of the University of the Virgin Islands, for example, has recently sponsored a training program in metadata collection procedures for geospatial biological and environmental information for environmental information specialists from across the northeastern Caribbean, including public, private, local, national and non-governmental organizations. Because this information is being catalogued in a standard format, the

United States Geological Survey agrees to provide computer facilities to make this information available over the World Wide Web to students, researchers, planners, and managers from the next island or around the world.

With improved access to high quality environmental information, it becomes easier for planners and developers to incorporate environmental considerations in their development plans. This, combined with a permitting process that emphasizes environmental concerns, will stimulate competition among investors for innovative, effective and environmentally sustainable tourism developments.

Mitigation Strategies

This section lists five priority goals to enable regional and national planners and policy managers to mitigate the negative environmental effects of coastal tourism:

- link tourism development to the country's integrated coastal area planning and management initiavies;
- develop sustainable, long-term tourism strategies with strong environmental protection elements;
- protect existing natural coastal areas;
- restore natural areas;
- apply voluntary tourism industry standards and training.

These strategies may overlap, but are not directly comparable to the best management practices for tourism facilities which are being assessed in another publication of the Caribbean Environment Programme.

Work Within an Integrated Coastal Area Management Program

Tourism development is simply another of the myriad of investment opportunities which are competing for space and resources in the coastal zone. Tourism development needs to be fully integrated in public policy formulation and resource management programs. Because of the glamour and exoticism associated with many elements of tourism there is a tendency to separate tourism planning considerations from other coastal area planning and management. This is a major mistake in both the planning process and public policy.

Using the definition of Integrated Coastal Area Management as developed by Jens Sorensen (UNEP, 1996) as:

- a dynamic process that continues over time,
- involving a governance arrangement to establish policies for making allocation decisions,
- a governance arrangement that uses one or more management strategies to rationalize resource allocation,
- management strategies that rely on a systems approach recognizing connections among coastal and marine activities, and
- having a boundary that crosses from the sea to the interior of the shoreline, it is clear that good tourism planning and policy management requires a framework of effective coastal area management.

Strategic Planning for Sustainable Tourism

Strategic planning for tourism is not, as implied in much of the literature, the search for a tourism "carrying capacity" for a given island. As pointed out by Paul Wilkinson (1990):

To achieve progress toward a strategic plan for accommodating tourism and environmental considerations, national planners need to:

Assess the importance of tourism in terms of its contribution to total income, growth of income, and foreign exchange earnings;

Identify the stage of tourism development, or where the national tourism industry stands within an evaluation framework such as the "Limits of Acceptable Change"; and

Identify the unique indigenous elements of the local tourism product, to understand potential conflicts and complementary interests with environmental protection.

Building or reviewing a tourism development strategy provides a means to re-evaluate public attitudes and government policies for tourism development, and it also provides improved guidance for developers.

6

Second Homes as a Part of New Rural Life Style

Second Homes-The Economic Impact on Rural Communities

There is concern in some quarters that second homes have a negative impact on the economy of rural communities. In some parts of the UK, local strength of feeling about this has occasionally erupted into arson, for example, with a number of second homes being burned down in Wales.

The main issues that create controversy are twofold. Firstly, there is the argument that second home owners drive up prices in rural areas, pushing them out of the reach of local people and exacerbating the problem that there is not enough affordable housing for low income local families. This is clearly an area that needs a balanced approach and well thought out strategy to help solve this very real issue.

The second common concern is that second houses are unoccupied for a large part of the year and this deprives local businesses of potential custom, sometimes badly affecting their viability. Another aspect of this is that local schools can become short of children, sometimes forcing local schools to close. Indeed, on some areas very popular with second home owners, the area can feel like a ghost town out of season, without the community vitality and vibrant local economy that characterises some other rural areas.

The problems seem to be focused on highly localised rural and coastal areas, the kind of attractive areas that are popular for second homes. For example, in North Cornwall, one in three properties is thought to be a second home or holiday home,

In general, the more remote rural areas have the greatest concentrations of second homes as a proportion of all the housing stock, intensifying the problem of creating a sustainable and robust local community with a thriving local economy.

Although second and holiday homes contribute to an uplift in property prices in rural areas, it is important not to view their economic impact in isolation from other factors contributing to changes within rural communities and especially pressures on local housing markets from other groups such as commuters, retirees, or people wanting a lifestyle change.

One way that second home owners can help avoid any negative economic impacts on the local community is to maximise the extent to which the second home does not stand empty.

By renting a second home out as a holiday home for part of the year, when it is not in use by the owner's family, it ensures that money is brought into the local economy as the family renting the holiday home will inevitably spend money in the local shops, restaurants and at local attractions. This is clearly a positive impact on the local economy and far better for the local community than having a second home stand empty. Yet many owners of second homes resist renting out their home to holidaymakers..

There are a wide variety of reasons for this. It is often not as simple as whether or not the owner of a second home would like to make a profitable return on their property.

Some second home owners simply do not want strangers in their home and this is a strongly felt emotion they are not likely to overcome.

Others do not want to get involved in what they see as complex property management issues, involving a lot of work and practical difficulty. For these owners, the answer is often to hire a holiday homes services specialist that can take away the hassle and arrange everything on their behalf, making the whole process of renting out a holiday home very straightforward.

If a holiday homes services specialist is engaged, they can arrange all aspects of property management, cleaning services and key holder services as well as sometimes a holiday concierge service. This means that the second home owner can benefit from a stream of income from the property, all the gain without the pain. In addition, the impact on the local economy is positive as the holiday home rentals bring money into the local shops, restaurants and attractions as well as necessitating the employment of local trades people, such as plumbers, electricians, painters and carpenters.

The impacts, both positive and negative, of second homes and holiday homes touch on a diverse range of factors that affect the sustainability of rural communities. One thing is clear-renting out a second home as a holiday home has a more positive impact on the local economy than leaving it standing empty for long periods.

New Countryside, New Rural Life

Demonstrating the top leadership's ambition to build a "new socialist countryside", Chinese Premier Wen Jiabao presided over a State Council executive meeting on June 30, focusing on rural taxation reform and further relaxing farmers' financial burdens. A statement from the meeting promised to transfer more funds to the local governments after rural taxation reform cuts out a large chunk of their tax income, while proposing the establishment of a mechanism to monitor farmers' debts.

The meeting might sound too profound for housemaid Li Yuanyuan. Yet the chubby girl from Xiangyang County of Central China's Hubei Province believes that "the central government now is trying to help us peasants, who work very hard all the year round, but earn little. " Landing the job of housemaid in Beijing five years ago, Yuanyuan can earn 800 yuan (US$100) a month, compared to her family of five making about 10,000 yuan a year by growing rice and wheat in a small plot. "You see, I alone can make that much in Beijing," says the 20-year-old.

Bidding to bail out millions of peasants like Li Yuanyuan, China earlier this year set out the plan called "building a new socialist countryside" to redress the chasm dividing the country into two parts: the affluent urban east and the less developed or even underdeveloped rural west. The plan is believed to signify a grand shift in infrastructure and investment priorities from urban to rural areas.

Reorienting government investment to create a "new socialist countryside" was declared as a "major historic task" for China's 11th Five-Year Development Program (2006-2010) in Premier Wen Jiabao's government work report to the latest annual National People's Congress

(NPC) session held in Beijing from March 5-13. The president of the School of Agro Economics and Rural Development at Beijing-based Renmin University of China saw the plan as a practical and realistic move "because the strategy is based on solid and extensive research in rural areas." "It's certainly one way to help raise farmers' incomes. Not until there is a substantial increase in their incomes can we possibly boost domestic consumption, which has already obstructed economic development as a whole," says Prof. Wen Tiejun, a noted expert on rural China. A recent survey on what peasants are expecting from the creation of the new countryside was conducted by the School of Journalism & Communication, and the Sociology Department, Nanjing University in East China.

The surveyors collected 940 questionnaires from 10 ordinary villages and 10 specially-chosen pilot ones across the country, plus 156 in-depth interviews. The findings indicated that 54.6 percent said the most important thing for them is to increase their incomes. And 19.5 percent planned to look for a job in the city. The survey also found 81. 9 percent said the annually agriculture taxations are not so heavy. Yet, their actual incomes are declining as the price of fertilizers, pesticides and seeds going up.

Although China is traditionally an agricultural power with more than half of the population still farming, industrialization and urbanization have overshadowed other sectors on the government agenda in the past decades. As a result, observes Prof. Wen, rural China has not kept pace with the development of urban areas. The new countryside plan indicates that the government is to pay equal, if not more, attention to the countryside as to the cities, and is to revitalize rural China through science and technology, Prof. Wen says. "Whether or not the countryside can get prosperous will have a great, far-reaching impact on the building of a harmonious society."

The official criteria for the new countryside, in Premier Wen's words, are "enhanced productive forces, higher living standards, civilized living style, an orderly and clean environment, and democratic administration." "This vision has defined the new countryside plan as a systematic and comprehensive policy, which clearly reflects the government's thinking on how to deal with the 'San Nong Wenti' — problems confronting China's agriculture, countryside and peasants," says Prof. Wen. But Li Changping, who served as the party chief of

Qipan Township of Hubei for 17 years, does not see anything special in the strategy. "The new countryside is not just as simple as building new roads, new houses and new toilets," says Li, now a recognized rural development expert.

The 43-year-old Li earned his reputation as "China's Most Notable Party Secretary at Grassroots Level" after he wrote a letter to the former Premier Zhu Rongji in 2000, complaining that "peasants are too miserable, the countryside is too depressed and agriculture is too much in danger." Soon after that, Li had to resign from the post of township Party chief. He now works as a consultant for the charity Oxfam International, Hong Kong. Prof. Wen disagrees with Li. In his view, the new countryside plan has touched upon some "fundamental problems". One is the emphasis on a good interaction between urban and rural areas and on the construction of harmony in rural communities. For instance, while organic farming is encouraged, the countryside can supply cities with safe food and also keep its own development sustainable.

Second, the plan highlights the efforts to perfect social security systems in the countryside. There have been rural residents who became broke and impoverished once a family member got sick, or a child went to a higher learning institution. "You have to have a sound social security system to tackle these problems," Prof. Wen says. Third, the plan aims to build rural areas into desirable communities for comfortable living: not just attractive to conventional rural dwellers but also urbanites. Prof. Pan Wei, director of the China and World Research Centre at Beijing University, describes the new drive as China's "second rural revolution" since 1979, comparing it to the launch of the household-based system of contracted responsibility.

That reform of 27 years ago resulted in two significant changes in farmers' lives: increase in their incomes and growth in their purchasing power. That in turn led to township enterprises emerging as a new force where state companies failed to meet demand.

Rural development in the 1980s was designated to have industrialized the countryside. The three key elements of agriculture — land, labour and capital – were consumed to achieve that goal. Rural enterprises set up by peasants absorbed surplus farming manpower, shifting them into non-agricultural work without uprooting them from the countryside. Villagers who put money or technology became shareholders in village factories, and a group of peasant entrepreneurs came to the fore. An unprecedented increase in peasants' incomes helped narrow the urban-rural income gap. But only a small part of the rural communities, mainly in the east, sustained the momentum of development and remained affluent, experts say. The vast bulk of countryside had remained stagnant as urban expansion soared during the 1990s.

The central government has decided to spend 339.7 billion yuan on farmers this year, an increase of 14.2 percent on last year. Most of the money will be allocated to bettering rural schools, improving access to health care and public works like road construction and irrigation works. Rural infrastructure facilities lag far behind. Nearly seven percent of rural schoolhouses are in danger of collapsing, meaning more than one million pupils cannot go to school regularly, according to the Guangzhou-based Southern Weekend.

But while the increased spending must be welcomed, it's important to remember the base is low. Rural development forms 8.9 percent of China's entire budget, says Prof. Pan Wei of Beijing University. "It's a drop in the ocean. That is to say the new spending only amounts to an additional seven dollars per head a year." He suggests "developing peasants' own cooperative organizations and helping them get into profitable fields like buying and selling, financing and supermarkets."

Through their own organizations, peasants can negotiate effectively with other economic bodies and establish a stable contractual relationship. China has already set up 30 pilot cooperatives. Social services in the countryside are also in a precarious state. "You cannot deploy a doctor or a teacher to every single village. Therefore, we must prepare rural people with some necessary social skills to survive urban modernization, a must for a nation's modernization," says Prof. Ding Yuanzhu with the Macro-Economic Research Institute of the State Development and Reform Commission.

Building a new socialist countryside in the final analysis is all about building new cities in rural areas, or so believes the CCTV pundit Song Xiaojun. "The idea of a new countryside is about hope, materially and culturally. People mostly live on hope or expectation." "The city and the countryside both are children of the government. Now the government calls for rich urbanites to energetically support their long-overlooked rural brethren. That's a hope for the vast countryside." A vegetable vendor in north Beijing agrees with Song. Her home village, says Li Xiuli, is "boring and dull." Li, 27, had never been to a cinema before she came to Beijing from her home in North China's Inner Mongolia Autonomous Region five years ago. "The closest cinema was 30 kilometres away in downtown Ningcheng County. Here in Beijing, everything is entertaining. Supermarkets, malls, TV programs and the like. "However, Prof. Wen Tiejun says, international experience indicates that urbanization alone cannot save the countryside. Take a look at Japan's new countryside. The government spent 2 trillion yen on re-partitioning agricultural land during the course of its urbanization. Consequently, Japan's small-farmer economy lost its competitive ability and became dependent on increasing government subsidies to survive.

Therefore, privatizing agriculture land is not the solution. "The problem China really needs to solve now is the systematic contradiction: separation of the urban and rural regions," says Ding Yunzhu, adding, "Again, the new countryside plan is the key to addressing the problem."

A New Rural Lifestyle-Keen Vendor, Make an Offer

Whether you want a large, new and modern family home or a quieter rural life with some income, 'SNOWHAVEN' will satisfy your needs. The home is on a 2.2 ha block and was designed and built to the highest standards with quality fixtures and fittings throughout. The over-sized clay bricks have a sandstone appearance, the windows and doors are double-glazed, there is in-floor heating in the kitchen and bathrooms, granite bench-tops in the kitchen, a gas fire in the lounge room, reverse cycle air conditioning in the main bedroom, and both the external and internal walls are insulated. The home comprises a very large master bedroom with an adjacent bathroom and is quite separate from the rest of the house. The second bedroom, with a kitchenette and disabled bathroom, and third bedroom are accessed from a large air-lock entrance and can be divided from the remainder of the house. The living and community areas are large and comprise a kitchen with walk-in pantry and views of the mountains. A breakfast bar divides the kitchen from the living/dining room, where the gas fire is located. There is also a lounge room, formal dining room and laundry with a third toilet. The home is completed by a 2.4 metre wide covered veranda on all sides, which provides weather protection whilst not interrupting the 360 degree views. Outside there are two 9m x 7m sheds: a garage, with automatic doors, which includes an "artist's" studio and bathroom, and a steel shed with concrete floor, insulated roof, plumbing and power nearby. Water, a very important item in The Snowys, is collected in a huge 100,000 litre storage system from all roofs, and supplemented by a shared bore measured at 4,000 litres per day. Located on Glenrowan Estate, approximately midway between Jindabyne and Berridale and only 50 kilometres from Cooma and the NSW ski resorts of Thredbo Village and Perisher Blue, and sitting at nearly 1300 metres above sea level, this home has views of the Snowy Mountains to the west and the Monaro plains to the east. All in all, a very attractive rural package which has easy access to the ski fields, Jindabyne, Berridale and Cooma, with Canberra only 160 kilometres away. The bed and breakfast licence provides options and flexibility not usually found. Contact us for further information or to arrange an inspection.

Second Home Development in Nordic Countries

Together with the associations for local authorities in Sweden, Finland and Norway, Nordregio Academy will provide the research community as well as local and central authorities with an opportunity for experience transfer and learning. The seminar will summarize current research on second home development in Nordic countries, in particular research that helps us to better understand societal driving forces, to clarify the relations between recreational home ownership, tourism and local development and to identify the main similarities and differences between the Nordic countries in these issues.

The seminar will treat four major themes:

- New lifestyles have expanded the scope and geographic scale of living and working. Increasing mobility impacts how people interweave home, work, and leisure. Do new lifestyles really bring added value to rural areas?
- Recreational commodities or natural reserves: how should open areas be viewed, and how can development preserve desired traits while exploiting them? How can countryside homes be sustainable?
- Goods and services targeting the part-time population: the economic impact of second home development and local economic restructuring. What are the possibilities and what are

the limitations? " Local development strategies: by accident or design: the characteristics of successful and less successful development strategies.

Cost of Living in Philippines, Rural Area, Rural Lifestyle

I believe, as I have said in the recent past, that the best place to find information on budget is in the archives. Of this List.I can live well in our island at about $900 to $1000 a month. We have cable, hot water, DSL, eat well and have an old car that is paid for. We owe nothing in credit cards and enjoy life here to the fullest. Originally when I got here, the peso traded 50 to a dollar. Then the rate went to 56 then down to as low as 40 to a dollar.

Prices within the local economy have also increased. Factor lower peso/dollar rations and domestic inflation and we see about 25% or so lose in the USD buying power. Yesterday I got a thousand pesos of diesel fuel for our old car. I waited as the attendant of the station raised the price one peso a litter. That is up about 9 cents a gallon by rough count. Someone with a calculator could correct me. But, the price of domestic fuel is increasing often. Poultry and pig feed are also up. Transportation costs are also up. In 2003 it cost me 4 pesos to take a tricycle or jeepney from my home to the buyan. Now that same ride costs me 10 pesos. Fuel is down from nearly 60 pesos a litter to about 33 pesos a litter on out island South of Luzon.

Tailors charge me more. Repair and replacement of a zipper was about 30 pesos a year ago. Now it is nearly 40 pesos to replace the same zipper. Shoes are about 500 to 700 pesos a pair. I plan to purchase 4 to 6 pairs before I return to Houston.

Clothing is still relatively cheap, but I see more ready made and less tailor made than when I first came her 38 years ago. Eggs in the market are 4.5 pesos each, a bit higher than in a supermarket, on sale in Texas. Milk is high and few purchase it on any regular basis. Tomatoes were 30 pesos a kilo or about 60 cents a pound. I saw roma tomatoes for 48 cents a pound in an ad that I used to teach ESL students before I left Texas. Carrots, cabbage and other fresh vegetables are cheap, but by standards here, the local populace has problems putting such fare on their tables. Beans, squash and okra are common and cheap, at least here. I bought roasted and salted peanuts yesterday, 60 pesos for 1/2 kilo. Good puluton. Labour, for a yard worker or laundry women is about p150 a day. Minimum wages are about p250 to p260 a day, but no one pays anywhere near that amt. Pork now sells at p110 live weight and about p190 dressed. Chicken is about the same. Beef, tough as hell and requiring steel teeth, is available for about p160 a kilo.

Bovine and Carabobo beef are only killed once a week in our area. Correction, we get chicken for p150 as we resell it at the store. Regular price is about 180 a kilo. Chicken in Houston is as low as 48 cents a pound, whole fryer, on sale. I ordered 3 kilos of ground pork for next Saturday. The sukie will also provide 3 liters of casings at no cost, cleaned of course, [the casings that is]. We will make sausage and then stuff the casings. I make so darn good sausage too. I expect to purchase vegetables at the flea market here on the island every week. We usually purchase charcoal for resale and because we have a car, we do not have to factor in transportation as we were going to the market after all. [Poor business logic, I know!] Overall a tank of gas is about p565. When we came here a few years ago the same tank was pressing 400 ps a tank. With the current economy, less dollars are coming into the country from abroad. Natives are encouraged to take any job possible regardless of returns on their efforts. Some are not listening and are returning to the islands of paradise and have no plans of returning to overseas employment.

I see various government projects in the works, but far less than in the past. There are a few sewers going in, but not nearly the projects that were in full swing a few years ago. Overall, we got about half a tank of LPG gas yesterday. That will last us about two weeks.

Our gas for cooking may last until we head home. We supplement with some charcoal that we purchased at the chungy market yesterday. Power is high and we spend about 4to 5 k a month. Water is about 350 pesos a month. We have a small ice business and use more than others might. The water is drinkable from the tap, but we still use filtered water for our usual consumption at our table. We spend about 200 a day on food. We could spend less but it is fiesta and we have relatives coming from the mainland and from abroad. Now lets get to the important things.

Beer is about 19 to 22 pesos a bottle, depending on the type you choose to swill down. Rum is 21 pesos for a 250 cc bottle. Pop cola is 7 pesos and coke about 10 pesos a small bottle. Ice is 2 pesos a block. We sell a lot of ice and have problems keeping up with the supply. We would add a second reifer, but then the supply would be above the need and the price may fall. We pay about $40 for health care, [USA], a month, we are giving up on vonage as the majic jack works so well for us. I am hoping to make a few faxes one way and return before doing away with vonage, but my mind is pretty well set.

Internet is about p1995 on our island, for unlimited use, DSL. We hear it is cheaper on other islands, but we have not gone out to compare prices prices on our island. We get good service and know the tech well. He is a presonal friend. We are grateful for our high quality internet, [while the power is on], and we enjoy internet at home. We could use a cafe for much less but then we would have to factor in the transportation. We own our home. We built the structure for about $7500 about 6 years ago. Prices are up about 100% since that time.

Imagining Rural Life: Schooling as a Sense of Place

In American and British education literature, "rural" designates an isolated region, often the now-fragmented remnants of a once flourishing farming community. Rural areas are characterized by low socioeconomic status (SES), disconnected from metropolitan areas and low in population density. Families have often lived in rural areas for several generations; newer families moving in are uncommon.

Research of the 1980s and 1990s tells us that members of rural communities frequently express concern for the continuation of their lifestyle, which is threatened not only by out-migration of young people to metropolitan areas, but also by declining economic opportunities and closure of local schools through consolidation.

The region discussed in this ethnographic study contradicts the above definition of rural. Rural in this case involves previously urban families migrating to homes surrounded by land undeveloped with buildings and industry other than farming. The families of this study, in contrast to other rural families, migrated to the area from more populated regions, including large cities. Some families moved to the region from across the continent. Most importantly, many of these families represent a higher SES than "old-timers" and have chosen to live in the area not because of occupations in farming, mining, timber, or other historically rural occupations, but in search of a quality of life presumed to be found in the country. My purpose is to explore how these families construct their rural identity by building a small school.

Sense of Place

Significant scholarship has emerged in the arena of place and identity. Perin's (1977) seminal work on cities and suburbs in the United States provides scholars with a means of exploring those cultural values we take for granted. In her discussion of homeowners and renters, suburban sprawl and zoning regulations, she reveals cultural values of self, identity, and social relationships through our identification with place.

Hummon (1990) builds from Perin's work to consider how place exists within cultural notions of community. Through our place of residence, Hummon argues, we form our world view and our understanding of other persons as well as ourselves. Perin and Hummon consider the typically unobserved effect of place on ourselves and our world views; they seek to bring those effects to the surface. In his widely cited work, Orr (1992) argues for all persons, scholars and lay persons alike, to develop a more active understanding of place, including an intentional involvement with a place.

Attending to place and the interrelationship between all of its parts comprises the fundamental work of living "sustainably." Orr contrasts "good inhabitance" with mere "residency." The former requires "detailed knowledge of a place and a sense of care and rootedness," whereas the latter requires only "cash and a map".

He demonstrates that some people achieve a deep connection with a place, while others merely pass through (albeit potentially for a duration of many years). Those who establish a deep connection, in Hummon's (1990) and Perin's (1977) conceptions, may define their identity through that place.

Of the authors discussed, Orr may provide the strongest statement on place as he observes a moral necessity for actively engaging in one's place. Place, particularly a rural place, becomes more than an opportunity for learning-it is the central cohesion point of a life interconnected with other beings. He raises the philosophical question of what constitutes an ethical life. If a person has the financial resources to purchase a home and property, and that person chooses to have nothing to do with their neighbours (or the land itself), is that person merely fulfilling their right in the American dream? Or is that person living unethically? Orr makes his opinion abundantly clear: to live alone is a fiction. Our lives are inextricably interconnected, and to imagine otherwise demonstrates a lack of awareness of the wholeness of our world. Orr's philosophical and ethical concerns for place provide a potent backdrop for the people and region in the current study. To attune to wholeness and connectedness means, necessarily, to move beyond culturally prescient individualism in which parents make educational decisions only for the benefit of their own children, rather than for the benefit of all. Orr and other authors do not ignore the contested nature of place as people construct different meanings of place and themselves in it. According to Lutz and Merz (992), "different individuals in the same geographic place may have different views of or sense of community".

Lutz and Merz go on to ask whether "without rural schools can there be rural community?". Certainly the studies exploring the effects of school closure suggest the answer is negative. While these and other studies explore the impact of school closure (primarily as a result of consolidation), the current study considers the impact of a school opening. I explore whether the introduction of a school might have both constructed a new rural community as well as disrupted the existing rural community.

In the process, I consider the nature of our modern communities. In this postmodern society, our communities are made up largely of replaced persons who come from different backgrounds and experiences. They replace themselves in new locations where they feel they can live a particular desired lifestyle and seek connection there. In the process, what they share within their group—sameness-gets privileged over their differences. Between the group and outsiders, however, differences enable group members to put up walls to keep out those who hold different cultural values and practices.

Those walls limit possibilities for growth and change, but the walls do not resolutely hold. Supposed differences are illusory and often permeable. A "sense of community" emerges, therefore, not out of what a group of people share in common, but out of the common enemy, outsider, or other. It is a reactive sameness, rather than a shared constructive experience. My particular concern is with the cultural construction of rural community that has been deemed in jeopardy.

Reborn Rural Community

The American ideology of small towns and rural regions perceives these places to be simpler worlds that are slower paced, less prone to change, and more "direct, personal, and comprehensible" than urban locales). That ideology also includes images of rural decline such as the dust-bowl devastation of the 1930s, family farm foreclosures, and the gradual encroachment of suburbia onto former farmland.

All of these images suggest that rural places are not as up-to-date either technologically or culturally as urban centres. In addition, much rural literature suggests that small towns and rural centres are in danger of disappearing. The context of fear elicits an impulse for conservation rather than change, which accords with American cultural assumptions of rural regions as conservative and urban regions as progressive. A different construct emerges as some rural regions have begun to comprise an alternate ideology. From this perspective, such regions may be places of new possibility.

In reaction to perceived dangers, stresses, and the frenetic lifestyle of city life, middle and upper-middle class Americans have begun to look to small towns and rural regions. Exasperated with their city lives, these people have begun a reverse migration back to the land. With the influx of new money and energy, rural regions undergo a renaissance that is fuelled by families who believe and want to enact the "nostalgic and romantic image of rural living". While that image may be mythical for more traditionally rural families, its salience is evident in the migrations occurring today.

Significantly, not all rural regions share salient demographic, economic, and cultural features. To differentiate these regions, Gjelten (1982) proposes a typology of rural school settings that includes the concept of a "reborn" rural region. I "Disgruntled city dwellers" flock to a reborn rural region, bringing with them urban values.

These regions "are mostly in the scenic and tranquil rural spots, where there is much to attract a refugee population from the city". Urbanites admire the lower property values, lower crime rates, larger open spaces, and cleaner environment found in such rural areas. In addition, they expect to find a slower pace, less material lifestyle, and more personal interactions than they experience in cities.

Urbanites Grasp Nostalgically for a Putatively Lost Way of Life

Today's urbanites are missing something. We don't have the sense of community and perma-'The other rural regions Gjelten (1982) defines are stable rural, depressed rural, high growth rural, and isolated ruralnence our ancestors had. Qualities once taken for granted-trust and honesty, regional and ethnic heritage, clean air and friendly neighbours-are special treasures. As the news highlights the emerging global economy, many of us simply hunger for a supportive local network. We need to feel *connected.* When these urbanites move to the "outland", they bring with them economic resource-to purchase, for example, an ailing farmhouse and restore it. In the process of restoration, they infuse capital into the local economy through purchasing of the home, hiring carpenters, and other crafts people, and making purchases in hardware stores and other local shops. "The newcomers have money, and are using it to transform the rural town into a new suburb-better schools, paved roads, rising real estate values and property taxes to match". In a region of otherwise declining farm values or the loss of other industries such as mining, these urbanites may help keep local businesses alive.

These Transplants May also Take Advantage of Business Opportunities

The new people moving in (to the reborn rural community) have probably *chosen* the community and therefore are likely to bring with them a positive attitude and a level of enthusiasm that may easily overshadow the spirit of the long time residents. If this energy can be harnessed to work for the betterment of the school, and it often can be, amazing improvements can happen. Many of the newcomers have talents and skills that can be put to good use in the school, whether the people work as paid teachers or as unpaid volunteers. The newcomers bring new cultural values along with their money. Urban Americans prefer moving to a small town or rural region that is nevertheless close to an urban area where they can take advantage of a city's resources when they choose. Transplanted urban values include geographic mobility (the ability and the expectation of relocating one's residence), diverse financial resources (investments as well as occupations), culinary tastes, and expectations of privacy. Prospective migrants are cautioned to be aware of local values and to adjust themselves to local ways by working with established cultural norms, not against them. While urbanities may adapt their values to more closely fit the local customs, in the process they also change those customs, a point that will be developed more fully below.

Gjeiten (1982), however, suggests that urban transplants may hold a romanticized and nostalgic view of rural life which they then perpetuate. Nostalgia involves a "symbolic management of the present" that simplifies and ennobles particular practices and values while withholding others. In the region of this study, newcomers started school-based "traditions" which they felt expressed their conceptions of rural life. "Most bring their city ways with them, but they are also enchanted by the country, and as converts to the rural lifestyle, they are among the most zealous defenders of many traditional rural customs and institutions". Local parades, tree-lighting ceremonies, and crafts-making are only a few of the "rural traditions" practicedby relocated urbanities. Such practices suggest a culturally conservative and paternalistic attitude of newcomers towards the rural way of life. Newcomers institute their versions of rural traditions, rather than adapt to customs already established.

The changes brought by disgruntled urbanities are not necessarily positive. New landowners may disrupt generations-old hunting traditions when they post "no hunting" and "no trespassing" signs. Urbanities likely bring different religious traditions that clash with existing practices. Economic disruption can also result as urbanities purchase homes and land for premium prices and commence upgrades. When property values rise, "the next generation of natives can't afford to live in their hometowns". Newcomers are likely to sell their rural homes and move again, whereas rural families may remain on the same farm for generations.

For those who remain, property taxes rise with property values. "Urban" values can create problems in traditional rural communities. In some reborn rural communities, there may develop a schism between the natives and the newcomers. There may even be two separate communities, each with its own set of values and ideas. As conflict develops between the groups, communication may diminish, and people may associate only with each other. In his discussion of 15 "small places" around the United States, Rawls (1990) compares small town newcomers with weeds that, like dandelions, "tend to take over". Despite advice to adjust to local ways, "the intention today appears to be to improve small places rather than adapt to them". What constitutes improvement or imposition may well differ according to one's cultural perspective.

According to Perin (1977), newcomers prompt "status renegotiation" as their arrival affects the social position of old-timer residents. She observed how such renegotiation is carried out in zoning hearings and homeowners' associations.

Perin's study focused on urban movement to then-newly suburban environs in which the newcomers' arrival signified their own increased status. From the perspective of the "old-time" suburban dwellers, their status is threatened by newcomers. Similar renegotiation may occur in reborn rural regions. Established status hierarchies based on relationships, history, and age may be disrupted by income, profession, and education.

Participant Observation in Oakleaf 2 My study in Oakleaf was conducted over 11/2 years as part of a study of the local school. During that time, I volunteered at the school 4 days a week, substitute taught, and visited school members in their homes and other sites in the region. I attended and participated in as many school and community events as possible, such as a Thanksgiving pageant, camp-out, and roadside cleanup day. Much of the data were collected in 21 semi-directed interviews with local residents, excerpts of which appear below. Interviews were conducted at the individual's home, workplace, or at the school, according to the interviewee's preference. Interviews lasted from 45 minutes to 21/ 2 hours. I used a prepared list of questions to prompt the interview, but followed each person's lead as they recounted stories and shared artifacts.

Oakleaf Country School Oakleaf is located in the Piedmont region of the southeastern United States. Oakleaf refers to a crossroads area marked by an elementary school, a post office, a grocery, and a doctor's office. It is located about 15 miles from Springfield, a university town of about 45,000 residents.

The Oakleaf area lies in a particularly picturesque part of the county, which covers about 750 square miles and about 75,000 residents. The school is situated on two and a half acres of gently sloping hillside donated by a local wealthy landowner.

Oakleaf Country School is a nondenominational independent school founded in 1984 by parents. At the time of the study, 55 students attended kindergarten through fifth grade, in addition to approximately 20 preschool students who attended on either a 2-or 3-day schedule. The school first occupied one room and building; it has been expanded as the enrolment has grown to the present four classrooms, library, director's office, kitchen, reception area, and two sets of bathrooms.

Depending on enrolment, the school employs four fulltime teachers as well as one half-time preschool assistant, and part-time art, physical education, music, and language teachers. The paid administration consists of a full-time director, an office and financial manager, and an administrative assistant. Parents and community members make up the nine-member volunteer Board of Trustees.

The curriculum has been constructed by the teachers and parents over the years and may be characterized by a lack of textbooks and a proliferation of projects. Although the school day is scheduled according to subjects, the project-based curriculum often involves the integration of subject matter. Further, teachers frequently bring their multigrade classes together for joint projects. The overall mood is relaxed, but focused. Teachers and students frequently call class meetings to discuss issues of discipline, social interactions, or other misunderstandings.

They express the belief that time spent discussing and negotiating noncurricular concerns promotes a more positive and trusting environment for everyone. Instead of report cards, teachers write lengthy evaluations on individual students as well as the class as a whole. The concern is to evaluate each student's individual progress rather than to rank the class or the school. While the location of their homes contributes to Oakleafers' rural self-conception, the school provides a symbolic and experiential centre of the newcomer rural community.

The parents' motivation for founding the school rested on three concerns. First, public school redistricting announced in the 1983-1984 academic year required their elementary age children, including kindergartners, to ride the bus 45-60 minutes (one way) to school; the parents felt this distance too great for young children. Second, parents preferred their children to attend a smaller school than the new elementary school formed by redistricting. Third, parents wanted to playa greater role in their children's education than they believed was possible in the local public schools. They described feeling pushed out of the process of educational decision making because they were not education experts.

For example, parents felt that the school board dismissed their desire to keep a small school because they could not prove that small schools were better.'

The physical setting of the school, school rituals, the school curriculum, and other school activities contribute to the rural construction of the school place. Newcomer families, whether they live in the nearby town, in a renovated farmhouse, or a subdivision, connect to a rural identity through the school. One family that lives in town their rural environment: You sense that different and unique.

The first time you set foot on the grounds you're looking at these log buildings that have been assembled. The whole atmosphere is a country school. And then you sort of associate the values of a country school as being solid and having a little more relaxed feeling about learning-relaxed in that it's not as dictated. I mean, those were all of the associations I had of a country school: being more connected to your place, your environment, and just the awareness of the trees, the fields and the views to the mountains.

Just that whole sweep of view. You want to believe that it will have some influence on the kids when they're out playing on the playground, they're hearing the cows. It's all that sort of pastoral, romantic notion of things. Set in that pastoral landscape, the country school focuses many family events throughout the year. Although no longer a parent-run school, parents continue to be closely involved with day-to-day events of the school.

Through parents' involvement, the school is not only a place for children, but also houses the activities and needs of adults as they work together. Some of the effect of the school emerges as a gestalt. Asked about the affective qualities of the school one parent commented, When you drive by and you see the little Fourth of July parades, or other things. It kind of adds to that. You think, "Oh, that's really nice." "Nice" because of opportunities for children and adults to socialize. In a statement reminiscent of distant prairie homes, one parent stated that her children rely on the school for social activities:

> *It's neat for the kids in this community to have a school that's here, because they are country kids and so it's hard to have playmates and things like that. They don't all have neighbours. So this is kind of their neighbourhood and I think that's really important for them.*

By overemphasizing the distances between homes, this parent justifies the role of the school as a "neighbourhood" locus. She reinforces the rural quality by *not* mentioning daily car trips between houses, after school soccer clubs and dance lessons, frequent sleep-overs, as well as activities in town that provide children opportunities to play together. According to residents, Oakleaf Country School provides a rural sense of place through its "character." The two original school rooms are log buildings, the driveway remains unpaved, and the playground is mostly open field. I think I ended up being comfortable with Oakleaf initially from just the atmosphere of the place. The whole character of the place. The scale, the log buildings, the big oak trees in the playground, the views all around, it was just wonderful that you could see all around at the views from the windows. We being architects, and being very tuned into how the setting is and how it affects you, I think that was probably what initially caught my attention first, was the whole atmosphere of the place. The scale of it.

Schools members reveal great pride in the log buildings, which visually distinguish the school from others in the area. In fall of 1998, school members decided the students should have a playhouse on the playground and tapped in to the nostalgic sentiment in their announcement to parents and friends: "15 years ago, parents themselves built a log schoolhouse. Come back to [Oakleaf] with tools (or not!) and help us 'bam-raise' a genuine old log playhouse for new fun on the playground". In the earliest years of the school, parents supplied most of the labour to build the school. This invitation to barn-raise reminds school members of that fact.

While few families in the region ever participate in actual bam-raisings today, these families know the phrase and its connection to rural and older ways. Yet they do not wish to simply return to the past, as the "genuine old playhouse" will be used for "new fun."

Supported by the physical setting of the school, Oakleaf's rurality emerges in school rituals, curricula, and activities. At the fifth graders' graduation and other annual events, students sing the first two stanzas of the Shaker traditional song "Simple Gifts:"

'Tis the gift to be simple, 'tis the gift to be free 'Tis the gift to come down where we ought to be And when we find ourselves in the place just right 'Twill be in the valley of love and delight.

* When true simplicity is gained.
* To bow and to bend we shan't be ashamed.
* To tum, tum will be our delight.
* Til by turning, turning we come 'round right.

The song contrasts markedly with the substantial materialism of students' families. Whether they live in reno vated farmhouses or newly built homes, they enjoy wellequipped kitchens, computers, fancy cars, and landscaped gardens. The school provides a refuge of simplicity as many material and popular culture items are not allowed in the school. Teachers (and parents) do not allow students to bring fashionable toys and clothing, particularly logo-ed items, to school. For these replaced families, the enforced simplicity of the school symbolizes the imagined rural life as simple and uncomplicated.

The edict lies strongest against any forms of weapons including play guns and images of guns. One young boy in his first week at school drew a picture of a rifle, an image that is forbidden. His teacher allowed the image, however, not only because he was new and still learning the rules, but also because the drawing was of a hunting rifle and illustrated the boy's story about a hunting trip with his uncle.

Hunting, while not condoned, is tolerated reluctantly because of its prevalence in local rural culture. Founding and later families expressed some desire to tap into that culture: "We were coming to have our children just be a part of it and relish being a part of the community, to learn that this is their roots." "Their roots" does not refer to their particular family histories, but to a nostalgic remembrance of past generations' lives.

Other "rural activities" at the school include day hikes and overnight backpacking trips in the nearby mountains.. Students keep a small vegetable garden on the school grounds. Once a year, students, teachers, and parents spend a day of fishing, painting, and crafts before camping out at a local 4H camp. The school hosts a May Day celebration in which students dance around a may pole festooned with flowers and garlands. These and other events link students to the local place through an emphasis on the outdoor environment and, at times, the daily life of the community. While the school serves as the locus of newcomers' rural lives, that school is situated in a larger landscape. A few families moved to Oakleaf specifically because of the school's reputation, but most school families moved to the area before choosing the small school. Replaced urbanities name many reasons why they move to the Oakleaf region, including privacy, safety, a slower lifestyle, the physical setting, a "positive place" in which to raise children, and, in general, a desire to live in the country.

They seek an improved quality of life that represents a retreat and a contrast from urban life. As one couple said, "We wanted to live in the country after living in the city for so long." A move to Oakleaf is a move to a better quality of life, according to these parents. They purchase larger homes and more property than they could afford in most cities. Notably, these newcomers have "picked" Oakleaf and its neighbouring town Springfield. They have the financial means to choose a particular location and a lifestyle of retreat.

The region these families chose is one of the more affluent in the county. While the median value of a singlefamily home in the county is $111,200, within the Oakleaf census block the average house value is $229,300 (1990 Census). Throughout the county, but especially in Oakleaf, local residents, newcomers as well as old-timers, report a significant rise in home values during the past 10 years. They "read" the economic status not only in their tax bills, but also in material goods. Residents observe a rise in family incomes evidenced by the higher quality of vehicles parked in the school lot. One parent commented that "there are more BMWs now."

Although many Oakleafers purchase homes in subdivisions, they consider their lifestyle to be rural, not suburban. House designs mimic subdivision homes built around Washington, DC and San Francisco suburbs to the extent that the same developer may have built the homes. Home lots, however, are larger than typical subdivisions surrounding cities. In addition, Oakleaf subdivisions lie adjacent to farms and estates, not on the edges of cities. In their more remote locations, former urbanities enjoy a degree of privacy hitherto unknown, while benefiting from positive interpersonal relations with neighbours.

My husband wanted to be somewhere he could run up a power saw at midnight and no neighbours would complain. And I wanted to be someplace the kids could walk to neighbours' houses. And there would be people wanting them to be visiting. (A parent) Many newcomers share this parent's desire to be a part of a community, which she expresses as a place that provides both privacy and cooperation. Privacy results not from a lack of interaction with others, but in a quantity of physical space separating one home from the next.

In sharp contrast to the close proximity of urban neighbours, the low population density in Oakleaf ensures a buffer between houses. Yet the distances are not so great that a child could not walk to a neighbor's home to play. Significantly, this parent notes that her children would be welcome as "there would be people wanting them to be visiting," a further allusive contrast to an impersonal city in which neighbours may not know others on their block, or in their apartment building.

These relocated urbanities express the desire to "get away" and "escape," yet they are not seeking lives of solitude. They seek a community of active engagement with others, and report that they have found it in the rural lifestyle of Oakleaf. Newcomers seek to escape the city without giving up all city conveniences. Oakleaf's particular location suitsthese families well. Although a family may live on 20 acres that backs up against a wilderness area, they are only 20 minutes from Springfield. Cultural events such as restaurants and the arts, as well as professional opportunities, are readily available in Springfield. Many families also work in town, enjoying an easy commute along two-lane country roads. Oakleaf seems to offer the best of both worlds, as one newcomer couple explains:

> *Although the school's role as the locus of rural culture imagines rural life as simple and romantic, this representation satisfies transplanted urbanities. Oakleaf newcomers embrace the school as an idealized rural setting in which everyone works together to construct buildings and enact rituals according to the seasons. Yet this nostalgic rural image does not speak to the lived experiences of rural oldtimers who have experienced crop failure, mining accidents, and loss of farm land in this and other rural regions. As newcomers construct their imagined rural lives, they displace the rural lives of old-timers. An Oakleaf parent who married into an old-timer family describes the older way of life through vignettes: 'Who walk into the store and don't expect you to drop everything and wait on them immediately, or come out to the gas pump when you're in the middle of waiting on five people. These folks have the respect to know they have to wait their tum, that it's all going to be there in the end.*

There's an influx of middle class, upper middle class people that build $400,000 houses and have two cars. Twenty years ago Oakleaf was a town where lower middle class and probably 40% or 50% of the people at that time, their parents were born here. And 30% of the people still farmed on a part-time basis. You know, raised cows or had a huge garden or even a field that they cultivated. So that's been lost.

Old-timers in Oakleaf shop at the local grocery and deer check station that is stocked with bare necessities, defined by one old-timer as beer, ammunition, baby diapers, and feed for cows. The dark, overstocked store contrasts with the well-lit, clean school next door. These two buildings represent the two communities which live intertwined.

The school is the centre of the newcomer rural life, and the store is the centre of the old-timer rural life. While some newcomers may stop by the store, they are not wholly welcome as they don't "take their time" and "wait their turn." Likewise, some old-timers may send their children to the country school (about 5% of the annual enrolment), but usually withdraw them at the end of preschool in favor of the bus trip to the public and free kindergarten.

While the buildings symbolize the community rift, economics appears to be the underlying cause of the strain. With the influx of newcomers, a higher economic standard of living has been introduced. At one time, many locals were employed in farming. Today, newcomer residents enjoy business, law, and other professions. They do not work their land, but work in an office.

Newcomers recognize the economic shift: Some old-timers may have been considered well-off financially, but they were not considered different from "regular folk." As one Oakleaf parent who married into an old-timer family recounts, old-timers who were well-off financially were also integrated into community life: "grandfather owned a big farm. He was the affluent member of the community. A 300 acre farm. He was just a regular guy 'How many groundhogs did you shoot this year?'"

Attracted to the area, the number of newcomers has risen each year, causing property values to rise. Significantly, newcomers benefit in this environment. In comparison to the metropolitan area we came from, and grew up in, this is heaven. Plus we have the advantages here of having, because of the university, cultural things and-Good medical facilities-perfect advantages because of the great outdoors, and, you know, the city is not too far.

Oakleaf newcomers usually buy small farms or homes situated on several acres of land. Some families buy old farm houses that they refurbish; others purchase newly built homes, often custom-designed. While they may keep a few cows or horses, or pasture the land to qualify as a farm for tax purposes, no newcomer family considers itself a farming family. Tending a garden or keeping a horse are pasttimes, not careers, as primarily white-collar professional occupations provide their primary income. In Oakleaf, newcomers continue their professional occupations such as health care providers, architects, university professors, investment bankers, designers, and engineers. However, while Oakleaf newcomers do not consider themselves farmers, they did move to the area to live what they consider to be rural lives.

It sounds pretty crass, but one thing that I like about the school being here is it does put a very good light on this community, and my property value just zooms right on up there. I mean, we bought the piece of land we have for $30,000-25 acresand the bank tells us that with our $75,000 house on it that it's now worth close to $300,000. Well, I think that this school is one of the factors that makes the property values go up.

This newcomer parent enjoys the rising property values because she, like other newcomers, expects to sell her property and move in several years. At that time she will enjoy a strong return on her property investment. Old-timers who have lived in the region for generations do not expect to move on. Rising property values for them signify increased property taxes. The same parent observes that, "a lot of the old-timers don't like that because their property values are also going up and they haven't done anything.

It's not their fault that all these old hippies and nouveau riche or whatever are moving out here. If you're just standing there, then your taxes are going up." Because of rising property values, younger generations of old-timers can no longer buy land. "Foothill county is no longer the place to go if you want to homestead." Higher land prices are less of an issue for newcomer families who typically arrive in the area after establishing a successful career and a healthy bank account elsewhere.

Throughout these economic changes, the culture has shifted as well. "I'd say it's kind of a rural area but it's changed, is slowly changing into a semi-rural, gentrified suburb." A suburb, with its closer connections to city than country implies busyness and hurriedness, qualities which are not valued among the rural old-timers. Furthermore, suburbs imply shopping malls and national chains of stores, rather than locally-owned businesses such as Jaeger's Store.

While the school founders were still planning the building, some locals expressed concern that the school would trigger a process of gentrification and development, and that a "McDonald's" was sure to follow. One parent remembered those early days: [There was a zoning hearing] to allow a school on this property, which had just been a cow pasture. And there was opposition. Some of the neighbours complained that traffic would be increasing in the area, that it would change the rural area, or the rural character of the community that allows the school, and a lot of other things would come in.

The rural lifestyle may become "lost." [A parent] wrote to a Bob Dylan tune, some funny song about how people are moving, you know people are moving and it's changing. I think [Oakleaf is] becoming a much more affluent area than it was when the school started. Newcomers' greater economic power puts old-timers at a disadvantage. The strongest objections raised to newcomers may echo the sentiments of a colonized people.

My husband and his family moved into a Black neighbourhood on a road where there was no traffic. They used to sit on the porch and watch the seldom-seen cars go by. Now it's a highway and their Black neighbours are clearly in the minority. Or at least, the farmers are in the minority. There is, it's not an animosity, but there is a feeling among the natives of this area that they have been put on a reservation.

Disrupting and Excluding Rural Ways Oakleaf newcomers construct their rural identity through the local independent school. The school place symbolizes those rural qualities desired by newcomers: beautiful and peaceful open land, hand-constructed buildings, and land-focused rituals such as May Poles. Yet rurality is romanticized and nostalgic, in which families enjoy open pasture but few rise before dawn to milk a cow. The imagined rurality is not wholly naive as newcomers are fully aware that their reborn rural region has many elements of suburban or even urban life.

It really has a suburban flavor in that a lot of the people, most of the people that live out here do not make their living off the land. And that's the difference. There are a lot of big farms but principally the owners do something else. So that feels different to me than the rural which I really grew up in. We had a dairy farm and we worked the land, and so I felt like that was rural. But again, here, since most of the people that live here don't use the land to earn a living, it doesn't feel rural, like I'm used to. The kids get very upset when somebody says they live on a farm.

Despite the apparent disjunction between newcomers and old-timers, newcomers assert their construction of a rural identity is in solidarity with old-timers. While newcomers could have brought in shopping malls, modem construction, and other indicators of nonrural life, they chose to adapt their lifestyle to be more in accordance with existing rural values. They contrast their adopted lifestyle against the long-established rural gentry who send their childrento elite private day and boarding schools. However, the reborn rural community presumes the perspective of the newcomer and implies that changes are good. Progress and growth become the normative assumptions of rural place.

What happens to those residents who are not part of the new community? Old timers are not a part of redefining the rural region; they are excluded from the process. While each year two or three old-timer families send their children to the school, they assert that they are not part of the school community. Their exclusion is partly by their own choice, partly because they don't feel as welcome, and partly as they don't have the income to support private school tuition. These families usually leave Oakleaf Country School at the end of preschool. In several ways, oldtimers' lifestyles have been disrupted and they lack the economic and political ability to assert themselves. Their way of life is changing without their input or consent.

The people where I live put up "no hunting" signs. My road was prime hunting grounds for the old people who were hunters. The whole hunting shelter area is shot [because of no-hunting signs]... I think there were more deer killed on our road last year by cars than by hunters. So the older families either are finding that they cannot build here because it's so expensive, or they cannot hunt where they used to hunt, or something. Some way that they had is being disturbed.

Conclusion

Throughout the newcomers' construction of a rural way of life, they develop a community which, by its nature, excludes old-timers. In education literature, as well as everyday discourse, community typically refers to culturally prevalent notions of positivism and simplicity: "In ordinary speech for most people in the United States, the term *community* refers to the people with whom I identify in a locale a community is a group that shares a specific heritage, a common self-identification, a common culture and set of norms".

However, Young also provides us with the necessary counterpart to a group banding together. She continues: In the United States today, identification as a member of such a community also often occurs as an oppositional differentiation from other groups, who are feared or at best devalued. Persons identify only with some other persons, feel in community only with those, and fear the difference others confront them with because they identify with a different culture, history, and point of view on the world. Oakleaf newcomers gain *within* their own group through the construction of a rural community. At the same time, their actions negatively impact old-timers who are, by definition, excluded.

Aware of this exclusion, the Oakleaf Country School and its newcomer families have been and continue to be concerned to establish links with the old-timer community.

Their efforts are emblematic of wanting to dispel their own outsider status and provide value, not merely hegemony. The results of their efforts have been mixed. "I think that most of the community has accepted the school. I wouldn't say that the older faction of this community has embraced it. But accepted it." A sigh of fatigue and powerlessness may be heard in the old-timers' acceptance of a new rural identity of which they are not a part. The effect of Oakleaf Country School on the old-timer community may resemble efforts to construct charter schools in both rural and urban areas. Our nation's history has been one of internal migration, as well as immigration, and we are therefore familiar with cultural clashes between those who came before and those who have just arrived.

These communities change as economic bases shift and bring in new populations. While much of rural school literature has explored the effects of school consolidation and closure, the impact of a new school opening does not appear to have garnered much study. Such an omission is understandable given the lengthy and extensive history of communities losing their local schools. However, given the conjunction of a back to the land movement, charter school legislation, and an economy that increasingly allows whitecollar professionals to work in rural areas rather than urban areas, the cultural tension between newcomers and old-timers is unlikely to go away and may instead increase.

Rural identity may be increasingly constructed in local schools, as Oakleaf newcomers built their own elementary school to symbolize and centralize their cultural notions of community. Rural school researchers, like their urban counterparts, need to attend to the cultural shifts and tensions which frequently accompany population changes. Who will control these new schools? In the case of rural schools (and, thereby, rural identity), they may be taken over by newcomers with more financial resources than those folks who have lived in the regions for generations.

In the meantime, newcomer rural identity in Oakleaf is not about conservation, but about expansion. It concerns a selective retreat from urban bustle to a nostalgic and romanticized lifestyle. The newcomers' rural lifestyle appropriates rituals and visual trappings of rural life, without the less savory (in their eyes) aspects such as shooting groundhogs, chopping firewood, or milking a cow. In their designer homes, these newcomers look out on the rural landscape and simply enjoy the view.

Advantages of Rural Life

When considering living in a rural community there are several things that come to mind. You must understand that jobs are limited so it is best if you are lucky enough to have a job that doesn't require you be in the office everyday. Being a consultant is business that requires travel is good. You are on the road most of the time going from client to client, as a rule of thumb.

With the internet playing a large part in today's business world it is more feasible to live in a rural community. Most of your work can be done online; however, from time to time you will have to make an appearance in the home office. There are also more jobs becoming available online that do not require travel. The biggest set back of these type of jobs is you must be disciplined and a self starter.

More companies are hiring data entry persons that can work exclusively from home online. The medical field is more open to outsourcing their billing so that is a real possibility. Once you understand that living in a rural area you will have to find a job that allows you to do most, if not all, of your work from home.

The advantages of rural life can be wonderful. In a small town most everybody knows everybody and believe me that has some tremendous advantages. The schools tend not to be overcrowded so your children get more one on one help due to smaller classes. There is a lot to be said for smaller classrooms. I speak from personal experience. My three children have all gone to a small school all their lives and I must say it has helped them excel. My oldest graduated second in her class last year and received enough scholarships to pay for her school totally, with five dollars left over. My second oldest is a senior this year and he will graduate first in his class and he is being recruited by some of the best schools in the country, not just a couple of them, many top schools are trying their best to get him to go to their school.

My family likes very much the small town life. We have good friends here and it is a tight community. One advantage is if you forget to lock your doors at night you probably won't have a problem with someone breaking into your home. We tend to watch out for each other. I am not saying this is Mayberry by any means, but it is peaceful and we do not have to deal with traffic and pollution.

It is not all roses by any means. For example, the grocery store is 35 miles away so you learn to make a list, and with gas prices what they are, you try your best to limit those trips to town. We have very few fast food restaurants around close by, which I consider a blessing, home cooking is always better.

The Green Party believes that the pressure for one-off rural housing has become more acute during the last decade because of the rapid escalation in house prices. In Government, with the introduction of our new housing policies, we anticipate that this pressure will gradually abate as housing becomes affordable again.

We believe that the best way to maintain and increase population numbers in rural areas ? based on the evidence of the recent census results-is to support villages, as villages have held their population better than scattered communities in the open countryside. Areas of population loss as indicated by CLAR maps match areas with poor or nonexistent village and town structure.

This lack of village structure, which could have been the focus for new service jobs or small industries, is the main reason these areas suffered more population loss than others. Therefore, we believe that the best way to address population loss in weak areas is to create new villages or village clusters and to actively prevent further dispersal of settlement.

We believe that whatever perceptions exist concerning the lower quality of life in villages and towns as compared to the countryside, is not because of their ?alien? form or higher density, but because of their growing association with decline, disadvantage and poverty. Not long ago, villages were highly valued as centres of trade and enterprise and recognised as important contributors to Irish nation building. Since the 1980s, as the percentage of social housing relative to private being built grew higher in villages and towns than the average for the county, so negative perception grew. This perception has led to the low take-up of both local authority housing and affordable services sites in many villages.

In Government the Green Party will do the following:

- We will support rural housing being concentrated in clusters around existing village settlements so as to ensure sustainability. We will ensure that shops, schools and other services will be located within walking distance of everybody so that we can cut down on car usage.
- In order to encourage sustainable development in rural areas we will encourage local authorities to buy or to Compulsorily

Purchase land-banks around villages and to provide serviced sites at cost to residents of the area and to people who wish to work in the area.

- As stated elsewhere in our policy we will discourage the building of holiday homes in rural areas by the introduction of an Annual Site Value Tax on second homes.
- We will support the preparation of village framework designs or Strategic Development Zones draft planning schemes for small rural villages. The Green Party believes that many small rural villages are a very low priority for Area Development Plans because of their small size, their very specific needs and the necessity to plan larger settlements under greater development pressure. But, if small villages are to play their allotted role in the National Spatial Strategy (NSS) to provide housing with rural quality of life for locals and non-locals, action cannot wait until other priorities are met.

Most small villages in Ireland comprise one main street or a set of crossroads. With the rise in private car use, many of these approach roads are now major traffic routes and are unattractive or even dangerous roads on which to site further houses. The other development pattern seen in villages is the suburban cul-de-sac estate in a single field, unrelated and disconnected from the existing village. We believe that it is vital if we wish to provide an alternative to scattered housing in these areas, that existing small settlements, however modest, expand to provide pedestrian accessible, high quality and affordable houses while retaining and improving their distinctive rural character.

We support three-dimensional, costed Framework Designs for modestly-sized development schemes being prepared and submitted for Outline Planning Permission in the normal way. This might require an agreement to amend or vary the County Development Plan if the villages have no prior designation for development. The Framework Design should have a simple and limited brief that does not require elaborate statistical information or research-that is to lay out new access roads, public spaces and sites for services, buildings and utilities.

Alternatively, Part IX of the 2000 Act for Strategic Development Zones should be used specifying the economic, social and environmental importance of the development of small villages for rural housing provision. In that case, the Framework Design would correspond to the Draft Planning Scheme outlined in Section 168 and would be processed under the relevant sections.

More rigour would be called for in the development of the Framework Design (or Draft Planning Schemes as they would become) under these circumstances as appeals to an Bord Pleanala are precluded under Part IX. Funding for the preparation of Framework Design or Draft Planning Schemes can be recouped under the development levy system. The local authority need not carry out or commission the Framework Design directly. A number of agents are capable of this task including the local Leader or Partnership Company, a good local development association or a Community Land Trust. Planning and Engineering advice should be provided by the local authority, and it should monitor the entire process closely to ensure statutory and local development requirements are met.

We will promote a number of new sustainable settlement pilot projects in areas of weak settlement structure. We will provide a revolving development fund for this purpose, available to a range of potential development agencies including local authorities, Partnership and Leader Companies, Housing Associations or other not-for-profit Companies such as Community Land Trusts.

An example of a sustainable and innovative new model of village renewal is the 'Farm Village' model developed by Sustainable Communities Ireland and currently being developed at Cloughjordan village in Co Tipperary and also similar initiatives by Blackwater Resource Agency in North Cork, a Leader Company and Freshford 20/20, a partnership of local orgnaisation and Kilkenny Co. Co. This model includes the provision of on-site sewerage and water treatment infrastructure, on-site generation of renewable energy to provide at least 50% of the energy needs of community facilities, employment and enterprise units, community transport vehicles, community gardens and open spaces.

This approach will see the model 'farm village' being integrated with the existing village as part of a carefully planned extension that will reinvigorate the entire area. We are completely opposed to the current trend of developing large, sprawling, surburban-style estates on the outskirts of rural villages which often do not have the level of services or infrastructure to cope with a significant increase in population.

We believe that Ireland is at a critical period of development at present and that if the wrong policies on rural housing are adopted now, major problems will arise in the future. It has been claimed that scattered rural housing is part of our heritage and should be facilitated, not restricted. Before the famine, in 1841, census figures show that about 90% of the population lived in rural areas.

However, the first ordnance survey map dating from the time, shows people did not live in scattered single rural houses but in 'farm villages' or clachans, consisting of clusters of 15-20 houses with open countryside around them. After the famine, the Congested Districts Board, and its successor, the Land Commission, moved people out of these villages into single houses as it was felt disease spread more quickly in crowded conditions. The splitting up of the big estates under the land acts continued this pattern of scattered housing.

Irish society has changed considerably since then. We are now an industrial nation with tourism a major employer, and farming is no longer the mainstay of the local economy. We believe that any settlement strategy for the 21st century must take into account the fact that modern living requires external services including piped water, electricity, and telephones. As these services are normally provided next to the public road, that is where the majority of new one-off rural houses are sited.

The result is ribbon development along rural roads, especially those leading out of towns. People also want to live where they can have a good quality of life and ready access to work, shops, schools and other services. Rural houses are in demand to a large extent because of the lower site prices but this does not take into account the higher long-term costs of commuting to work, schools etc. usually requiring a second family car. There are other costs that are not so obvious. An Foras Forbartha, in a study carried out in the mid 1970?s showed that it is more expensive to provide services to rural houses but the extra cost is often borne by the community, not by the individual.

In relation to the issue of one-off houses in the countryside, we wish to see the current social imbalance of housing development in villages versus the countryside being addressed.

In Government the Green Party will:

- Ensure the provision of affordable rural housing that is rural-generated as opposed to urban-generated. Urban-generated rural housing is housing that is built in rural areas for people who are working in towns or cities many miles away. This kind of development tries to get around the unaffordable cost of housing in urban areas but pushes the price of rural housing up for everybody. In contrast, rural-generated development meets the real development needs of rural areas.
- Promote rural planning policies that give preference to those who make an economic contribution to the rural community in which they wish to live, and who will participate in, and contribute to, the life of the local community. We will actively encourage a range of alternative rural enterprise through the planning process including organic agriculture, renewable energy projects, cottage industries, local specialty food production etc. We support the right of individuals who wish to establish new rural-based enterprises or businesses to be treated favourably within the planning process, subject to sustainability criteria.
- We will ensure the inclusion of a category of individual entitlement to planning permission in the open countryside based on functional or social need within sections of County Development Plans dealing with settlement strategy in rural areas. Functional need will relate to where proposed householders need to live in a rural area because their work requires proximity to it-for example in the case of guards, nurses or schoolteachers-and where there is no existing suitable accommodation available. Social need will cover where proposed householders are caregivers of established rural residents and where there is no existing suitable accommodation available. New holiday homes will only be permitted in existing or new sustainable settlements.
- Conditions will be attached to planning permissions for a new house (subject to the criterion of functional and social need) on an existing farm so as to minimize environmental impact, that it be sited near the farmhouse and that, in as far as possible, it share one upgraded sewerage treatment system and

one road access point. This measure would reduce applications from landowners purporting to need a new house for a family member but which is built at some distance from the existing family home and all too frequently sold soon afterwards. (Informal research by planners in co Meath showed that 50% of permissions granted for family members are being lived in by unrelated people 5 years later).

- We will support the widespread use of Section 47s by local authorities in relation to one-off rural housing in order to control resale within a 10-15 year period, and the use of planning conditions for local occupancy. We will introduce a form of Capital Gains Tax for houses built under family/social need that are resold within this period, to discourage speculation or abuse of this planning opportunity.
- We will ensure that rural planning decisions focus to a much greater extent on the environmental impacts of a dwelling, rather than purely on its visual impact. We will ensure that planning conditions ensure the maximum use of the most environmentally sustainable building materials. New homes will, in as far as possible, be constructed using sustainable natural materials and will use timber frame construction and natural cellulose or wool insulation in order to ensure better standards of insulation. New houses will be encouraged, through tax incentives, to take advantage of passive or active solar energy or wind power. Measures including conserving the use of fresh water by recycling surface water runoff, that is grey water for uses where fully treated water is not necessary. Where houses are to be located in rural areas, a landscaping planting plan based on native species will be required, rather than the typical quick-fill screening.
- We will introduce an Annual Septic Tank levy to cover the costs of monitoring and inspecting septic tanks. Although the one-off house owner provides his/her own sewerage treatment, this does not relieve the local authority of the considerable costs in monitoring and servicing the facility. Sewerage sludge must be collected once a year and treated in licensed facilities but this is not happening at present because of a combination

of lack of awareness and the lack of suitable facilities. This neglect has had a negative impact on water quality. The government is upgrading and chemically treating Group Water Schemes, which have consistently failed to meet minimum EU drinking water standards, because of agricultural and septic tank contamination in rural areas. In Government, we will require that septic tanks and percolation areas should be in accordance with the most up-to-date European and national guidelines available. Tax relief will be provided on the installation of alternative wastewater treatment systems such as reed-bed systems.

- Planning permission conditions for new homes in rural areas will require that each householder minimises and manages waste, including creating a composting facility and organising the separation and collection of individual waste streams.
- We will ensure that local authorities make schemes available such as exist in other countries whereby grants are provided for new or older converted houses to assist in making them more sustainable and minimising their resource use.
- We will address the current imbalance of investments in land and property in Ireland that is fuelling an asset price bubble in housing and in farmland. We will provide incentives for Irish people, both on an individual basis and in companies and communities, to invest in alternative productive assets. In the light of coming fossil fuel scarcity, the most productive assets are likely to be renewable energy generators. As our best renewable energy resources are in rural areas, hydro, wind, biomass, slurry and eventually tidal power, this policy will diversify investment from the larger cities and towns.

The Government's own policy framework for renewable energies, published in the Green Paper on Sustainable Energy in 1999, gave a strong endorsement for the community ownership of wind farms, but despite the establishment of a Renewable Energy Strategy Group in 2000 to develop strategies for the increased deployment of wind energy, little has been done since to increase community participation. In Government the Green Party would act to remove the barriers to the fulfilment of this policy. Other renewable energy resources, in particular biogas digestion in the midlands of the country, have great potential for community ownership and investment. We believe that Community Land Trusts as outlined earlier in this document could manage the collective investment of communities in natural renewable energy resource built up through goodwill royalties as in Scotland or through individual Credit Union savings and borrowings the main reason we moved here, and I think you may agree. We lived in Austin Texas and the year before my oldest was to start school a third grade kid shot and killed another kid in the very school that my children were going to be in. Don't get me wrong violence is everywhere but in our little town there has never been a school shooting. Call me crazy if you like, but I didn't have children to send them to school only to be in danger of possibly being shot.

Rural life isn't for everyone, and for that we are glad. If everyone moved here then we would have all the problems associated with living in a large city. However if you are looking for a peaceful place to raise a family I highly recommend the small town life. It has been very good to us and I don't see myself ever living in a large city again.

7

Second Homes Ownership and Demand

The Future of Second Home Ownership

With the entry level single family home in a resort towns like Aspen commanding $5 million it becomes clear that the traditional second home ownership model might face some competition from an unexpected rival.

Not all second homes are created equal. With the baby boomer generation approaching retirement there will be an increased demand for homes away from home. The low use of second homes and the costs associated with owning and maintaining vacation homes has given rise to a new breed of property types over the last few years.

Worry free vacation home ownership is at the top of the agenda for most second homeowners. The affluent demand top-notch services and amenities. With time an ever-rare commodity it is crucial to accommodate the travel patterns and flexibility demanded. Many short trips rather than long extended stays have become the norm.

A simple look at costs involved in owning multiple vacation homes makes the substantial financial commitment obvious that comes with the travelling lifestyle. Homes want to be serviced and maintained, services are to be provided and taxes are due to be paid.

Owning a slope side condo in Aspen ($4 million) a cottage in the California wine country ($3 million) and a beachfront property in Cabo San Lucas ($5 million) is used as an example to highlight the costs involved. A total investment of $12 million at 7% represents an interest cost of $840,000 per annum with maintenance, utilities and taxes adding at least another 3% ($360,000) to the yearly tally. The total annual cost of this vacation property lifestyle is at least $1.2 million. With the average second homeowner spending less than 30 days at his vacation property the properties are not utilized to their true potential. In addition that usage number decreases with the number of vacation properties a household owns. These economics have created an alternative vacation ownership model. Why own all these properties if you are using them only a fraction of the year?

Fractional ownership was created out of a need to reduce costs for the owners. Over time it has become apparent though that the inflexible fractional schemes do not serve the owners well. Flexibility is king when you do not own 100% and cannot come and go, as you like. The next evolution of this concept is club vacation property ownership. This in turn has now lead to the creation of super luxury clubs with owners having exclusive access to a multitude of properties at various locations. Membership is often limited to a few hundred families with properties offered for use worth several hundred million Dollars. The biggest benefit is the complete usage flexibility with no set schedules. Owners have a certain time allocated to them but can use it at their discretion.

The clubs offer a worry free lifestyle. Full maintenance of all aspects of the facilities, all taxes included, luxury services and a fun group of people to hang out with if desired. Club memberships like this can be acquired for as little as $1.5 million. That represents an opportunity cost of only $84.000 with annual dues adding another $50,000. A total expenditure of $134,000 can offer the same privileges and better services with less hassle than full ownership. It will become apparent to the seekers of full service luxury vacation properties that financially as well as practically the top end of the luxury vacation resort clubs offer a great alternative to the full ownership model.

Second Home Ownership

The idea of owning a summer home by the lake or a cabin in the woods has slowly ingrained itself into the traditional American value of owning a home. An aging Baby Boom generation and a long period of low interest rates have been primary factors for the continued increase of second home ownership.

The National Association of Realtors reported that slightly more than 1 million homes bought in 2005 were vacation homes. This accounted for 12.2 percent of all home sales in 2005. According to a survey released by the realtor trade association in May 2006, half of vacation homes are located in resort or recreational areas, 18 percent in small towns and 16 percent in rural areas. Considering the SOSA region fits all three of those descriptions, second homes are a prevalent feature in many of the counties. Second-home development contributes to the consumption of agricultural lands in the Sierra through land use zoning changes. In communities where the second homes are prominent feature of the housing landscape, increased property values and land values can push average wage earners out of the community.

In 2000, second homes in the Sierra counties of California and Nevada made up 5.6 percent of the region's total housing units, significantly higher than the state average of 2 percent for both California and Nevada. However, second homes dominated the housing landscape in several counties, especially Alpine (61.8 percent) and Mono (49.8 percent).

Download Data Second Home Ownership

The popularity of second homes is prominent in the Sierra foothills near Yosemite National Park (Tuolumne County: 21.3 percent and Mariposa County: 18.8 percent) and just north of the park in Calaveras County, 24.2 percent. The northern Sierra counties of Plumas, 26.7 percent, and Sierra, 23.9 percent, also had a significant portion of its housing market devoted to second homes.

Simply looking at the raw number of second homes, the region connecting the Sacramento metro region and Lake Tahoe contains the highest concentration of second homes. El Dorado, Nevada and Placer counties account for 35.1 percent of all the second homes in the Sierra Nevada counties.

Case Study: The Social and Economic Effects of Second Homes Northwest Colorado Council of Governments. While ranchettes contribute to rural sprawl with their tendency to fragment large chunks of land, other residential trends, such as second homeowners, contribute to the rise of residential land usage.

Using assessor databases from four counties – Eagle, Grand, Pitkin and Summit – the Northwest Colorado Council of Governments

(NWCCOG) created a housing unit database to determine the prominence of second home ownership on the region's economy and its housing availability. Download The Social and Economic Effects of Second Homes 2004.

Located in the rural mountainous region of Colorado, the counties are home to several world-renowned ski resorts, have a strong historical ranching background and are now dominated by the tourism and service economy sectors. NWCCOG discovered that 60 percent of the housing units in the four-county study area were second homes. The percentages vary from a low of 49 percent of the housing units in Eagle County, 55 percent in Pitkin County, 63 percent in Grand County to a high of 67 percent in Summit County.

Second homes take up large amounts of land in Colorado's mountain resort areas where developable land is already in short supply. As a result, the second homes' property values and the land surrounding them rises and potentially drive up the price of homes beyond what the average wage earner in the county can afford.

Over time second homes become a large and often dominant part of both the physical and economic landscape. The irony of second homes is they create a demand for construction, maintenance, and operations employees, yet rising home prices drive employees out of the immediate area. As the number of second homes increase, the demand for workers increases as well.

Rising housing costs make it difficult for the workers to live within a practicable distance of their place-of-work. Employees are forced to live in nearby towns with reasonable housing prices, creating bedroom communities coupled with second home communities.

NWCCOG is a voluntary association of five counties and 21 municipal governments in north central Colorado. NWCCOG was the fastest growing region in the state from 1990-2000, with a population growth at 73 percent, more than double the state's population growth.

Multiple-Home Ownership and the Income Elasticity of Housing Demand

Traditional models of the income elasticity of demand do not account for the possibility that households may own two or more homes. Although estimates of the number of second homes and the share of households who own them vary, it is possible to use existing surveys to narrowly define second homeowners to exclude those who may own additional properties purely or mostly for investment reasons and then model their housing choices.

This topic is of interest because it stands to reason that households that divide their consumption of housing services among two or more properties may make different choices about their primary residences than households that own a single home. For example, those splitting their consumption among multiple homes may allocate less, all else equal, to their primary home and make decisions about the locations of their primary and second homes that have implications for urban form and the operation of land and housing markets.

This paper examines the determinants of the ownership of multiple homes and the influence of multiple-homeownership on the income elasticity of housing demand. It explores the impact of owning multiple homes on the income elasticity of demand for just primary residences, as well as total housing consumption. To the extent feasible in the datasets used for this analysis, homes owned for purely investment purposes are excluded from the analysis because such investments are little different from investments in other non-housing assets. Homes that are not used by their owners at least in part for seasonal or occasional use do not produce a flow of housing services that they consume. If the intention is not to use them, there is little reason to expect ownership of such homes to affect the income elasticity of demand for primary residences.

Of course owning a home always has an investment element to it because dollars invested in the home have opportunity costs and homes are typically leveraged investments. But the twin consumption and investment motives for homeownership are well established and have not prevented household level estimation of the income elasticity of housing demand.

Both the American Housing Survey (AHS) and the Survey of Consumer Finances (SCF) are used to model second home demand but only the AHS is used to model the income elasticity of demand. A logistic regression is used to analyse the determinants of the demand for multiple-homeownership while log linear models are used to estimate the income elasticity of demand. We model the impact of the log of estimated permanent income on the log of value of primary homes for single and multiple home owners separately, after controlling for demographic characteristics, and with or without a dummy variable for having investment savings of $20,000 or more. The regression is then repeated to estimate the impact on the log value for the total of all homes owned by households with more than one home. These models test for possible differences in the income elasticity of demand for primary residences subject to the possibility of owning a second home for consumption purposes.

The paper begins with a literature review on the extent and determinants of second home demand. With few empirical investigations of second homeownership to review, this part of the review is brief. The literature on estimating the income elasticity of housing demand is far richer. But much of it focuses on the proper way to measure income for the purposes of estimating the elasticity of demand, as well as other appropriate controls. Our interest is in the impact of second homes. Hence, we also indicate how allowing for multiple ownership might influence elasticities and advance hypotheses about the likely influences on the choice to own a second home. This section is followed by a discussion of data and methods, model findings, and conclusions.

Literature Review

Despite the growing market for second homes, there are very few studies of the determinants of demand for second homes or the propensity of persons to own second homes. While there are numerous studies on the income elasticity of demand for housing, our review found no studies that examined the impact of second homes on the income elasticity of demand either for primary residences or for all residences owned at least in part for consumption purposes.

Propensities to Own Second Homes

Previous studies of the propensity to own second homes have not used formal probability models to estimate the independent influence of different variables on the odds of owning a second home. Using US government data, Di, McArdle & Masnick (2001) explored the characteristics of the owners of second homes, as well as locations, definitions and measurements of second homes. The paper found that second homes are owned primarily

Are Fractional Ownerships Replacing Second Homes?

In this current economy, Americans are scaling back on luxury items like vacations, while others are defaulting on second homes that were purchased for tax reasons and the prospects of major profits. For those unwilling to give up their vacations and uneasy about holding onto cash, fractional ownerships may be an inexpensive option.

The fractional ownership market emerged as an ideal investment in 2008 because it allowed investors to (partially) own high-end properties in a luxury resorts for a low price and without any maintenance responsibilities. For example, a three-bedroom unit in Vail, Colorado — a popular fractional ownership location — may cost $4 million to purchase outright. But an investor who is interested in securing vacation time and confident that the unit will appreciate over the long-term may only have to pay an initial $400,000, plus yearly fees of approximately $10,000, which cover maintenance and services costs.

Though fractional ownership may seem like a great way to secure top-notch lodging and make enough money on the sale of the fraction to make those vacations essentially free, there are many caveats that go along with fractional ownership.

The Pros

Like Real Estate Investment Trusts (REITs), fractional ownerships offer investors the opportunity to own an asset that they may otherwise never be able to afford. With fractional ownership, however, not only are you able to invest in a high-quality asset but you can actually enjoy that asset while you own it — something that's difficult to do if you're part of a REIT that invests in office buildings.

Another perk of investing in a fractional ownership is that many of the hospitality chains that offer this investment are upscale resorts with five-star amenities. By paying the yearly fees, owners are not just covering the costs of repairs and upkeep, they are also paying for high-end services that are not normally offered to hotel guests. Owners can have groceries purchased and stocked, family pictures displayed and dining reservations made. Some resort communities even offer free spa treatments and rounds of golf to its owners.

One advantage that many fractional owners believe they have over second homeowners is that, instead of paying for a mortgage that would cost the same whether they lived there all year long or only visited for one week, fractional owners only pay for what they use. "Fractional ownership allows you to buy just the amount of time in a vacation home that you can actually use," said Dr. Richard Ragatz, president of Ragatz and Associates, a research firm that focuses on the worldwide resort industry. "Research shows that the typical household uses their wholly owned vacation home no more than four to five weeks a year. The rest of that time it sits idle, accumulating maintenance costs, taxes and repair fees."

Most fractional owners are allotted anywhere from two to 13 weeks a year, depending upon the number of owners. Timeshare investors are typically allowed a maximum of two weeks per year, which usually must be used consecutively. Another advantage fractional ownerships have over timeshares is that owners receive a deed for their fraction of the property, allotting them a share in the property's equity. "The day after you buy a timeshare you've lost, on average, 55 percent of what you've paid for," Ragatz said. With a fractional ownership, you're able to share in any profits the property makes due to appreciation, just as a second homeowner would. Ragatz also noted that there is a large difference between where an investor's funds go in a fractional ownership versus a timeshare. His research shows that 75 percent of a timeshare investor's money goes toward the timeshare company's administration, marketing and sales efforts, meaning only a quarter of these funds actually go toward the property. In the case of a fractional ownership, 65 percent of the money goes directly into property.

Speaking of marketing, Ragatz also believes that the demand for fractional ownership is growing because of the small supply. There are only 254 properties in the world that offer fractional ownership. Right now, only 60,000 fractional owners exist due to this low inventory. "There is very high interest in fractional ownerships," he said. "Because there was significant untapped demand when most of these properties were being built. When the economy comes back fractional ownerships will take up a huge demand."

The last benefit of fractional ownership is an important one, especially during a credit crunch. Though the lending atmosphere remains hostile across all property types, banks have historically been more willing to lend to second-home and fractional ownership investors, as opposed to timeshare and condo hotel investors, because the former two have the potential for appreciation. It is also easier for fractional owners to obtain a loan because they only need to supply a percentage of the property's overall price — usually 10 percent to 25 percent, or $100,000 to $500,000.

Cons

A common problem that besets any investment with multiple participants is that they must be in agreement before any action, such as selling the property, can be taken. Sharing costs and responsibilities, such as abiding by the rules of the property's Homeowner's Association or charter, can also prove problematic. If one investor fails to keep the property in working order or damages the unit, the group will receive a bill that must be divided amongst them. Remember that just because a fractional owner does not have to perform routine maintenance or change the sheets does not mean that the investment and use of the investment is free of responsibility.

A group of fractional owners may also suffer if one member fails to make his monthly mortgage payment. Again, the group must decide how to get the mortgage payment up to speed and whether that will affect that owner's usage or share in the property. Note that most developers offering fractional ownerships have laws in place that allow an owner accused of a violation to contest the violation, which may result in resolution or the selling of that owner's share. In such times of economic instability, it is not inconceivable that there may be a point in time when one or more investors are unable to make their portion of the fractional ownership payment. To prevent such instances from dramatically affecting the other owners, experts recommend that the group create a back-up fund that each contributes to equally that can act as a form of insurance in case an owner fails to make his payment or wracks up other fees and expenses.

Another common issue amongst group members is usage of the property. Like a timeshare, the owners of a fractional ownership must still work out a reservation system that ideally allows all owners to use the property during on-and off-seasons. Rules about who, other than the owner, can use the property should also be ironed out before any contracts are signed. Many investors purchase this property so that both themselves and their families and friends can use it, but many investors are not comfortable with people who have no vested interest in the property or its upkeep utilizing it for their pleasure. To the other owners, this is more of a risk, as friends and relatives may not be familiar with— or choose to respect — all of the property's rules, resulting, again in added fees for the group.

Even with the most scrupulous owners, however, a fractional ownership can still fail. And poor management is usually to blame. Part of the appeal of fractional ownerships is that they are relatively worry free because the developer's management and maintenance teams take care of its general upkeep and any other tasks the owners may require. However, poor management can result in a dirty unit, unappealing appearance and nonfunctional amenities. Though a management company can always be taken to court, most investors know that this can be a long, drawn out and risky process, especially if the contract affords the management company significant control over the unit and how it is maintained. For fractional ownerships inside resorts, poor management can not only result in a less than ideal unit, but also in a bad reputation that chases away guests and other potential investors. If this occurs, it is unlikely that the fractional owners will be able to sell their share or the entire property for a profit, if at all.

Investing in a fractional ownership with reputable investors and a fabulous management company still does not guarantee success. Like all homes, vacation properties are subject to economic upheaval and the normal ebbs and flows of the real estate market. So even though you're investing less money into a fractional ownership than you would a wholly owned vacation home, the success of both investment vehicles is tied to many factors, including its maintenance, location, size, amenities and surrounding neighbourhood.

"There's no real investment opportunity in a fractional ownership any more so than there is with any other property," Ragatz said. "The anecdotal evidence shows that the appreciation of a fractional interest is the same as with the whole ownership of a vacation home." Ragatz also noted that many individuals have changed their mentalities when it comes to buying real estate, thanks to the housing bubble burst and the recession. "People don't buy for appreciation anymore," he said. "They buy for use. They feel that they're much better off spending $200,000 on a permanent, very high-end, quality vacation than on something that sits vacant most of the year."

Whether you're goal is to invest in future vacations or a small piece of high-end real estate that may appreciate over time, the key to any successful fractional ownership is understanding the terms of the contract. That all begins with the developer, as a legitimate developer and owner will allow the owners to negotiate the level of control they want over a property and how much they're willing to pay for that. After that, it's all about choosing a fractional ownership that will be surrounded with financially sound, responsible investors. For every investor knows that a partner can make or break an investment.

The white, middle aged homeowners with high incomes, and that 40 percent of second homes are mobile homes, but it did not look at wealth of second homeowners. Looking at wealth, Gutierrez (1999) searched to find any evidence of a wealth effect on the demand for new second homes, but concluded that the data were too unreliable to draw definitive conclusions about whether the wealth building and economic prosperity of the late 1990s were associated with any increases in second home development in areas with large second home shares. Kochera (1997) reported rapid growth in recreational properties in the mid 1990's, but also large numbers of unexplained "other" second homes not used for recreation or investment purposes. More recently, Carliner (2002) reviewed data on second homeownership from the decennial Census, AHS, HVS as well as surveys of homebuyer preferences from NAHB and NAR, and found that second homeownership is strongly associated with age of homeowners. He concluded that although the market still appears to be largely misunderstood, studies indicate that demand for second homes has been holding up and may accelerate somewhat with increases in income and wealth of homeowners and as more baby boomers enter age cohorts with traditionally higher second homeownership rates.

In summary, research on the propensity to own a second homes have shown descriptively that age, race, and income are associated with second homeownership, while wealth, though not examined on a household level, has been generally assumed to play a role. No econometric research has been done to study determinants of second home ownership, nor, as discussed below, have studies been done to measure income elasticity of housing demand in the context of with and without considering second homes.

Estimating Demand Equations

There is a very rich body of research on the income elasticity of housing demand. Demand for housing is an embodiment of a consumer's decision as to how much housing to consume. Standard theoretical models posit that demand for housing is a function of household income, the price of housing services, and the price of all other goods and services. The standard theoretical equation for the housing equation is a log-linear model:

Second Homes Become Yesterday's Dreams

Homeowners are pulling at their purse strings and pulling up their metaphorical drawbridges as they stay put at home. New statistics reveal that the number of second home purchases both at home and abroad have slumped as the recession takes hold.

Falling Demand

There have been big falls in both the number of second homes in much of England and in average prices in traditional second home owning territory. In Westminster-where 6.5% of properties are registered as second homes-there has been a fall of nearly a quarter in the number of registered second homes, according to the latest analysis by Savills Research.

Other areas have shown significant, though smaller, reductions in second home ownership. In South Hams, in Hampshire, there was a 5.9% fall in second homes and in North Norfolk there was a drop of 3.4%. Other holiday home hotspots have seen years of growth grind to a halt, with increases in second home ownership in East Anglia and the South West dropping to a mere 0.7%. Second home ownership in England reached a record high of 245,000 properties only last year.

Good News for Some

The reduction in holiday home ownership is at least good news for younger first time buyers in areas where they have traditionally been priced out of the market-and for would-be second home purchasers who still have cash. In Devon, house prices have dropped 24% since they peaked in mid 2007. In Cornwall, they have fallen 21%.

It is a similar story in other desirable areas. In the Cotswolds, prices have reduced by 18.6%; and in Suffolk, Norfolk and Dorset by 15%. However, locations close to London that are suitable for weekend retreats rather than holiday homes have retained more of their price. "There is clearly a significant difference between the working week pied à terre in central London and the classic weekend retreat or holiday home, but both qualify for a second home designation", says Lucian Cook, director of residential research at Savills.

It's Different in London

"We are certain that falls in registered second home ownership in central London locations are not wholly attributable to redundancy or financial concerns as we have not seen an associated rise in property for sale. Rather, we believe that the reasons are more prosaic. For example, owners need a permanent home to secure a parking permit, which may well have triggered them to forego the benefits of a second home registration and re-register their property for full council tax."

In areas where it is possible to commute to London, prices may have been protected to an extent by people choosing to relocate from the capital, adds Cook.

But in resort towns such as Salcombe in Devon and Rock in Cornwall-where 40% of dwellings are second homes and prices rose exponentially in recent years-the house market is now quiet, says Cook. He expects "turnover and prices to remain suppressed for some time to come".

Quality Counts

There is also a marked difference, Savills found, in price performance according to the quality of the home. The most attractive properties have fallen in value by less than 12% since their peak, while the least attractive have lost more than a quarter of their price.

Comparable demand trends can be observed in the overseas house buying market. The agency Look a property reports enquiries for overseas homes is down 90%. Chief executive Aaron Turner says the "market is looking pretty dead". He adds "people are no longer serious about buying overseas".

However, it seems that the old virtues of good publicity and pretty pictures can still counter other trends, even in a recession. Mamma Mia is not only the highest grossing film in British history, it has also sparked a flood of enquiries for home buying in Greek islands. One property agency has reported a 120% rise in potential buyers visiting Greece to view homes for sale and a nearly threefold increase in expressions of interest.

In this equation, x_i is the annual real expenditure on housing services, y is income, p_H is the relative price of housing, p_0 is an index of the price of all other goods, and *u* is a disturbance variable. Using a log form, $\hat{a}_1$ is the true income elasticity and $\hat{a}_2$ is the true price elasticity of demand for housing.

The Debate on Current vs. Permanent Income

When it comes to housing demand models, household income is thought of two ways: current income, which is a highly transitory measurement for earnings in a single year, and permanent income, which is a long-term concept of what household income will be into the future. This concept is shown in equation, where Y_i is current income, Y_i^P is the permanent income component of current income, and Y_i^T is the transitory income component of current income.

As a durable good with high transaction costs, it is generally argued that decisions on housing consumption are based on a household's permanent income (Y_i^P), and therefore the transitory income component of a household's current income (Y_i^T) biases demand models that use current income (Y_i), and results in underestimates of demand elasticities.

A review by Carliner (1973) found that demand models attempting to use measurements or proxies for permanent income have achieved significantly higher income elasticities than those using current income. Polinsky and Ellwood, 1979, revisited several studies and showed that, when substituted for each other within the same housing demand equation, permanent income elasticities average about 50 percent higher than those for current income. Polinsky and Ellwood used metropolitan housing sales price and income data to estimate their own measure of permanent income elasticity and found estimates ranging from 0.80 to 0.87. Since then Goodman & Kawai (1982) have found permanent elasticities to be 100 percent greater than current income elasticities.

Though it is generally agreed that permanent income is the appropriate measurement for household income within a demand model, there has been much debate over how to correctly estimate permanent income, and also how to treat current income in the process. Reid (1962) approximated permanent income by using a restricted sample of households with stable incomes and using current incomes as a proxy for permanent incomes. Models by Muth (1965), Winger (1968), and DeLeeuw (1971) used city median incomes as proxies for permanent income, arguing that averaging incomes across metro areas eliminates transitory elements. Other studies, such as Carliner (1973) use a multiyear average of a household's past four years of incomes to approximate permanent income. More recently, Goodman and Kawai (1982) define permanent income as the predicted value of a regression of current household income on the determinant variables of permanent income, with the residual being transitory income.

Incorporating Demographic and Other Household Characteristics

Housing demand models have grown to include a number of demographic variables in attempts to measure differing "tastes" for housing consumption among a cross section of households with differing characteristics. There has been much disagreement as to the significance of demographic factors within demand models. In a review of several studies, Hansen et. al. (1998) suggests that exclusion of demographic variables likely to be correlated with permanent income, such as race, age, sex, and household size, will bias estimations of income elasticity, and that the direction of this bias is most likely upward. However, an earlier empirical study by Carliner (1973) finds income elasticity measurements from regressions using demographic terms are higher than those without. Another empirical study from Follain (1979) found income and price elasticities not sensitive to the presence of socio-demographic variables, and a third empirical study by Goodman (1990), found demographic interactions relatively insignificant for populations close to general population means but highly significant for populations away from means, such as those at very low or very high incomes. In light of this diverse array of findings, we felt it necessary to include demographic variables within our model, and that age, race, and family type were the most appropriate factors available within our dataset.

Controlling for House-Price and Non-Housing Cost Indexes

The standard demand model in equation (1) generates price and income elasticities of housing demand based on the utility of housing consumption relative to all other goods. Goodman & Kawai (1984), following examples from DeLeeuw (1971) and Polinsky and

Ellwood (1979), estimate a demand model with demographic and housing characteristic variables but without a non-housing cost index, choosing instead to apply various fixed-effect coefficients within the Ordinary Linear Regression. Due to limited geographic data in the AHS dataset, our model uses this fixed-effect approach to control for relative differences in both house-price and non-housing costs based on regional location as well as metro / non-metro area location.

Where h_i is the value of housing consumption and Z_{ji} is a vector of our 12 geographic dummies to control for the relative price of housing and non-housing goods to the individual, as well as demographic and other housing characteristic dummy variables that potentially affect the demand for housing and control for fixed-effects on housing consumption within the model.

We use housing value as our measure of housing consumption (h_i) in our equation. Researchers generally agree that housing consumption for homeowners is best approximated and more easily obtained as a standardized measurement of total housing value, rather than as annual expenditures on homeownership. The common method, used by Goodman and Kawai (1984), involves hedonic regression, whereby a household's housing value is taken as a function of neighbourhood and resident characteristics. The housing price index can be determined by the price of a standardized unit of housing according to the hedonic regression, and housing consumption can then be measured as housing value divided by the price of a standardized unit. Including geographic and socioeconomic characteristics within our fixed-effects model enables us to standardize housing value somewhat within the demand model; though using separate hedonic regressions would clearly be superior. Therefore, h_i, in our model is approximated simply as the total value of housing.

Controlling for Other Effects: Wealth and Elderly Status

Wealth variables seem not to have been included in previous studies, although it may have an impact on the propensity of second home ownership and influence on income elasticity estimates. Also, although age has often been included in studies of income elasticity, its effect may not be linear and its interaction with income is very possible. The lack of these variables in previous studies encourages us to include them in our study.

Measures and Magnitude of Second Home Demand

This paper is not intended to reopen debates about the level of income elasticity of housing demand. Instead, it explores whether ownership of second homes influences the income elasticity of demand for primary residences or for the aggregate value of all homes that are owned, at least in part, for consumption. This is increasingly relevant given the apparent increase in second homeownership in recent years.

Statistics on the extent of second homeownership and the number of second homes are often inconsistent. These inconsistencies mostly reflect differences in methods of data collection, especially in how questions about the purpose of vacant or additional owned properties are asked, but also as a result of differences in sample sizes, sampling procedures, and weighting procedures across surveys.

The AHS, Housing Vacancy Survey (HVS), and decennial Census each contain estimates of the number of second homes based on interviewer efforts to determine the status of vacant units. The AHS and the HVS produce estimates of second homes (defined here as homes for seasonal or occasional use and homes occupied by those with a usual residence elsewhere) that are closer to each other than to the decennial Census, which consistently estimates a far smaller number of second homes. However, the AHS produced higher second home estimates than the HVS in the early to mid 1990s and then lower estimates thereafter. The HVS registered a strong 20 percent increase in the number of second homes from 1995 to 6.8 million in 2005 while the American Housing Survey reported a smaller but still substantial increase from 5.8 million in 1995 to 6.2 million in 2003.

Many surveys ask households questions about whether they own additional properties and then ask them questions about these properties. These include the AHS, the SCF, the Survey of Income and Program Participation (SIPP), the Panel Study of Income Dynamics (PSID), and industry surveys such as one of new homebuyers conducted by the National Association of Home Builders (2000) and by the National Association of Realtors® (NAR) of homebuyers and homeowners. A recent NAR survey of 2005 homebuyers found that about 12 percent of all homes purchased were characterized by their owners as for vacation use and 28 percent for investment purposes. The intricacies of how all the other household surveys are conducted are well summarized by Carliner (2002) and the US Department of Housing and Urban Development (2004). Suffice it to say here that the SCF is the only dataset to ask questions about second homes on a regular (every three year) basis. Like the HVS, it shows growth in second home demand over the past decade (Chart 1). However, for all age groups except those now in their 60s, all of the growth was in households reporting timeshare fractional ownership in a second home. Overall, the SCF shows an increase of about 600,000 homes for "seasonal/ vacation use" and in time shares of fully 1.8 million. Assuming that fractional ownership averages 2 week per year, then a 1.8 million increase in timeshare owners translates into onlWhile the figures shown here suggest that second homeownership rates among homeowners peak in their 50s and 60s at about 6-6½ percent, and rates of time shares peak at about 5 percent, these may be undercounts. The reason is that when SCF respondents are asked what type of property they own, they must choose from "seasonal/vacation home," "time share ownership," and a host of structure types including single-family house, condominium, residential, trailer/mobile home, farm/ranch, etc. It is likely that some of those who own homes for occasional use on weekends or for work do not consider them for seasonal or vacation use. Indeed, many of those responding with a structure type do not derive any rental income from their second home, suggesting that in some cases they are at least in part for consumption uses.

With an even greater number of households headed by younger boomers growing into the 50-59 age group by 2015 than the number of households headed by leading edge boomers currently in that age, and each generation accumulating more household net wealth and higher median incomes than previous generation at similar age, demand for second homes are likely to continue to grow in the coming decade.

Hypotheses

The literature and economic theory suggest the following hypotheses with respect to the likelihood of owning a second home and the impact of owning a second home on income elasticities for housing:

A) *The likelihood of owning a second home will be increasing with permanent income, current income, wealth, and age:* Higher incomes and wealth allow consumers to allocate more of the household budget to housing consumption and investment. Lifecycle factors suggest that even after controlling for income and wealth, second homeownership might be higher for older aged households as they approach or reach retirement and look towards more leisure time. But the impact of the presence of children is more ambiguous because on the one hand it may increase the utility derived from a second home, but on the other may be a drain on the household budget. Geographic location of the primary residence might also have an influence, but again is ambiguous. With most owners having second homes within driving distance of their primary residences, living in a lower cost area could increase the likelihood of owning a second home because the costs of buying a second home are lower. On the other hand, these same areas tend to have lower price appreciation and therefore leave owners with less housing wealth to leverage up for second homeownership.

B) *The income elasticity of demand for primary residences will be lower for those with second homes than for those with just one home:* There are several factors that lead to this expectation. First, households that have a preference for owning second homes divide their housing consumption among more than one property. Because they split their consumption between two homes, one would expect the income elasticity of demand for just their primary home to be lower than for owners of only one home. This holds true whether the initial decision on how much to spend on a primary residence was made with the intention of buying a second home or if instead, over the lifecycle, a homeowner decides to adjust their housing consumption upward by investing in a second home rather than trading-up to a higher valued home or improving their primary residence. Second, second home owners have higher average incomes and housing consumption levels relative to owners of just one home. Indeed, their average income is very close to that of owners in the upper income quartiles of a just a single residence. Therefore, second home owners may be closer to being fully housed. In this case, uses of an incremental dollar other than housing may maximize their overall utility. As a result, increases in income may not in turn result in as large a percentage change in consumption in their primary (or secondary) homes. Lastly, owners of a single home with no desire for second home ownership may have more of an incentive to maximize the quality and consumption value of their sole home, while those with a propensity to own second homes may under-consume their primary house in favour of second home ownership.

C) *The income elasticity of demand with respect to all houses owned by second homeowners will be lower than the elasticity of just their primary property:* With consumption split, spending on the primary home will take precedence over spending on the secondary home, and therefore lower elasticities of secondary home demand will drag down overall elasticities of demand which incorporate both primary and secondary home consumption. Given the same income distribution, the income elasticity of demand for the primary home (eP) relates to the elasticity of the second home (eS) as a ratio based on the way in which consumption of these two goods relate to each other, based on the formula1:

D) *The income elasticity of demand with respect to all properties owned by those who have second homes for consumption purposes will be lower than that of single-home owners*: This is because, similar to the reasoning in (B) above, second homeowners, being on average older with high levels of wealth and income and high levels of housing consumption already, are less likely to be under-housed than the generally lower income owners of a single home. Therefore, income increases are not matched by the same increases in housing consumption seen by the generally lower income owners of a single home only. This may be tested and seen through decreasing elasticities of demand among single-home owners as income levels increase.

E) *Models that do not include the value of second homes and do not control for second homeownership are likely to produce biased estimates of the income elasticity of housing demand*: This is because the ownership of multiple homes is expected to influence the income elasticities of demand in the ways stipulated in (A)-(D) above.

Data and Method

We use the AHS and SCF to provide empirical evidence on determinants of second-home ownership and AHS to explore income elasticity of housing demand when second homeownership is considered.

The AHS is conducted by Census for HUD every two years at the national level, and only twice (in 1985 and 1995) did it have a supplemental survey on second homes. In these years, respondents were asked about other residential properties they owned in addition to their primary homes.

For these properties, up to 6 such properties are surveyed. For each recorded property, it asks respondents about why they hold such a property and asks them to mark all the reasons that apply. In our paper, we only look at those properties that are marked for recreational use in order to narrow the field as much as possible to households that self-report homes that they view, at least in part, as providing them a flow of housing consumption services.

The regular AHS survey contains detailed household information including current household income, age, race/ethnic background, the education level of household heads, and family type. Unfortunately, geographic detail in the dataset is lacking. While about 100 metropolitan areas are specified, in most cases the number of observations is far too few to create a meaningful hedonic price index. Instead, to control for differences in the costs of housing and non-housing goods across areas, we rely on the interaction of the 4 census regions and 3 types of metropolitan status (cities, suburbs, or non-metro). This provides 12 variations—an admittedly crude control for housing price differences across the country.

The AHS also has a dummy variable on whether the household has investment savings of $20,000 or more. This is a crude proxy for the level of non-housing wealth of a household. This could have an impact on the income elasticity of housing demand but the current literature overlooks potential wealth effects on income elasticity. Particularly for the propensity of second-home ownership, it may have some influence as a determinant.

Exhibit 1 shows basic descriptive statistics on the variables from the AHS we use to model propensities and elasticities. Because AHS top-codes the value of primary homes at $375,000, we drop these roughly 3 percent of cases in all of our elasticity models to avoid using exactly the same value for all records with house values at the top code. Importantly, the second home value is not top-coded, so models of the total value of properties owned by people who own a home under

$375,000 in 1995 are not right-censored on second-home value. We also exclude a couple of hundred cases (less than one percent of the entire sample) in our elasticity models involving owners of multiple homes where no information on the value of second homes was provided.

The SCF is conducted by the Federal Reserve Bank every three years. The most recent survey is 2004 and was just released in March 2006. The survey was originally designed to measure all kinds of debt that people take on, and thus has very rich information on liabilities vs. assets and therefore the net wealth held by each household surveyed. Because of the imbalances in wealth holding and distribution, the SCF over samples wealthy households. Roughly half of its sample is a set of wealthy households and the other half are households distributed across a greater spectrum of household wealth. Because of that, we have to use a weighted sample in modeling work.

One of the benefits of this sampling procedure is that it insures better accuracy at the level of aggregate household net wealth. Therefore, one of the advantages of using the SCF data to model the probability of owning a second home is that SCF data provide the most accurate and detailed wealth information of any household survey. With this data, we are able to obtain non-housing wealth as a variable that omits home equity, which is too closely correlated to our dependant variable of home value and would induce bias our model. This is more precise than the AHS dummy indicator of savings in excess of $20,000.

The biggest limitation of the SCF data is that it has a small sample size of less than 5,000 households. Because of that, the released file for public use does not have any geographic variables. This prevents us from controlling for any house price variation across even regions or metropolitan status. It also prevents meaningful estimation of permanent income. For this reason, we only use SCF data to model the propensity of owning a second home.

The SCF also has some intrinsic problems embedded in the questionnaire design. As noted above, the coding system is such that some households may have chosen structure type categories such as single-family or multi-family units even though the home they own is for their own seasonal or occasional use. Exhibit 2 displays some descriptive statistics of homeowners in the SCF data. Because we run models on weighted samples, both un-weighted and weighted statistics are displayed. The two different datasets have different estimates on the share of vacation home owners among all households. While 2004 SCF data indicate a 3.7 percent vacation homeownership rate, the 1995 AHS data show a 3.3 percent rate. That is not surprising when considering the growth of vacation homes during the decade and differences in how questions about the purpose of second properties are asked. In both data, we exclude timeshare units from our count of recreational second homes.

With the compelling theoretical and empirical arguments for using permanent income rather than current income as the appropriate correlate to estimate income elasticity, in our preferred AHS models we use the Box-Cox square root transformation in a two-step method first estimating household permanent income as described in Appendix A and then plugging in predicted values into the propensity and income elasticity of demand regressions. We did not estimate permanent income in SCF data because it lacks any kind of geographic information control for regional wage differentials. Thus, in our models using AHS data we put in permanent income while in our propensity model using SCF data we put in both current household income and the education level of household heads, which is often a proxy indicator for permanent income.

In our elasticity models, we run non-elderly and elderly samples separately, as we suspect they may have statistically significant differences in elasticity with respect to permanent income, especially since our predicted values for permanent income are apt to have larger residual errors for older people because the correlation of current incomes and the right-hand side predictors is weaker for retirees. We also run models with and without the wealth variable to see how it affects other coefficients, especially income elasticities.

In Model 1, we estimate the elasticity among those who own only a single home, using the value of primary home as the dependent variable. In Model 2, we estimate the elasticity of demand for just the primary residence among those who own more than one home, again using the value of primary home as the dependent variable. This is our principal test of the hypothesis that the income elasticity of demand for primary residences will be lower for second homeowners than others because they split their consumption among multiple properties.

We estimate the income elasticity of demand using total value of all homes owned by owners with second homes as the dependent variable to test the hypothesis that it will be lower because a percentage point increase in income will bring about a smaller percentage point increase in a larger combined first and second home total value. In Model 4, we estimate the income elasticity of demand just for second homes among second homeowners to test the hypothesis that it will be lower than the primary home demand elasticities, indicating relatively low income elasticities for second home demand, preference for primary home consumption, and most importantly, the negative influence of second home ownership on demand elasticities for total housing consumption. In Model 5, we present a single model of housing value for all homeowners with a dummy variable indicating ownership of a second home. This is included to provide an unbiased estimate of the income elasticity of housing demand that incorporates the possibility of second home ownership.

Lastly, we perform a secondary test of the hypothesis that, because they have higher average incomes than the general population of homeowners that own just one home, second home owners have lower elasticities of demand for primary residences. To accomplish this, we divide the owners of one home into income quartiles to see if the income elasticity of demand is in fact lower among owners with average incomes similar to the population of second home owners.

It should be noted that our data do not include geographic controls for second home location. Therefore, since our models proxy housing consumption with house value, uncontrolled-for location-based differences in appreciation levels of second homes may bias measurements of income elasticities based on current second home values. Although most second homes are within driving distance of the first home and may have similar rates of appreciation, if a significant number of second homes bought at the same price point had significantly different appreciation rates, then the current value does not equally reflect total home consumption. In the end, we assume that second home location and appreciation rates have some effect on income elasticities and owners' adjustments to housing consumption that lie beyond the scope of this paper.

The functional form of our propensities models is logistic and the form of our elasticity models is log-linear. Hence the variables in propensities infer differences in the odds of owning a home conditional on each individual variable holding the others constant. The coefficients on income in the log-linear models can be interpreted as the elasticity of housing demand with respect to income and assumes constant elasticities across all values of the dependent variables.

Second Home Ownership Debate Key to Building Rural Community Balance

Second homes can have a significant impact on rural communities. They are likely to stand empty for long periods, which has a detrimental impact on local life and the viability of key services including shops, schools and public transport. Demand for second homes can often result in local people being priced out of the housing market, causing significant social problems.

These impacts are likely to be worse in areas where second homes make up a significant percentage of housing stock, such as coastal locations and areas of high landscape value.

The issue has been raised repeatedly, including by Matthew Taylor's *Living Working Countryside* review and the work of the Affordable Rural Housing Commission, the Commission for Rural Communities and the National Housing and Planning Advice Unit (NHPAU).

The Taylor review of how land use and planning can better support rural business and deliver affordable housing was presented to the government last July. This sparked much debate. However, it is widely recognised that there is a lack of evidence on the social, economic and environmental consequences of second home ownership.

The NHPAU's *Rapid Evidence* Assessment of the Research Literature on the Purchase and Use of Second *Homes*, also published last year, warned that a failure to plan for second homes will affect those "at the margins of homeownership in certain areas because of the impact of further undersupply".

The Taylor review focused on two issues — how to nurture a healthy rural economy and how to ensure an adequate supply of rural housing. Taylor set out the importance of the planning process as an "engine of regeneration" and as a key tool in providing a "positive, lasting legacy of places in which people actually want to live". In his report, Taylor recommended that the government examine the options for revising secondary planning legislation to limit changes of use of full-time homes into second homes. He advised trialling this in a community that is already feeling the impacts of a high rate of second home ownership.

However, the government rejected his recommendation over concerns that it would be difficult to implement through the system and would interfere with the "legitimate rights of second home owners". Instead, it called for more innovative ways of providing affordable housing.

The RTPI rural planning network is debating the issues through its online thinkpiece on planning for second homes, which aims to gauge views to feed into RTPI policy. The network is asking its members to consider a number of questions.

These include identifying the positive and negative impacts of second homes on rural communities and helping planning authorities to find the right balance between these, bearing in mind that such areas and communities are diverse.

It also asks whether the government's response to the Taylor review tackled the symptoms rather than the underlying causes of the problem. Have we reached a point where the absence of planning control over the growth of second homes is causing significant harm, outweighing the personal right to own a second home? If this is the case, should the planning system intervene to ensure that balanced judgements are made? The government is calling for fresh approaches to the provision of affordable housing in rural areas. So what current examples of good practice are there? Should Taylor's recommendation on change of use limits be followed? How will new afforable housing sit next to older, more traditional rural properties that are currently used only as second homes?

These are just a few of the issues that provide rural planners with a unique set of challenges in the delivery of sustainable communities. It is important that we work to bring together the different sectoral and professional interests to ensure a coordinated approach to development — a course that the network aims to promote.

Home Ownership Issues

The current climate of economic uncertainty is extremely worrying for the 68 per cent of households in England who own their home.

As house prices increased over the last decade, so did the numbers of borrowers who took out risky mortgage loans that stretched them to their financial limits. At the same time, growing numbers of people found themselves priced out of buying altogether. Now that house prices are falling, and market conditions are bringing insecurity to many households, the Government's policy of increasing home ownership in this country is looking increasingly unrealistic and out of date.

Shelter welcomes Government initiatives to provide more affordable housing through low cost home ownership schemes, alongside the delivery of more social rented homes. Yet Shelter believes the sector's most pressing issues include providing better protection for home owners at risk of repossession and better regulation of the industry.

How Many People Really own Their Home?

In reality, only a minority of households can afford to buy their homes outright. By contrast, most people need to buy their home through taking out a mortgage loan secured against their property. So, although on paper over 14.6 million households in England (68 per cent of the total households) already own their home, over half of these still have an outstanding mortgage. That means these homes can still be repossessed if households become unable to keep up with their mortgage repayments.

Issues with home Ownership

The Current Affordability Crisis

The most conspicuous problem with the UK property market in recent times has been spiralling house prices, which have sparked a situation where many people cannot afford to buy. Even now that prices have fallen, home ownership is still out of reach for thousands of households.

There are many reasons why house prices rose so rapidly. On the supply side, levels of house building have failed to keep pace with high levels of demand. On the demand side, smaller households, the popularity of buy-to-let as an investment, and second-home ownership all contributed to a situation where more and more people were competing to buy a relatively small number of properties. If the underlying problem of the shortage of housing is not addressed, this cycle of boom and bust is destined to repeat itself.

The Risk of Home Repossession

Even if you can get on the ladder, you're still not guaranteed to be in a secure position. Many people were given mortgage loans many times their annual salary. This resulted in hefty repayments that stretched households to the limits of what they could afford. In these circumstances, there is a big risk of borrowers being unable to meet future repayments. This in turn raises the threat of a home being repossessed when borrowers are unable to remedy the situation, potentially leading to homelessness for that individual and all their dependants.

Sale and rent back schemes can potentially offer a way for people struggling to meet their mortgage payments to keep their homes. However, some practices in this area give cause for concern, and unscrupulous companies can evict former owners after six months and then sell the property for a significant profit.

The Council of Mortgage Lenders has predicted that mortgage repossessions will rise to 65,000 over the course of 2009. With increasing turmoil in the sub-prime market, where mortgages were often given to borrowers with bad credit histories at premium interest rates. This is a trend that looks set to continue, particularly for those households that have taken a second mortgage on their property.

The Impact of the Right to Buy Scheme

In 1979, council housing tenants were granted the Right to Buy their homes. In response, more than 1.75 million council tenants bought their homes in England, in many cases spurred on by private companies seeking to exploit the Right to Buy for commercial gain. This was later followed by the Right to Acquire, which granted the similar privileges to housing association tenants. Overall, this has caused a massive reduction in the size of the social housing sector in England, leading to longer waiting lists and a rising number of people living in overcrowded accommodation.

Protection of Council Houses in Areas of High Demand

Shelter supports the Government's action to stem the loss of council houses in high-demand areas and address the problem of the commercial exploitation of the Right to Buy. Once it is operating successfully, we believe the Social Homebuy scheme should replace the Right to Buy and the Right to Acquire which have decimated the supply of social housing stock. Alongside this, more needs to be done to expand the number of social rented homes in the UK.

How to Address These Issues

Shelter is not opposed to home ownership, and on the contrary, we believe home owners need greater protection. We are opposed to a situation in which people's homes are insecure and at risk of being lost.

We believe that if the Government wants to achieve its objective of increasing the proportion of the UK population who own their homes, then it is essential to improve the safety net and advice available, so that people are helped to keep their homes and avoid homelessness. Shelter believes it is not acceptable for individuals and families alone to bear the brunt of unexpected shifts in the economy or shoulder the risks inherent in an increasingly volatile housing market.

Low-cost Home Ownership Schemes

Faced with a growing affordability crisis, Shelter welcomes the Government's commitment to provide more affordable housing through low-cost home ownership (LCHO) schemes.

These are typically shared ownership schemes, where the property in question is part-owned by the resident and part-owned and managed by a housing association. People living in shared ownership housing pay a mortgage for the part they own and rent for the part they don't.

Improved Mortgage Advice and Safety Nets

Shelter believes the safety nets and advice available to home owners need to be improved so that people are helped to keep their home and avoid homelessness. We believe that the current state safety net should be replaced by a reformed system, funded through contributions from lenders, individuals and the Government. In particular, we believe the Government should closely examine the Joseph Rowntree Foundation's proposals for a Sustainable Home Ownership Partnership. This involves a block insurance fund which would pay out on a time-limited basis to homeowners in danger of repossession.

Pre-action Protocol

The pre-action protocol sets out the steps that should be taken by lenders to ensure that repossession is only used as a last resort. It gives borrowers at least 6 months to resolve their arrears or to negotiate new mortgage agreements before possession proceedings are commenced against them.

Shelter both campaigned for and welcomes the protocol as a way of helping people to keep their homes. The drop in the number of repossession claims since the introduction of the protocol in November 2008 is a positive indication that it is having some effect. However, there is the danger that repossessions will resume once the initial 6 months have elapsed.

The pre-action protocol also only represents guidance for best practice, there are no sanctions for lenders who fail to follow this procedure. Those people with second charges are particularly vulnerable as they are not covered by the protocol at all.

If the courts were able to enforce the pre-action protocol, and impose penalties on those who do not follow the protocol, it would then be more effective at helping people who are in arrears to keep their homes.

Campaign Demands

Shelter calls for:

- lenders to use repossession only as a last resort.
- tougher enforcement of FSA rules on responsible lending behaviour.
- FSA regulation of buy-to-let mortgages and second charge lending.

Information on Second Home Purchasing in Breckenridge and Summit County

If you're thinking about purchasing a second home in Breckenridge or Summit County, this web site offers valuable information to help you in this momentous decision. Your second home can be a place for you to get away from it all, develop and enjoy your hobbies, renew your spirit, and do the things you love.

But before you make the decision, there are some important practical issues to consider mostly having to do with the financial aspects of second home ownership. The major decision is whether you want your second home purely as a vacation home, or are you looking for an investment property? The tax ramifications are different for these two uses. A vacation home is one that you use for at least 14 days per year (or, if it is rented, at least 10 percent of the total number of rental days). An investment property is one that is used less than 14 days, and owned primarily to generate rental income. In both cases, you have the probability of appreciation as it relates to your overall financial goals.

The tax ramifications of these two types of ownership are very different:

	Vacation Home	***Investment Property***
Mortgage Interest	deductible	not deductible
Rental Revenue	tax free	must be reported, taxable
Rental Expenses	n/a	deductible
Property Taxes	deductible	deductible
Utilities	n/a	deductible
Home insurance	n/a	deductible
Depreciation	n/a	allowed

In an investment property, in some cases, rental losses can be used to offset other income, dependent on the amount of other income and your own usage of the property. It may be possible to use funds from your retirement savings accounts to purchase an investment property. It is also possible to schedule "fix-up or maintenance days" which are not counted as your own personal usage. You should consult an accountant for these rules and information.

Whatever the choice, it is possible to use the equity in your permanent residence to purchase or make the down payment on your second home. Once you've decided on the Vacation versus Investment property, you can consider all the reasons why you've chosen Breckenridge or Summit County as your second home location.

A 2006 survey of current homeowners (both local and second homeowners) by the Northwest Colorado Council of Governments (NWCCG) reported the following about second homeowners in Breckenridge. All responses are listed in order of importance.

Why did you purchase in Breckenridge? Recreational amenities, proximity to ski resort, scenery and surroundings, intend to vacation here, investment potential, small town atmosphere, climate, air and water quality, friendliness, proximity to front range, rental income, more affordable than other mountain resorts, intend to retire here, proximity to friends/family, and proximity to airports. How important are community services? Open space/trails, parks/trail system, recreation centre, arts/cultural, public transportation, library services, Division of Wildlife, medical services.

Most important recreation? Downhill skiing, walking/jogging, hiking, mountain biking, golf, fishing, picnic areas, swimming, Nordic skiing, playgrounds, snowboarding, tennis, sailing/boating, ice hockey/skating. What is most important? Recreational opportunities, parks/trails and open spaces, public safety, appearance of town, opportunities to attend cultural events, transportation, sense of community, shopping alternatives, health services, education (K-12), traffic, adult education, job opportunities. These responses probably match-up pretty closely with your own decision to purchase a second home here.

According to the National Association of Realtors (NAR), if you're a typical second home purchaser, you are a baby boomer in your late 50's with a belief in diversifying your assets, and you earn around $120,000 annually. In their 2006 report, the NAR reported that of all home purchases in 2006, 36 percent were for second homes, with vacation home sales up 4.7 percent over 2005. 24 percent of these second home purchases were in resort areas. Of all home purchases in 2006, 22 percent were for investment properties, and 7 percent of them were in resort areas.

All this information is provided to let you know that you're not alone in considering a second home purchase in Breckenridge or Summit County. Because of this, when you consider the supply/demand ratios, you can anticipate that prices will continue to escalate (appreciation) because Summit County is approaching "buildout" where all the property available for development has been developed.

Home-ownership at the Crossroads?

- There are early signs that home-ownership in the UK is changing and that this might have long-term consequences for the housing market and wider economy.
- The total number of home-owners has broadly stagnated since 2005. Meanwhile, strong growth in Buy to Let activity has

disguised a fall in the number of owner-occupiers buying with a mortgage over recent years.

- Housing issues have become a core area of Government policy, but in many respects the housing market is increasingly dominated by the structural mismatch between supply and demand. Measures to address these imbalances are necessarily longer-term in nature.
- Innovation by lenders has broadened the range of households that can take out mortgage products and the options to help keep people in their homes if they experience financial difficulties. Although lenders are increasingly basing underwriting decisions on assessments of individual affordability, the need for prudence means that affordability pressures for many households have intensified over time.
- Such pressures are particularly acute for young adults, resulting in many choosing to rent privately rather than to buy and a growing share of first-time buyers relying on parents or other relatives to help out financially.
- But house moves may be becoming more difficult for existing home-owners, with less trading up activity and increasing signs that the housing market is becoming more polarised and fragmented, and functioning less well than in the past.
- The housing market continues to be underpinned by strong fundamentals, but a number of trends will challenge the future shape and functioning of home-ownership in the UK.

Andrews (2006) provides insights into why this has happened. He points to factors such as credit constraints (the lack of a deposit) and student debt slowing the transition to home-ownership, the substantial costs of transactions in the context of significant job mobility of younger households, as well as a shift in the income distribution where younger households faced a relative decline in incomes. The upshot is non-graduate and single person graduate households face particular difficulties entering the housing market.

As Smith et al (2005) argue, the long term consequences of these changes in entry to home-ownership are potentially enormous and require further research. First time buyers (FTBs) have been crucial in absorbing properties from last time and existing sellers, so helping to maintain the liquidity of the housing market. FTBs have in the past made up nearly 50% of annual transactions, whereas now are about 30% of the market. This attracts much comment but it is important to recognise that because home-ownership has been growing over time the volume of moves by existing home-owners increases and the proportion of transactions by first-time buyers almost inevitably declines. But, we should note that the actual number of FTBs has fallen, from a peak of 613,000 loans in 1986 to 369,000 in 2005, a 40% reduction over 20 years.

With an ageing population it is no surprise to note that the number of 16-34 year old persons has also been in decline through the 1990s albeit it is now recovering. This reduction has obviously contributed to the falls discussed above but as Holmans notes, it is the behavioural factors that outweigh demographic trends. Tatch (2006) reminds us that some CML Housing Finance transactions reported as FTBs are in fact returners to the market (it is estimated such households make up about one fifth of stated FTBs). Given that they are typically older and wealthier their presence has a distorting effect on the statistics. Tatch also highlights the increasingly important role of financial assistance from parents and other relatives in helping those under 30 onto the housing ladder.

What all this suggests is that there may now be significant groups of households-including many young, single people, those on lower incomes and those without generous parental support-that face great difficulty in achieving or to all intents and purposes are excluded from home-ownership. Wilcox (2005) analyses the capacity of working households aged 20 to 39 to purchase at the lower end of the market. In 40 local authorities, 40% of younger working households could afford to pay more than a social sector rent but could not buy at the lowest decile point of local house prices. If such exclusion persists over a number of years, we run the risk that the home-ownership rate might begin to fall significantly as it has in other countries.

8

Fractional Ownership of Second Homes

Consumers who want the luxury of having a second home at the beach or in the mountains, but don't have the money to plunk down on the choicest properties, now have an appealing alternative: half ownership. Like other shared ownership ventures, Halfshare.com gives customers the chance to get a piece of the good life, but at a much lower cost. Unlike traditional timeshares, which pioneered the concept of fractional ownership, Halfshare.com buyers aren't purchasing time in a hotel or resort, but an actual home—and all the benefits that go with owning it. Along with sharing costs, buyers share profits if the value goes up. And depending on the terms both owners agree to, the property may generate rental income, too.

Getting started is as easy as logging onto Halfshare.com, where members can browse listings of available properties throughout North America. Halfshare.com can match them with other prospective buyers based on tastes, backgrounds, interests, hobbies and lifestyles through the Buyer Match Plan. Potential co-owners can arrange to meet one another online, by phone or in person to determine if they'd make a good match. Once buyers select a property, Halfshare.com's Tenants-in-Common Agreement takes care of all the details, formalizing legal concerns and each owner's rights. "It spells out what is expected in terms of financial arrangements, seasonal time sharing, rental revenues, re-sale, property maintenance and repair, among other pertinent details."

Although the real estate market is currently in a bit of a slump, demand for sandy beaches, mountain air, cultural attractions and picturesque scenery isn't likely to wane any time soon. Which means that making vacation homes affordable, fraction by fraction, could be a worthwhile start-up in almost any region frequented by tourists looking to make themselves at home. (Related: One-stop shop for transumers and Fractional supercar ownership.) Springwise and its network of 8,000 spotters scan the globe for smart new business ideas, delivering instant inspiration to entrepreneurial minds.

- Folding camper reborn as stylish pop-up lodging.
- Home-repair bidding site prescreens contractors.
- Online yoga classes, real fellow students included.
- Roaming eyewear store visits customers at work.
- Wheelchair redesigned for better form & function.
- Club Bounce caters to the big & beautiful set.
- Crowdfunding an Irish startup via Twitter.
- Ticket price forecasting for live events.
- Spillproof cooking coach: a touchpad made for kitc.
- Computer tasks for workers in the developing world.

Fractional owership has certainly been growing rapidly and there are now over 250 fractional developments in North America, plus many more when you add in all the shared individual homes. At the high end the most luxurious fractionals are often referred to as private residence clubs. For lots of background informatin on these, the amenities and services they offer.

The same in South Arica: The upward growth of 5* resorts allow for a great Fractional Ownership market. A new project that has just been launched and located near Durban called "Sabuti". Perhaps a viable idea but the company you featured doesn't seem to have any properties listed. I just looked at properties on or near water, and all the listing were sold in 2005 or 2006. So, is this company really making a go at it? For one, I noticed a fractional ownership cost starting at $750,000. How affordable is that?

It's an interesting web site – not sure what they charge for matchmaking service. It doesn't say. Using the analogy with dating agencies, they appear to operate rather like an old style personal matchmaker rather than an online dating agency. I recently found a website called yours2share that offers the "online dating agency" type of service free of charge. As well as allowing you to find like-minded people with whom to share the ownership of property and anything else that is high in value like boats and aircraft, yours2share is also interesting in that it helps people find partners for fractional rentals. This page explains it well. I think there is huge potential for people to get together and share things – just think about all the second homes and yachts that are idle for 11 months of the year. It's just a case of find someone like-minded with a compatible requirement – just what the web's made for.

Second Homes: A bright spot in the real estate market *Matt Mullins* It is no secret that the housing market is experiencing a major correction after its long run of excessive price growth, but the one bright spot in today's real estate market is the second home. According to the National Association of Realtors (NAR), second-home sales accounted for an astonishing 36% of all existing home and new home sales in 2006. Vacation home sales increased by approximately 5% this past year and accounted for 14% of all home purchases, while investment home sales and primary residence sales fell by 29% and 4%, respectively.

Second homes are one of the fastest growing sectors in the real estate industry and we expect it to rise over the next decade as America's 79 million baby boomers (born between 1946-1964, now ages 43-61) continue their quest for second homes. This attractive demographic is the country's largest generation. Baby boomers are still in their peak earning years, and today have more free time as they have become empty nesters. Boomers are seeking to diversity their investments, and looking for recreational amenities. At the same time, technological advances and flexible work environments have made second homes increasingly more attractive to the population as a whole. Temperance Landing (Schroeder,MN) People who buy second homes for their primary residence benefit from tax write-offs from mortgage interest, taxes, and insurance. Vacation home owners can avoid capital gains of up to $250,000 (single person) and $500,000 (couple) if they live in the house two of the previous five years prior to selling.

Many second home-owners plan to rent and/or let their children use their unit, with the long-term goal of making it their retirement residence. *Lutsen Resort– Cliff House Townhomes (Lutsen, MN)* Second Homebuyer Trends Second-home owners refer to householders that own one or more residential properties in addition to a primary residence, and who use these properties for either investment or vacation purposes. Today, the typical vacation home owner is 59 years old, according to NAR data. An overwhelming majority of vacation homebuyers are married (78% in 2006) and about 14% of vacation buyers own more than one vacation home. The median distance between vacation homes and the primary residence was 215 miles. However, 42% were within 100-miles and another 32% were 500 miles or greater. About half of second home owners' primary residences are in the suburbs. The following chart shows buyer motivation for purchasing a vacation home; while a significant number purchase the property for investment reasons (diversification, tax benefits, etc.), most want to have a vacation retreat for family and friends, a property to retire to at a later date.

Research indicates that nearly half of vacation homes are in resort or recreation areas. As illustrated in the following chart, most vacation home owners noted their interest in water sports as a primary motivation for purchasing a second home. Many of the desired features for a vacation home are to be found at destinations in northern Minnesota, with water sports, boating, fishing, and golf. The "New" Second Ownership-Fractionals Second homes are not just limited to full-ownership product types. Today in addition to vacation homes, second homes include fractional ownership, destination clubs, timeshares, condo hotels, even houseboats. In Minnesota, growth in the leisure market, paired with the high cost of vacation property, has resulted in a growing number of fractional ownership projects in northern Minnesota. Fractional ownership allows individuals to be able to share ownership and use a vacation home for a portion of the year, often without the difficulties and hassles associated with full ownership.

There is often a management company that handles the scheduling and maintenance of the home for the owners. Fractional ownership typically divides property in fourths, eighths, and 13ths. While similar to timeshares, fractional ownership provides direct ownership of the property with deed title to the land as well. In general, the prospective buyer of a fractional product has always wanted a vacation home and has the means to secure one, but the fractional product offers all of the benefits of second home ownership at a "fraction" of the cost. The value in the fractional purchase is looking better each year. Even buyers who can afford whole ownership see the added benefits of fractionals. Along with their ownership, they usually receive onsite concierge services, priority tee times, valet service, clubhouse access with indoor and/or outdoor pools, exercise facilities, steam rooms, saunas, onsite restaurants, and more. Most of these amenities do not come with the traditional lake cabin. The fractional buyer is purchasing a lifestyle. Although many fractional buyers initially desire to have their own private home, fractional ownership offers ownership to a much broader number of people and offers a reasonable amount of time for use of the unit. A disadvantage of fractional ownership is somewhat less convenience regarding use of the facility (owners are committed to specific weeks), which needs to be addressed by potential buyers. In the North Shore area-and most recently the Brainerd Lakes Area-there are a number of resorts that offer fractional ownership opportunities. Along the North Shore, recently completed projects include *Burlington Bay* in Two Harbors and *Larsmont Cottages* in Larsmont.

These developments have a majority of three-bedroom/three bath units with quarter shares ranging from $130,000 to $189,000. *Burlington Bay* also offers one-eighth shares starting at about $70,000. Other older fractional share projects along the North Shore include *Superior Shores* (Lutsen) and *Superior Townhomes* (Two Harbors). All of these developments are also available for full-ownership. *Trappers Landing (Walker, MN)* In the Brainerd lakes Area, the vast majority of vacation properties are full-ownership projects in which owners participate in a rental program that guarantees seasonal use and the ability to trade shares. The only "true" fractional ownership is *Trappers Landing* in Walker, which opened in 2007. *Trappers Landing* offers full, one-quarter, and one-sixth ownership options and also has a rental program. One-quarter share prices range from $99,000 to $174,000.

Raising the amenity bar Finally, most these new vacation developments are raising the bar with a higher-level of in-unit finishes and access to a wide variety of recreational amenities. Unit features typically include granite or Cambria counters, custom cabinetry, porcelain tile floors, ceramic tile baths, stainless steel appliances, and gas fireplaces. Many of the resort-style developments have a central lodge with a restaurant, pool, exercise room, sauna, meeting rooms, among other features. Outdoor amenities may include boat slips, outdoor grills, canoe rentals, lawn games, bonfires on the beach during the summer, and cross-country skiing and access to groomed snowmobile trails in the winter. *Second/Vacation Home Outlook* Despite our current housing market contraction, second homes will likely remain a bright spot in the real estate market over the next decade.

In Minnesota, 1.4 million of the state's 5 million persons are baby-boomers, a cohort far surpassing all other age groups. In addition, 55- to 69-year olds will account for over one-half of population growth over the next decade-the age group that is most likely to purchase a second home. Since whole-ownership second homes continue to increase in value, especially in desirable locations, fractional ownership developments are expected to become an attractive addition to one's real estate portfolio.

Second Home Ownership and the Affordable Rural Housing Debate

Currently, there are four separate organisations debating second homes in the context of affordable rural housing, each one of which has issued a Report:

* Affordable Rural Housing Commission.
* Commission for Rural Communities.
* HRH Prince of Wales's Rural Housing Initiative.
* Joseph Rowntree Trust Rural Housing Forum.

The Report issued in May 2006 by the Affordable Rural Housing Commission contained recommendations that could severely impact on second home owners, including further tax penalties. The proposed tax increases were referred to a fifth organisation, the Review of Local Government, headed by Sir Michael Lyons. In view of this, and the negative media comment which it generated, the Association of Second Homeowners felt it necessary to produce this Paper for submission to the Lyons Inquiry. Unfortunately, our approach to them of May 17th did not receive a reply until June 21st, at which time we were informed that submissions were required by July 31st, leaving insufficient time for the research normally required for a Paper such as this. In view of the importance to our membership, this timescale is unacceptable. This Report concentrates on the rural debate but we would like to remind Government that the highest incidence of second homes in the Country is to be found in London, as is the greatest concentration of homelessness, and the highest property prices. We wonder why four organisations debate rural housing issues, but not one is considering the situation in London, where the need for affordable housing is the most acute

Definitions and Types of Second Homes, Second Home Owners, and Affordable Housing

The debate surrounding affordable rural housing is often linked to second home ownership. It is therefore important to understand that the perception of what constitutes the average second home is often at odds with the reality.

Holiday Lets

Over half of our members own properties which are let to holiday makers through local 'holiday cottage' Agencies. They market and manage the properties in return for a commission – usually 20% of income, plus cleaning charges etc. The owners pay any service charges, and business taxes on the profits, before receiving the remaining income as a return on their investment. Not only are these properties essential to the wellbeing of the tourist industry in places such as the Lake District, Yorkshire Dales, Norfolk Broads etc., but they provide direct employment to the local people who manage and maintain them. The governments own Visit Britain initiative relies heavily on these properties to provide quality accommodation for visitors in key tourist areas. They are inspected annually and given star ratings against strict criteria.

Unaffordable Houses

In some of the most popular tourist destinations, stylish and expensive properties are often sold as second homes. Such properties cannot; by any definition, be described as affordable, and cannot therefore have any impact on the availability of affordable housing. They do, however, require managing and maintaining, so providing income for local enterprises and individuals. The owners require few local amenities, yet make a substantial financial contribution to local services through council taxes. They also spend freely on leisure activities – eating out and boating being two of the most popular – to the advantage of the local economy.

Purpose Built Holiday Homes

Many of our members own properties that were designed, built and marketed by local people, specifically as holiday homes. These developments were granted planning permission by local authorities in the certain knowledge that they were aimed at the second home market. They were built by local tradesmen, and sold through local estate agencies, often using national advertising to attract holiday home buyers. These properties are generally unsuited to, and never intended for, local people seeking affordable housing. They are often part of a development in communal grounds, for which owners pay a substantial annual maintenance charge, which is spent on local services. An example at one end of the scale would be high value houses and flats in a marina setting, and at the other, log cabins which can only be used eleven months of the year.

The Rose Covered Cottage

There is no doubt that this commonly held vision of an idyllic second home does exist. But if one discounts those that are used as commercial holiday lets, and the very expensive properties that could in no way be described as affordable, they are few and far between. It should also be remembered that they are usually sold to the second homemaker by someone in the local community, with the intention of making money from the transaction. Many older properties had been empty and unsold for some time before being bought by a second homeowner from a grateful local.

Long Term Ownership

A number of owners have enjoyed their holiday homes for generations. A member with such a property in West Sussex, tells us that his family is now afraid to admit to being holiday home owners when using local shops, blaming the anti-second-home publicity generated by some politicians as a cause of friction in the community.

The Amateur Investor

This type of owner uses savings to purchase a property which is intended to provide an income from letting. The income generated, after taxes and charges, is rarely more than that which could be achieved by investing in a bank or building society account. These form a significant part of an individuals savings and provision for future retirement. The amount of income received can vary annually, depending on occupancy levels, but investors look to achieve capital growth over the longer term, on which capital gains tax is paid.

The Professional Investor

This type of owner also invests for income and capital appreciation, but usually on a larger scale, often using external finance. Properties may vary between holiday lets in rural areas and buy to lets in cities. The investor runs the usual risks associated with property investment, and pays taxes on profits, as in any business.

The Holiday Maker

Holiday homes in Britain, rather than overseas, tend to appeal to people who enjoy pastimes such as walking, sailing, and watching nature. The properties are used by owners, their extended family, and friends. On average, the property owner and family will occupy the property for around 25% of the year, but will spend heavily on local facilities. This type of owner pays council tax at 90%, but uses few of the Council services this tax is intended to provide. Properties are often bought with a view to retirement, as a way of trying out the area before 'taking the plunge'. Many others have been owned and used as a holiday retreat by families for generations. The occupations of members who own on this basis varies dramatically. The thing they all have in common is a love of the area in which the second home is based.

A Report from The Affordable Rural Housing Commission defines affordable housing as: Non-market housing provided to those who's needs are not met by the market. It can include social-rented and intermediate housing, for example shared equity, and should normally meet the needs of future and eligible households, for example through restrictions on price, eligibility, and resale. It includes private sector and unsubsidized homes that meet the definition. It is difficult to see how second homes can be defined in such terms.

Tax, Representation and Other Issues

Many people complain about the political process, but do not stop to consider where they would be without it. Second homeowners know exactly what it is like. They are heavily taxed on their second property, but get no representation of any kind.

This leads to some opportunistic politicians, in both local and central government, either ignoring second homeowners, or seeing them as a soft target. In turn, this has led to the Council tax discount on second homes being reduced from 50% to 10% (the 10% was only left in place so as to identify a property as a second home). The reasoning behind the original discount was that second homeowners use few of the facilities this tax is intended to provide.

The reasoning behind the reduction, is that second home owners are accused of depriving local communities of affordable housing, and, it is argued, should therefore provide the funding for such housing. As can be seen from this Paper, second homeowners cannot be blamed for the lack of affordable rural housing, but we accepted the reduced council tax discount as a means of deflecting this unfair criticism.

Unfortunately, Councils saw the additional £90million raised from the reduced discount as a windfall, to be spent on whatever they liked.

Indeed, most local politicians seem unaware that it was intended for affordable housing. A report from the Commission for Local Communities, outlining the ways in which this money was being spent, described it as a 'wasted opportunity'. We would simply describe it as a waste of our money. Another Government Commission, for affordable rural housing this time, failed to identify the size of the need for affordable rural housing, yet recommended another tax on second homeowners, intended for the same purpose as that raised by way of the reduced discount. Significantly, this Commission did not see fit to include a second homeowner in its membership.

Had they done so, we would have pointed out that they estimate there are 90,000 second homes, so on average each property already pays around £1000 each year in reduced discount, specifically intended to provide affordable housing. We would also have said that until this money is spent on the purpose for which it was intended, we would like it to be returned, and considering our lack of political representation, imposing further taxes may constitute an attack on the civil liberties of our members.

As an Association, we are prepared to help in any way we can to address problems within the communities in which we enjoy our holiday homes. The Recommendation section of this Paper outlines the way in which we think the affordable housing issue should be addressed.

Although we have limited expertise in matters of Local Government, our membership includes many highly qualified managers who are familiar with problem solving techniques, all of which agree that the starting point has to be the quantification and qualification of the 'problem', not the imposition of yet more taxes.

Allocation of Blame

We do not consider it constructive to 'blame' anyone for the shortage of affordable rural housing. However, we cannot escape the fact that certain politicians are determined to do so, and that their fingers are pointing at second homeowners.

The Governments Affordable Rural Housing Commission has now proposed an 'impact tax' on second homes in popular tourist areas- which is where most second homes are located for obvious reasons- intended to provide affordable rural housing. This is, in effect, allocating blame for the shortage of affordable housing in these areas to second homeowners.

We Question the Thinking Behind This on two Levels

Firstly, a purchaser cannot be held to be responsible for the 'affordability' of a property. The price is set by the seller-the buyer wishes to pay as little as possible. Had Planning Authorities required developers to provide a percentage of affordable housing as part of every scheme approved in recent years, the problem would not exist.

Secondly, the availability of affordable properties is dictated by many different actors, few of which can be influenced by purchasers of second homes.

1. The 'right to buy' schemes have removed many 'affordable' properties from social housing stock.
2. Planning permission has been granted to local developers to create housing designed for the holiday market, rather than local occupation.
3. Pro-active planning policies could have cushioned local people by imposing local occupancy and agricultural occupancy clauses on appropriate developments.
4. Market prices have simply outstripped salaries, leaving first time buyers struggling in every area in the UK, not just those with heavy concentrations of second homes.

It would be unfair to blame the local people who sold properties to second home buyers for as much money as possible, but the same local community cannot now expect the buyers of those properties to replenish that housing stock.

To blame a local authority for its lack of planning foresight would be equally pointless, but to give that same local authority a bonus payment at the expense of second homeowners, as a means of rectifying those mistakes, cannot be justified.

2006 Housing Needs Assessment

Local Authorities recently produced a Housing Needs Survey, intended to show the current and future housing requirements in their areas, including that for affordable housing. These were mostly published at the end of June/beginning of July 2006. As far as we are aware, the findings have not yet been collated at a national level, and so the overall requirement for affordable housing, as portrayed by these surveys, has not yet been established. The timing is significant as it allowed little time for assessment and debate before preparing this submission by the end of July 2006. In the time available, therefore, we can only give our first impressions, based on reading a number of these reports covering the areas in which the Commission for Affordable Rural Housing advocates to the Lyons Inquiry that taxation on second homeowners should be increased. We have members with experience of major research projects. Although these were in the private sector, the techniques and methodologies used in all large-scale research projects are much the same. The Housing Needs Assessments were prepared following guidance notes issued by the Office of the Deputy Prime Minister.

We can only assume that guidance put the research companies involved in something of a straight jacket, otherwise we feel that they may have done things differently. Research is usually carried out using either quantitative, or qualitative methods. The first is fact based, the second is based on opinions and aspirations. As a general rule, it is dangerous to mix the two methodologies.

The way this research has been carried out allows a degree of opinion and aspiration into an otherwise quantitative questionnaire. Asking people what they *need* in terms of future housing, can result in them putting down what they *want*, which may be two different things.

If that happens, grossing up a 20% response would massively exaggerate the requirement. Also, we question the validity of a sample survey, given the emotive subject matter. Those people who took the trouble to complete the long questionnaire would almost certainly do so because they have a vested interest in the subject matter, or because they had time on their hands. The latter would lead to over-representation of older/non-working respondents. 'Weighting' the findings, however carefully, may not give a representative result. Our interest is limited to the lack of affordable housing, and any justification for charging second homeowners a tax on the lack of it.

If this survey is to be believed, there is a massive shortage of affordable housing, but most of the requirement is for rented accommodation, or shared ownership, because the market has outstripped the incomes of most first time buyers. Second homeowners cannot be held responsible for such a shortfall. Even in tourist hotspots, where the incidence of second home ownership is at its highest, second homes only account for less than 6% of housing stock, and, as outlined elsewhere in this report, few of those could be called 'affordable homes'. However, we do think it is essential that the requirement for affordable housing is qualified and quantified, and we think the obvious way to do this is being ignored.

Recommendations

It is essential that the requirement for affordable rural houses be quantified– and qualified. Although Parish Councillors are amongst the most vociferous critics of second homes, we believe that Parish Councils have a major role to play in this, starting with an assessment of the *real* need. As we have already said, we are skeptical about the findings contained in the recent Housing Needs Surveys, and we wonder why the Parish Council structure was not used to gather the rural data, rather than expensive and overly complicated research methods. Parish Councils have a finger on the pulse of their local community. They are therefore in a position to not only quantify, but qualify, the local requirement.

Housing Needs Return

A simple return from each Parish Council, listing those people in the Parish who currently need housing, broken down into:

A. The number of people who need new social housing.

B. The number of people who can afford to buy low cost housing at market rates, if this was to be made available.

C. Those who could afford a house on a joint ownership basis, if these were available.

Qualification criteria must be agreed, but would include essential employment, and long-term family residency. An assessment of future needs, over the next five years, would also be required. The Return would need updating each year. This is not seen as an onerous task. Indeed our limited research has shown a willingness to cooperate amongst all the Parish Councilors we have spoken to. Each Parish Council should be given the results of the Housing Needs Survey applicable to their area, for comparison purposes. Unfortunately, this data was not collected by parish, and so is not strictly comparable, but it would serve as a guide. The returns could be collated at District or County Council level, and the resultant requirement for low cost subsidised housing should then be submitted to The Housing Corporation, who would be responsible for allocating the funding we understand is already in place. However, the available funding is adequate for a demand in line with the needs estimate from the Commission for Affordable Rural Housing, but would fall far short of that which will emerge from the various Housing Needs Surveys.

Delivery

District planners would be responsible for encouraging the required affordable housing planning applications, and for controlling the supply of new market (not 'affordable') housing aimed at specific markets, such as second homes and holiday lets, by imposing occupancy restrictions on those planning applications, where it is thought to be necessary.

Once the need has been quantified, the capital requirement for affordable rural homes will become clear. We understand that funding for 3000 affordable homes each year is already in place, and second home owners now provide, through the reduced Council Tax discount, additional taxes sufficient for a further 700 affordable homes each year. 3700 new affordable rural homes each year would go some way towards resolving the problem. Although it is nothing to do with us, we believe thought should be given to the likely requirement for social housing that this Return would throw up, and how that will be handled. New social housing would need to be of a good standard if it is to be accepted by local communities. There is, therefore, a danger that any new supply of attractive social housing would entice people to move into rural areas with the sole aim of obtaining such a house, and some would hope to profit from the 'right to buy'.

Obviously, a mechanism must be found by which any such housing can be kept as social housing for local people in perpetuity. This Housing Needs Return would not be difficult to organise, and something of the kind should have been carried out before any recommendations were made by the various bodies who have so far 'assessed' the requirement for affordable rural housing (we find it truly amazing that the Commission for Rural Communities did not await the Housing Needs Survey before publishing their own report).

Because Parish Councils would be involved from the outset, their local knowledge should ensure that fewer NIMBY problems are encountered, as they will take care to ensure that the quantity and quality of the housing fits the location.

The Parish Councils could also play a major role in ensuring that affordable housing created for their local community, whether or not it be shared ownership, remains that way in perpetuity. In some areas, Parish Councils already have some say about the resale of houses built to be 'affordable' in perpetuity. These properties have to be sold at 10% less than market price indicated by professional valuation. Unfortunately, we are told that owners employ estate agencies who are prepared to over value the properties before discount. Obviously, a way to control this must be found. Other considerations are local schools and infrastructure. We know of one village in East Yorkshire where the local primary school was in danger of closing due to an influx of wealthy middle aged commuters.

The Parish and District Councils encouraged the development of desirable and well positioned affordable housing which attracted young families with young children. The village school is now in the process of being doubled in size. However, too many planning applications were granted (against the advice of the Parish Council), and the additional housing caused the water drainage and sewage systems to become overloaded, resulting in flooding and property damage. It illustrates the need for joined up thinking in these situations.

It is important that the Planners heed the advice of the Parish Councils in these housing matters. Planning departments, and Central Government, have been known to ride roughshod over Parish Council recommendations.Support would also be needed from Central Government in terms of regulation. The creation of affordable housing may need to fall outside of the usual planning processes.

Control

It could be argued that such a system would be open to allegations of abuse, and, for that reason, Parish Councillors would be unwilling to take responsibility for controlling the ownership of these affordable houses. However, we would point out that we are not talking about social housing, but affordable housing which people would be expected to pay for, at least in part, and which would also be subject to strict terms and conditions of occupancy, agreed in advance by whichever Government body is chosen to monitor progress. The numbers involved are not great, and so we do not see a need for layers of bureaucracy. The responsibility for ensuring that the scheme works would rest with the Parish Councils, who are subject to the scrutiny of the very local communities that this is intended to serve.

Second Homes and Holiday Lets

Existing properties are usually sold by members of the local community before they become second homes. Any attempt to control that situation, or prevent it, will result in a fall in property values affecting the community as a whole. However, controlling the supply of new developments which are obviously aimed at the second home market, is possible. Once again, the Parish and District Councils are key to this, and, again, Central Government must revise the appeal processes which allow such developments to proceed in the face of local opposition.

Local developers and local trades people may need to divert their activities from creating holiday homes to creating affordable housing, but it is about getting the balance right in each local community. Second homes should not be confused with holiday lets. Many of the areas with high concentrations of holiday lets, need a buoyant tourist industry to provide employment for the local community, and holiday lets are essential to that. It must be remembered that some holiday accommodation – hotels, guesthouses, and holiday lets – have lower occupancy out of season, particularly in coastal resorts. Critics often point to empty holiday homes in the middle of February, yet ignore the empty hotels.

Most holiday lets are owned by private individuals as an investment for income, and managed by local companies. If they were unoccupied for most of the time, the returns would become inadequate, market forces would come into play, and the investment would be sold. There will always be a faction who see holiday lets and holiday homes as a blight on their local community, and those who work in, and for the tourist industry, who see them as essential. It is, we believe, about managing the situation to create the right balance. Tourism is fundamental to the economy of many areas. Penalising holiday home owners could deflect much of this investment overseas.

Conclusion

Second homeowners cannot be blamed for the lack of affordable rural housing. There are simply not enough second homes in the context of overall numbers, for them to make any substantial impact on availability or property prices overall. Most are not 'affordable', and never were. Many are purpose built holiday homes. The affordable rural housing shortage has been caused by rising property prices, a social housing shortfall, and a lack of pro-active planning.

Bibliography

Andrew, N; Flanagan, S & Ruddy, J: *Tourism Destination Planning*, Dublin, Dublin Institute of Technology, 2002.

Apostolopous, Y and Leivadi, S: *Sociology of Tourism, The: Theoretical And Empirical Investigations*, London, Retailed, 1996.

Ashworth, G J and Dietvorst, A G J: *Tourism and Spatial Transformations: Implications For Policy and Plan*, Wallingford, CAB International, 1995.

Ashworth, Greg and Larkham, P J: *Building a New Heritage: Tourism, Culture & Identity in the New Europe*, London, Routledge,1994.

Baum, Tom: *We're all Going on a Summer Holiday: Images of Tourism Past and Person*, Buckingham, University of Buckingham, 1995.

Beeho, A & Prentice, R: *Conceptualising The Experiences of Heritage Tourists*, 1997.

Beeton, Sue:: *Film-Induced Tourism*, Clevedon, Channel View, 2005.

Belie et al.: *Tourism and the Inner City: An Evaluation of / Impact of Grant Assist*, London, HMSO, 1990.

Benefice, Brian G, and Cooper, Chris: *Geography of Travel and Tourism*, The, London, Heinemann, 1987.

Bolshevism, Germy: *Coping with Tourists: European Reactions to Mass Tourism*, Oxford, Berghahn Books, 1995.

Boniface, Priscilla and Fowler, Peter: *Heritage and Tourism: In the Global Village*, London, Retailed, 1993.

Bosselman, Fred P: *In The Wake of the Tourist: Managing Special Places in Eight Countries*, Washington, DC, Conservation Foundation, The, 1978.

Briguglio, L and Vella, Leslie: *Competitiveness of the Maltese Islands in Mediterranean in Tourism*, Chichester, John Wiley, 1995.

Brown, Dona: *Inventing New England: Regional Tourism in the Nineteenth Century*, Washington DC, Smithsonian Institution, 1995.

Brunt, Paul: *Market Research in Travel and Tourism*, Oxford, Butterworth Heinemann, 1997.

Burkart, A and Medlik, S: *Management of Tourism*, The, London, Heinemann, 1975.

Chambers, Erve: *Native Tours: The Anthropology of Travel and Tourism*, Prospect Heights, Waveland Press, 2000.

Chandler, Harry and Carter, John: *Chandler's Travels: A Tour of the Life of Harry Chandler*, London, Quiller Press, 1985.

Clark, Colin: *Tourist Services and Guidance: Heritage and Information*, Strasbourg, Council of Europe Press, 1989.

Coccosis, Harry and Nijkamp, Peter: *Sustainable Tourism Development*, Aldershot, Avebury, 1995.

Cohen, Erik: *Towards a Sociology of International Tourism*, 1972.

Dann, Graham M S: *Language of Tourism*, The, Wallingford, CAB International, 1996.

Davidson, R and Maitland, R: *Tourism Destinations, London*, Hodder and Stoughton, 1997.

Davidson, Rob: *Travel and Tourism in Europe*, Harlow, Addison Wesley Longman, 1998.

Ecotec: *Calderdale: Tourism Impact Study*, Calderdale, ECOTEC/Calderdale Council, 1990.

Edensor, Tim: *Tourists at the Taj*, London, Retailed, 1998.

Edgell, David L: *International Tourism Policy, New York*, Van Nostrand and Reinhold, 1990.

Elliott, James: *Tourism: Politics and Public Sector Management*, London, Retailed, 1997.

Fairgrieve, James: *Geography in School*, London, University of London Press, 1926.

Foster, Douglas: *Travel and Tourism Management*, London, Macmillan Educational, 1985.

Frechtling, Douglas C: *Practical Tourism Forecasting*, Oxford, Butterworth Heinemann, 1996.

Gamble, P. R: *The Educational challenge for Hospitality and Tourism Studies*, Tourism Management, 13, 1992.

Ghimire, Krishna: *The Native Tourist*: Mass Tourism within Developing Regions, London, Earthscan, 2001.

Goeldner, C. R: *The Evaluation of Tourism as an Industry and a Discipline, Paper Presented to*, International Conference for Tourism Educators, Guildford, University of Surrey, 1988.

Gunn, Clare and Var, Turgut: *Tourism Planning*, London, Retailed, 2002.

Hall, C Michael *Tourism Planning: Policies, Processes and relationships*, Harlow, Prentice Hall, 2000.

Hall, Colin and Jenkins, John: *Tourism and Public Policy*, London, Retailed, 1995.

Hall, Colin Michael: *Tourism and Politics*: Policy, Power, & Place, Chichester, Wiley, 1994.

Harrison, Lyndon: *Tourism Means Jobs*, Chester, Lyndon Harrison, 1996.

Harron, S and Weiler, B: *Ethnic Tourism*, Belhaven/Wiley, 1992.

Inkpen, G: *Information Technology for\ Travel and Tourism*, Harlow, Addison Wesley Longman, 1998.

Inskeep, Edward *National and Regal Tourism Planing*: Methodologies & Case Studies, London, Routledge/WTO, 1994.

Irwin, William *The New Niagara*: *Tourism, Technology, And the Landscape of Niagara Fal*, University Park, PA, University of Pennsylvania, 1996.

Jack, G and Phipps, A: *Tourism and Intercultural Exchange*: *Why Tourism Matters*, Clevedon, Channel View, 2005.

Jakle, John: *Tourist, The: Travel in Twentieth Century North America*, University of North Nebraska, 1985.

Jennings, Gayle: *Tourism Research*, Chichester, Wiley, 2001.

Judd, D R: *Promoting Tourism* in US Cities, 1995.

Karski, A: *Urban Tourism* - A Key to Urban Regeneration?, 1990.

Kotler, Philip et al: *Marketing Places*: *Attracting Investment, Industry & Tourism etc*, New York, free press, 1993.

Labarge, Margaret Wade: *Medieval Travellers*: *The Rich and Restless*, London, Hamish Hamilton, 1982.

Laws, Eric: *Tourist Destination Management: Issues, Analysis & Policies*, London, Routledge, 1995.

Leed, Eric J: *Mind of the Traveller, The: From Gilgamesh to Global Tourism*, New York, 1991.

MacCannell, Dean: *Tourist, The: A New Theory of the Leisure Class*, London, Macmillan, 1976.

Machin, Alan: *Retracing the Steps: Tourism as Education, Janus*, Fin, ATLAS / FUNTS, 2001.

Opperman, Martin and Chon, Kye-Sung: *Tourism in Developing Countries, London*, International Thomson Business Press, 1997.

Patullo, Polly: *Last Resorts*: *The Cost of Tourism in the Caribbean*, London, Cassell, 1996.

Pearce, Douglas: *Tourism Today*: *A Geographical Analysis*, Harlow, Longman, 1995.

Pearce, P L: *Social Psychology Of Tourist Behaviour*, The, Oxford, Pergamon, 1982.

Peters, M: *International Tourism*, London, Hutchinson, 1969.

Ringer, Greg: *Destinations: Cultural Landscapes of Tourism*, London, Routledge, 1998.

Ritchie, Brent: *Managing Educational Tourism*, Clevedon, Channel View, 2003.

Robinson, H: *Geography of Tourism*, A, London, Macdonald and Evans, 1976.

Robinson, M, Evans, E & Chalazion, P: *Tourism and Cultural Change, Sunderland*, Business Education Publishers Ltd, 1996.

Rogers, H Anthea and Slinn, Judy A: *Tourism: Management of Facilities*, London, Pitman: M & E, 1993.

Schwaninger, M: *Trends in Leisure and Tourism for 2000 - 2010*, Prentice Hall, 1989.

Scottish Tourist Board: *Visitor Attractions: A Development Guide*, Edinburgh, Scottish Tourist Board, 1991.

Seaton, A V et al: *Tourism: The state of the Art*, Chichester, John Wiley, 1994.

Shaw, G and Williams, A: *Tourism and Tourism Spaces*, London, Sage, 2004.

Stevens, Terry: *Island Tourism*: Malta, , WTO, 1993.

Trench, R: *Travellers in Britain*, London, Aurum, 1990.

Tribe, John *Corporate Strategy for Tourism, London*, International Thomson Business Press, 1997.

Urry, John: *Tourist Gaze*, The, London, Sage, 1990.

Van den Berg et al: *Urban Tourism: Performance and Strategies in Eight European Cities*, Aldershot, Avebury, 1995.

Van Harssel, Jan: *Tourism: An Exploration*, New York, Prentice Hall, 1994.

Veal, A: *Leisure and Tourism*: Policy and Planning, Wallingford, CABI, 2001.

Wahab, S A: *Tourism Management*, Tourism International Press, 1975.

Walle, Alfred H: *Cultural Tourism*: A Strategic Focus, Boulder, Co, Westview Press, 1998.

Wilkinson, Paul: *Tourism Policy and Planning: As Studies from the Caribbean*, Elmsford New York, Cognizant Communications Corporation, 1997.

Yale, Pat: *From Tourist Attractions to Heritage Tourism*, Huntingdon, Elm, 1991.

Zarkia, Cornelia: *Philoxenia: Receiving Tourists*-but *not Guests-on a Greek Island*, Oxford, Berghahn Books, 1996.

Index

A

Accommodation Capacity, 172.
Arrangements, 35, 144, 163, 199, 208, 315.
Associations, 40, 50, 51, 176, 177, 235, 250, 259, 261, 275.

B

Bay Islands, 235.
Business Development, 156.
Business Growth, 108, 158.
Business Travel, 168.

C

Campaign Demands, 309.
Coastal Degradation, 213, 233, 237.
Coastal Development, 97, 135, 137, 147, 226, 230.
Coastal Hazards, 136, 141, 149.
Coastal Management, 135, 136, 137, 198, 218.
Coastal Recreation, 134, 146, 150, 200.
Collaboration, 145, 149.
Commission, 8, 89, 138, 231, 237, 247, 274, 275, 304, 320, 321, 323, 324, 325, 327, 328.
Communications, 129, 214.
Contribution, 14, 26, 63, 100, 101, 104, 132, 140, 152, 167, 196, 217, 240, 276, 321.
Cultural Environment, 58.
Cultural Tourism, 66, 191.
Customer Service, 206.
Customers, 8, 205, 315, 316.

D

Demands, 13, 14, 22, 63, 99, 157, 173, 175, 309.
Destination Management, 204.
Development Strategy, 110, 164, 241.
Draft Planning Schemes, 274.

E

Economic Growth, 113.
Economic Impact of Tourism, 151.
Ecotourism, 136, 144, 145, 194, 206.
Electronic Databases, 12, 28, 29.
Entrepreneurship, 158.
Environmental Impact, 217, 220, 225, 227, 277.
Environmental Management, 198, 205.
Environmental Resources, 226.
Environments, 81, 137, 208, 214, 217, 224, 317.

F

Federal Government, 94, 95, 131, 136, 140, 142, 143, 148, 150.
Forms of Tourism, 1, 4.

G

Global Tourism, 129.
Governance, 240.
Growth of Tourism, 56, 131, 213, 234.

H

Health Benefits, 163.
Healthy Ecosystems, 136, 140.
Holiday Homes, 10, 12, 20, 22, 24, 34, 35, 36, 37, 39, 96, 97, 98, 99, 100, 101, 104, 161, 243, 244, 273, 277, 292, 321, 322, 324.
Housing Demand, 12, 13, 18, 22, 23, 39, 41, 284, 285, 290, 291, 293, 294, 296, 299, 300, 303, 304.

I

Information Systems, 237.
Institutions, 5, 105, 109, 128, 257.
Instruments, 236.
International Tourist Market, 131.
International Tourists, 131, 136, 147.
International Travel and Tourism, 129, 130.
Investment Property, 68, 69, 72, 83, 310.
Investments, 69, 83, 215, 229, 231, 234, 236, 237, 257, 278, 284, 317.

L

Labour Market, 41.
Laws, 9, 73, 84, 88, 93, 143, 202, 289.
Leadership, 130, 236.
Local Community, 55, 56, 58, 59, 62, 67, 110, 177, 188, 203, 204, 231, 232, 242, 243, 276, 322, 325, 327, 328.
Local Development, 237, 249, 274.

M

Maintenance, 18, 19, 73, 99, 139, 140, 142, 144, 146, 149, 150, 172, 182, 200, 203, 207, 217, 232, 280, 281, 283, 286, 287, 288, 289, 310, 315, 318, 321.
Majority, 29, 37, 38, 46, 48, 61, 71, 79, 179, 185, 206, 213, 275, 317, 319.
Management Measures, 177.
Marina Development, 184.
Marine Environment, 139, 152, 166, 198.
Marine Resources, 139, 213, 230.
Market Research, 40, 41.
Mass Tourism, 58, 61, 93, 223, 227, 232.
Mechanisms, 15, 24, 193.
Methodological Challenges, 18, 22, 24, 34.
Mountain Biking, 311.

N

National Policy, 140.
Natural Environment, 56, 64, 66, 67, 136, 161, 166, 167, 180, 187.
Natural Resources, 134, 233, 234, 236, 237.

O

Observations, 16, 300.
Occupations, 65, 252, 253, 257, 266, 323.
Opportunity, 84, 123, 179, 180,

181, 183, 208, 249, 253, 277, 281, 284, 286, 289.
Organizations, 107, 118, 147, 151, 233, 235, 238, 239, 247.
Outdoor Recreation, 50, 51.
Ownership, 4, 9, 12, 14, 15, 16, 19, 20, 21, 22, 26, 34, 35, 41, 69, 70, 78, 82, 100, 106, 156, 161, 163, 226, 249, 279, 280, 281, 282, 283, 284, 285, 286, 287, 288, 289, 290, 291, 292, 295, 296, 297, 299, 300, 303, 304, 305, 306, 307, 308, 309, 310, 312, 313, 314, 315, 316, 318, 319, 320, 322, 326, 327, 328.

P

Performance, 229, 292.
Place Attachment Concepts, 43.
Planning Network, 305.
Policy, 11, 12, 15, 16, 17, 18, 19, 20, 21, 22, 24, 25, 26, 27, 28, 29, 30, 33, 34, 42, 67, 95, 96, 99, 109, 111, 131, 134, 137, 140, 147, 162, 167, 186, 187, 197, 198, 202, 218, 224, 233, 236, 237, 239, 240, 245, 273, 279, 305, 306, 312.
Politics, 59, 92.
Powers, 15, 20, 166, 172.
Production, 11, 19, 24, 142, 192, 205, 207, 213, 276.
Projects, 7, 8, 11, 17, 81, 137, 138, 143, 169, 170, 191, 205, 209, 218, 220, 228, 236, 251, 259, 274, 276, 318, 319, 326.
Promoting Ecotourism, 145.
Promotion, 7, 131, 135, 149, 162, 207, 209.
Protection, 67, 77, 92, 103, 132, 136, 138, 139, 142, 145, 152, 166, 198, 219, 225, 230, 239, 241, 248, 306, 308.
Provision, 3, 23, 94, 96, 97, 98, 99, 100, 101, 104, 136, 137, 156, 162, 171, 172, 173, 175, 179, 181, 182, 184, 189, 190, 193, 194, 199, 200, 201, 206, 207, 211, 274, 275, 276, 305, 322.

R

Rafting, 46.
Recreation Properties, 77, 105.
Recreation Second Homes, 75.
Recreational Turn, 84, 88, 90.
Relationship, 2, 43, 44, 51, 55, 56, 59, 61, 64, 66, 86, 114, 116, 118, 119, 120, 121, 122, 123, 125, 126, 127, 162, 187, 247.
Research, 2, 11, 13, 15, 16, 17, 19, 21, 23, 24, 25, 26, 27, 28, 29, 30, 31, 32, 33, 34, 35, 37, 38, 39, 40, 41, 43, 44, 46, 50, 51, 54, 55, 56, 57, 59, 60, 62, 63, 64, 65, 67, 68, 73, 78, 89, 94, 109, 121, 126, 128, 138, 140, 143, 145, 151, 155, 156, 157, 202, 203, 226, 245, 246, 247, 249, 252, 274, 277, 287, 290, 291, 292, 304, 313, 318, 320, 326, 327.

Resource Management, 205, 238, 240.
Restaurants, 2, 61, 109, 113, 116, 174, 191, 192, 222, 223, 224, 243, 264, 272, 318.
Risk Management, 202.
Rural Coast, 175, 176, 177.
Rural Community, 254, 255, 256, 259, 268, 269, 271, 276.
Rural Housing Debate, 320.
Rural Lifestyle, 248, 250.
Rural Settlement Strategy, 95.
Rural Tourism, 96, 99.

S

Seaside Resorts, 10, 167, 171, 174, 197, 210.
Second Home Development, 249.
Second Home Tourism, 1, 3.
Second Homes Ownership, 280.
Security, 8, 9, 117, 136, 231, 246.
Small Business, 128.
Society, 17, 84, 88, 162, 164, 245, 254, 275, 322.
Strategic Context, 164.
Strategic Planning, 240.
Sustainable Development, 147, 231.
Sustainable Tourism, 147, 214, 240.

T

Technology, 87, 155, 156, 206, 218, 245, 246.
Tourism Activities, 4, 64, 148, 194, 215, 217, 224, 233.
Tourism Demand, 2.
Tourism Destinations, 135, 143, 232.
Tourism Development, 7, 56, 99, 215, 234.
Tourism Employment, 151.
Tourism Facilities, 216, 222.
Tourism Impact, 1.
Tourism Industry, 147.
Tourism Infrastructure, 136, 156, 158, 170, 195, 218.
Tourism Management, 135.
Tourism Markets, 176.
Tourism Organisation, 227.
Tourism Planning, 145.
Tourism Policy, 95.
Tourism Promotion, 131, 149.
Tourism Strategy, 159, 161, 162, 165.
Tourist Accommodation, 98, 99, 102, 172.
Tourist Destination, 7, 59, 61, 132, 135, 143.
Tourist Lifestyle Development, 59.
Trades, 243.
Traditions, 106, 257.
Transportation, 106, 119, 129, 195, 225, 250, 251, 252, 311.
Treatment, 100, 101, 222, 223, 229, 275, 277, 278.

V

Visitor Market, 168.

W

Water Recreation, 167, 171, 184.
Wildlife Tourism, 180.
World Bank, 220, 228.
World Tourism, 129, 147.

□□□